> "**Rather than letting the recession be a reason to let environmental ideals slip, it should give you a greater incentive to go green**"

Welcome to the second edition of the Green Living Guide. Much has happened since the first edition, Go Green the Easy Way, hit the shelves 12 months ago, and calls for serious action on climate change continue to grow unabated.

In November 2008, the UK government took Britain to the centre stage in the world's fight against global warming when it committed us to an unprecedented 80% reduction of greenhouse emissions by 2050 with the groundbreaking Climate Change Act.

Two months later, environmentalists across the world waved a keen farewell to the Bush Administration as President Barack Obama took up seat at the Whitehouse amid a sea of high hope and expectancy.

But whilst the world's politicians thrash out new policies and scientists look to technology for the right answers, it remains vital that we as individuals recognise and fulfil our own responsibility in tackling global warming and environmental destruction.

Times are hard as we continue to battle our way out of this recession. But rather than letting the economic downturn be a reason to let environmental ideals slip, it should give greater incentive than ever to go green.

The purpose of this guide is to provide you with the latest information and advice to help lessen your individual impact on the planet, and to show you that by being green you can actually save a lot of money in the process.

Over the next 200 pages we have covered the many different areas of our lives, from the food we eat to how we heat our homes, from the toys we buy our children to the way we choose to travel. **The Green Living Guide** provides you with the latest information and advice, and includes many new featured products and services to keep you up to speed with all things green.

We have searched high and low for examples of best practice in the UK today and hope these fascinating stories will provide you with ideas and inspiration.

While the aim of this guide remains primarily on cutting greenhouse gas emissions, much of the book focuses on the importance and implications of curbing environmental destruction and better management of the world's limited resources.

We hope that you find this book an invaluable guide to green living, and that you will dip in and out of it frequently throughout the year ahead.

Hugh Bowring - Editor

EDITORIAL
Author **Hugh Bowring**
Sub Editors **Nicola Tann, Jo Halpin**

ART & DESIGN
Art Editors **Sam Freeman, Nick Watts**
Designers **Aston Leach, Khoi Kieu**
Photography **Hugh Threlfall**
Repro **Linda Duong**

ADVERTISING
Advertising Director **Clare Williamson**
Marketing **Michelle Marsh**

MANAGEMENT
Bookazine Manager **Dharmesh Mistry**
(020 7907 6100 dharmesh_mistry@dennis.co.uk)
Production Director **Robin Ryan**
MD of Advertising **Julian Lloyd-Evans**
Newstrade Director **Martin Belson**
Chief Operating Officer **Brett Reynolds**
Group Finance Director **Ian Leggett**
Chief Executive **James Tye**
Chairman **Felix Dennis**

MAGBOOK™

The 'Magbook' brand is a trademark of Dennis Publishing Ltd, 30 Cleveland St, London W1T 4JD. Company registered in England. All material © Dennis Publishing Ltd, licensed by Felden 2009, and may not be reproduced in whole or part without the consent of the publishers.
Green Living Guide 2nd Edition, (previously published as 'Go Green The EasyWay')
ISBN 1-907232-06-0

LICENSING
To license this product, please contact Winnie Liesenfeld on +44 (0) 20 7907 6134 or email winnie_liesenfeld@dennis.co.uk

LIABILITY
While every care was taken during the production of this Magbook, the publishers cannot be held responsible for the accuracy of the information or any consequence arising from it. Dennis Publishing takes no responsibility for the companies advertising in this Magbook.

The paper used within this Magbook is produced from sustainable fibre, manufactured by mills with a valid chain of custody.

Printed at BGP, Bicester

Contents

CHAPTER 4
Work & Office

Page 128

Page 146

CHAPTER 5
Transport & Motoring

CHAPTER 6
Fashion & Beauty

Page 174

CHAPTER 1
HOME & GARDEN

Where to look

THE TREATMENT AND SUPPLY OF WATER IN THE UK CREATES AROUND 5 MILLION TONNES OF CARBON DIOXIDE EVERY YEAR

WATER

Every day the average Briton consumes around 150 litres of water. All this is drinkable water, processed through an energy-intensive treatment system – even though we use a quarter of it just to flush the loo! It is easy to take our stable water supply for granted, but without careful management, the survival of our wetland eco systems and the security of our precious water supply are at risk. Here we have plenty of advice on how to protect it

HOW CAN WE SAVE WATER?

01 WATER METERS

Saving water could also save you money. The average annual water bill rose by nearly 25% from £263 in 2002 to £330 last year. Water meters record the actual amount of water a household uses, in the same way that a gas or electricity meter records fuel consumption. Fitting a meter allows the homeowner to monitor water consumption and, since they are only billed for the water they actually use, encourages them to use less. Studies show that water meters lead to a 5 to 15% reduction in household water use. On the other hand, households with unmetered systems, pay a flat rate for their water irrespective of the amount they use. In the main this costs more.

To get a meter installed in your home contact your water supplier, which is obliged to install it free of charge within three months of your request. In certain instances it may be too technically difficult or prohibitively expensive to install a meter and the water company will apply an 'assessed charge' based on the amount of water the customer is likely to use.

02 GREY WATER

Greywater is the term for any wastewater other than that from toilets. A greywater recycling system collects wastewater from baths, sinks and showers, which is treated either with basic physical filtration or biologically (like in a sewage treatment work) and stored in a tank. This recycled water can be used to flush toilets, water gardens and sometimes feed washing machines, making up a significant proportion of domestic water use.

A domestic greywater system will cost in the region of £3,000 plus all the installation costs, so the payback period is likely to be long. There are greater financial benefits from systems installed in larger buildings, such as blocks of flats, since these can use more sophisticated and efficient treatment processes and can be maintained centrally.

Environmentally speaking, greywater recycling makes more sense. A decent system could potentially save a third of the water taken from the mains supply by a domestic property, significantly reducing the pressure on both water resources and the amount of sewage requiring treatment. However, greywater systems need energy to operate and this negates some of the environmental benefits gained from saving water.

> **"The average annual water bill has risen nearly 25% from £263 in 2002 to £330 last year"**

Did you know...?

As a rule of thumb, if there are more bedrooms in your house than there are people, you should think about getting a water meter installed. Just ask your water supplier to install one and they will do it for free.

◁ **Down the pan: using drinking-quality water just to flush the loo is a waste!**

03 RAINWATER HARVESTING

Rainwater harvesting is the process of collecting water that would otherwise go down the drains, into the ground or evaporate, so that it can be used in the home and garden. Harvesting systems can be installed in both new and existing buildings and can provide a medium-sized home with as much as 100m³ of water a year – equivalent to around eight showers every day. This water can be used to flush the toilet, water the garden, supply the washing machine and so on.

Storage tanks tend to be very large (typically between 1,000 and 9,000 litres) and are usually kept underground. They are connected to the house and outside taps by a separate pipe network. If the water level in the tank falls below a certain level, the system switches back to the mains water supply.

Although harvesting rainwater has significant environmental benefits, the initial cost of buying a good quality domestic system is between around £2,000 and £3,000, and plumbing and fitting costs vary. A typical system provides between 30% and 50% of a property's water use, so in financial terms the payback period could be long.

Rainwater harvesting: How it works

- Rainwater is collected from the roof drainage system via an underground filter (1). This removes the debris from the water and diverts about 95% of it into the storage tank. The remaining water goes to a soakaway or storm drain in the usual manner, as does the excess water from the tank. As water enters the tank it passes through a calmed inlet (2) which calms the flow of water and prevents disturbance of the float switch and any sediment.

- Water is then supplied by the pump (3) through a floating suction filter (4) to specific outlets; usually WCs, garden taps and washing machines. The pump is controlled by a combined pressure switch/ flow controller (5) that turns it on and off and gives dry-running protection.

- Mains water top-up is provided by a valve (6a) controlled by a float switch (6b). Water gravity-feeds to the tank through a 50mm pipe that then connects to the outlet pipe from the filter.

- Water is pumped via a pressure hose (7) up to the flow controller. Pipe and cables are ducted to the house through a drainage pipe (8).

- An overflow trap (9) provides a water seal against any foul odours from drains. (NB an anti-backflow version is available when connecting to a sewer.)

- An optional level gauge (10) gives a visual indication of tank water level.

For more information on this and other rainwater harvesting sytems, visit www.rainharvesting.co.uk

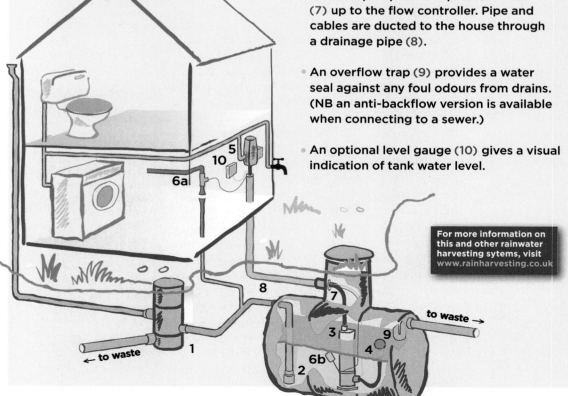

Good green buys

Aerated showerheads
These brilliant devices mix air with water to maintain the pressure of a normal shower while saving buckets of water. Available from Challis www.challiswatercontrols.co.uk and Mira Showers www.mirashowers.com. Prices vary.

Integrated toilet and hand basin
The award-winning Australian-made Caroma integrated water saving toilet and hand-basin is the first of its kind to feature a unique, dual-flush push button and spout arrangement that saves the water normally used when hands are washed in a separate basin. Visit www.sanlamere.co.uk for more details.

Eco Showerdrop
Calibrated shower timer which lets you know exactly how much water you are using with user-friendly graphics. A simple alert tells you when the recommended amount of water has been dispensed (35 litres as advised by Waterwise and leading water companies). Available from www.footprint-es.com, priced £9.99

WATERWORKS: How much water does it take for....

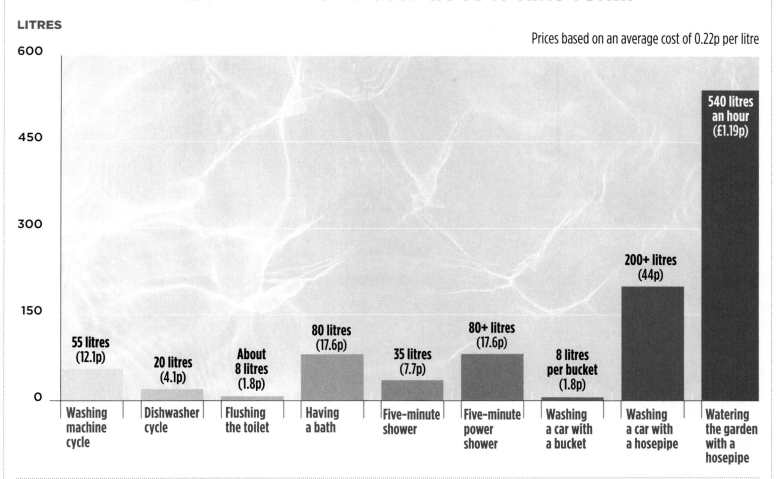

LITRES

Prices based on an average cost of 0.22p per litre

600

450

300

150

0

55 litres (12.1p)	20 litres (4.1p)	About 8 litres (1.8p)	80 litres (17.6p)	35 litres (7.7p)	80+ litres (17.6p)	8 litres per bucket (1.8p)	200+ litres (44p)	540 litres an hour (£1.19p)
Washing machine cycle	Dishwasher cycle	Flushing the toilet	Having a bath	Five-minute shower	Five-minute power shower	Washing a car with a bucket	Washing a car with a hosepipe	Watering the garden with a hosepipe

HOW WE USE IT

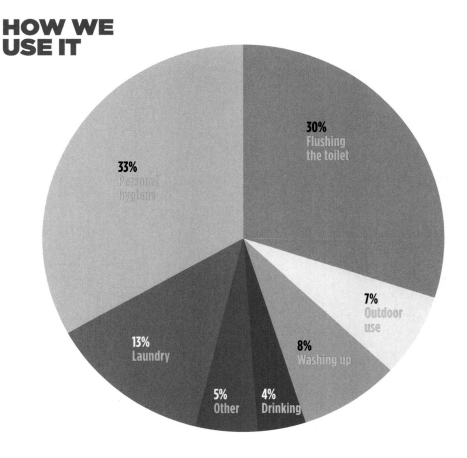

33% Personal hygiene

30% Flushing the toilet

13% Laundry

5% Other

4% Drinking

8% Washing up

7% Outdoor use

WATER WASTE

We've already learned that the average person in the UK consumes around 150 litres of water a day. However, according to the results of a WWF study published last year, if we take all the water used to make the products we use into account, this figure grows closer to a shocking 4,645 litres – which is 4.6 tonnes a day each! It takes about 13 litres of water to produce a tomato, about 170 litres for a pint of beer, in the region of 2,400 litres to make a hamburger and – wait for it – a gargantuan 4,000 litres of water to make a cotton T-shirt.

4.6 tonnes per day

WATER-SAVING TIPS

Dripping taps

Fix any dripping taps and leaks. Aside from being annoying, a dripping tap can waste as much as 5,500 litres of water a year and cost you £12, when often all they take to fix is a new washer. Fixing a leaking tap is a fairly simple DIY task – for an illustrated step-by-step guide, check out *www.diyfixit.co.uk* or consult any decent DIY manual. Otherwise call in the plumber.

Washing food

Wash fruit and vegetables in a bowl rather than under a running tap. You can even use the water left for watering house plants.

Shower

Try to shower rather than bath. A five-minute shower only uses approximately 35 litres of water compared with 80 litres for a bath (see chart on page 11). But remember, power showers are completely different – they can use more water than a bath in less than five minutes.

Water butts

Collect rainwater in water butts for watering plants. You may even want to consider investing in a rainwater collection system (see page 10).

Car wash

Use a bucket when you wash your car and not the garden hose. An average bucket uses eight litres compared to more than 200 litres when you use a hosepipe (see chart on page 11).

Water pipes

Burst water pipes can cause serious damage as well as waste water. Ensure your water pipes and external taps are lagged before winter.

Toilet

Get a plumber to install a low-flush toilet with the choice of a long or a short flush. While he's at it, get him to install low water-use spray taps and low-flow showers as well. For a selection of water-saving sanitary ware, try the Green Building Store (www.greenbuildingstore.co .uk). It is also worth trying a decent plumbers' merchants.

Drinking water

In summer, keep a jug of drinking water in the fridge instead of running the tap until it runs cold.

Household Water

Re-use household water (from the bath, for example) for the garden but be sure to use it within 24 hours or it might start to smell. Don't use water that has been exposed to powerful cleaners and detergents. To maximise your efficiency, you could invest in a greywater recycling system.

Taps

Don't leave the tap running while you brush your teeth or wash your hands – a well known old favourite, but it is such a good habit to get into. Running the tap uses up to five litres of water a minute and, according to the Environment Agency, if every adult in England and Wales did this, we could save 180 million litres a day, enough to supply nearly 500,000 houses.

Kettles

Don't overfill your kettle or saucepan. It's one of the most common pieces of advice but for good reason: using only what you need will not only save water and energy, but money too.

Water meter

Ask your water company to install a water meter. This is a free service and will most likely end up saving you money.

Dishwashers

Fill dishwashers and washing machines before you use them. Half-load programmes use more than half the water and energy of a full load.

x7

EACH YEAR THE AVERAGE PERSON IN BRITAIN THROWS AWAY AROUND SEVEN TIMES THEIR OWN BODY WEIGHT IN RUBBISH

WASTE & RECYCLING

Put bluntly, if everyone in the world lived as we do in the UK, we would need the resources of three 'Planet Earths' to support us. The principles set in the mantra 'reduce, reuse, recycle' provide the bedrock for sustainable civilisation in the 21st century. Here we've got loads of ideas for you to help make the most of our precious resources

REDUCE, REUSE, RECYCLE

Reduce

In the West, we've beome accustomed to a very wasteful lifestyle, constantly buying brand-new and disposing of not-very-old. Often when people think of saving resources, it is recycling that first springs to mind. But although recycling has a vital role in saving materials and energy, cutting down on waste in the first place is more important. Each year the average UK household throws away £424 of food. Most of that wasted food then ends up taking up valuable space in a landfill site rotting away to produce methane, which is a far more potent greenhouse gas than carbon dioxide. When you factor in all the energy, water, land, fertilisers, pesticides and everything else which goes into the production, transportation and packaging of that wasted food, and the environmental impact of greenhouse gas emissions, this waste of valuable natural resources quickly adds up. The production, transportation and preparation of all the food and drink we consume (and throw away) is responsible for a third of all greenhouse gas emissions.

By reducing our waste we are directly affecting climate change and easing pressure on the world's stretched resources. By the same token, if we choose to reduce our energy consumption by, say, getting up to turn the TV off at the wall, wearing a jumper so we can turn the thermostat down or biking to the shops instead of driving, we are starting to make real changes to our lives and the planet.

▼ Each year the average UK household throws away £424 of food, most of which ends up in landfill

Reuse

Of course, no matter how much we reduce our use of things, we are always going to produce waste. But what might be rubbish to one person could be highly valuable to another. Mobile phones, desktop computers, leftover paint and old clothes are just a few examples. Making the effort to find out whether another person or organisation might want your unwanted items is a great way of saving valuable resources, reducing carbon emissions and helping out the local community. There's also a good chance that if it's in reasonable condition you might be able to make some money out of it too.

If something is broken, there's a chance it could be repaired. Before you throw something out because it's no longer working, consider searching online or in your local phone book for repair services in your area. If you can't be bothered but think it could be repaired, then there may well be plenty of people willing to take it off your hands and do the work themselves (see pages 22 to 25 for plenty of tips on what to do with unwanted common household items).

Λ **Don't just discard broken gadgets: they could be just what someone else needs**

Recycle

Recycling reduces our reliance on landfill and saves limited resources and energy, helping to tackle climate change. Recycling aluminium, for example, requires only 5% of the energy it takes to make new aluminium – and produces only 5% of the carbon emissions. Recycling just one aluminium can saves enough energy to run a television set for three hours!

Today it is easier than ever to recycle our waste, and most communities now have some form of kerbside recycling scheme run by their local council to collect the most common recycled materials. By the end of 2010 every local council in England will be required to collect at least two types of recyclable waste from all homes, except under exceptional circumstances.

And of course, most areas now have access to recycling banks and larger household recycling centres which take a far wider range of materials and waste items.

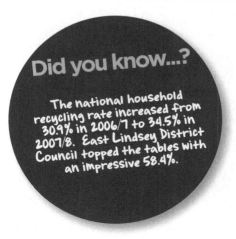

Did you know....?

The national household recycling rate increased from 30.9% in 2006/7 to 34.5% in 2007/8. East Lindsey District Council topped the tables with an impressive 58.4%.

Λ **Recycling not only saves materials, but energy too. Recycling one aluminium can saves enough energy to power your telly for three hours**

CHANGING HABITS
Limiting waste

☑ Buy second-hand.

☑ Buy quality goods that have been made to last.

☑ Keep it simple. Keep your recycling bin next to your other bin so it's as easy to recycle as it is to throw away. Alternatively, buy a bin with separate compartments for waste, recyclables and composts (visit www.homerecycling.co.uk for a wide range).

☑ When you go shopping, keep in mind everything you are going to end up throwing away and things you could reuse or recycle. Do you really need to buy those four apples in the shrink-wrapped package or are the loose ones just as good?
And make a shopping list so you only buy what you need.

☑ Your local council is responsible for the collection and disposal of waste in your area. To find out what kind of waste is accepted and how to dispose of it, visit www.recyclenow.com and type in your postcode. The website has very useful and easy-to-read maps plotting collection sites in your area.

☑ Buy refills where you can as this cuts down on packaging.

☑ Buy in bulk: it cuts down on packaging and usually saves money.

☑ Avoid disposable options where there is a long-lasting alternative (eg nappies, razors, napkins, cameras).

☑ Buy products with high recycled content.

☑ Rinse out food tins before you recycle them for hygiene purposes.

☑ Squash your cans and bottles so they take up less room. Use a can crusher if that makes your life easier (available from www.footprint-es.com, at £14.99).

☑ Reduce junk mail by registering with the Mail Preference Service. Visit www.mpsonline.org.uk or call 0845 703 4599.

☒ Say no to plastic bags. Take a rucksack or buy a bag for life (and re-use it!) when you go shopping.

MOBIUS LOOP
Indicates that a product can be recycled

MOBIUS LOOP WITH PERCENTAGE
Shows how much of a product is made from recycled materials

GREEN DOT
Indicates the supplier has contributed financially to the cost of recovery and recycling of packaging waste

EUROPEAN ECO LABEL
Shows the product has been produced in an environmentally friendly manner

WHY BUY RECYCLED?

One of the major factors limiting the scope for recycling is demand for the end product. There is no point investing time and energy collecting and recycling something if no one wants it.

Part of the solution is for governments and businesses to find uses for these materials and to limit the different types of material in the waste stream to those that can be recycled. But the consumer has an equally important part to play by choosing products made from recycled materials, increasing demand for recycled produce overall. Buying recycled sends a strong message to manufacturers and retailers and affects sustainability policies and practice.

⋏ **We create enough rubbish to fill the Royal Albert Hall every two hours**

What a load of rubbish

The UK creates enough rubbish to fill the Royal Albert Hall every two hours, and our landfill sites are filling up fast. But space is not the only problem. As rubbish decays it releases a toxic fluid called leachate that contaminates the land – and possibly even water supplies – if it leaks out, and a potent methane-rich landfill gas. Under an EU directive set up to reduce reliance on landfill, the UK is required to meet stringent cuts in the amount of biological municipal waste sent to landfill over the next 11 years, and failure to do so will result in tough fines – footed by the taxpayer. In response to the directive, the Government's waste strategy highlights the need for us to reduce our waste and for a substantial increase in re-using, recycling and

"As rubbish decays it releases a toxic fluid that contaminates the land and water supplies"

composting. However, ministers also want controversial 'energy from waste plants', or incinerators, to deal with more than a quarter of all household waste in England by 2020.

Environmental groups, including Friends of the Earth, vociferously oppose the use of incineration as a solution to the mounting waste problem claiming it destroys valuable resources, acts as a disincentive to recycling and has a negative affect on people's health by producing toxic chemicals such as dioxins, which can cause cancer.

WHAT MAKES UP WASTE SENT TO LANDFILL?

Plastic people

The world's consumption of plastic has risen from five million tonnes in the 1950s to around 100 million tonnes a year today, thanks chiefly to its increased use in the construction industry, automotive products and packaging. Making plastic requires huge amounts of fossil fuels (both as a raw material and to provide the energy for the manufacturing process) as well as plenty of other valuable resources – including vast amounts of water – and not forgetting that the process itself produces lots of waste and harmful emissions. There are many different types of plastic, and it can be confusing as to which types your council will accept for recycling. Below is a list of the most common types of plastic, together with their abbreviations (which should be stamped on any item containing them) and their typical uses. If you are unsure which you can put in your recycling bin and which should be left out, contact your local council.

PETE	HDPE	PVC	LDPE	PP	PS
Polyethylene terephthalate	**High-density polyethylene**	**Polyvinyl chloride**	**Low density polyethylene**	**Polypropylene**	**Polystyrene**
Drink bottles and oven-ready meal trays	Bottles for milk and washing-up liquids	Food trays, cling film, bottles for squash/water	Carrier bags and bin liners	Margarine tubs, microwaveable meal trays	Yoghurt pots, foam meat or fish trays, plastic cutlery

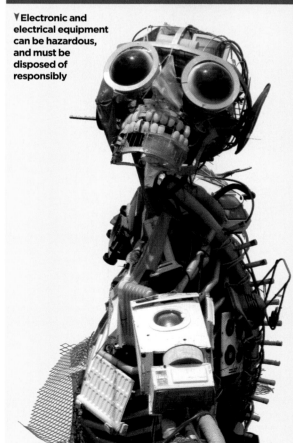

▼Electronic and electrical equipment can be hazardous, and must be disposed of responsibly

A word on WEEE

Electronic and electrical equipment is one of the fastest growing types of waste in Europe. UK households throw away around a million tonnes of it each year. By keeping waste electronic and electrical equipment (known as WEEE) separate from other rubbish it can be treated, hazardous substances removed and a large amount recycled.

Under new legislation, producers of electronic and electrical equipment now have to pay for the collection, treatment and recovery of it.

If you are making a like-for-like purchase of electrical goods, EEE retailers must dispose of the equipment you are replacing for free, regardless of where you bought it, or tell you an alternative site to dispose of it.

Alternatively, customers can take WEEE to their local Civic Amenity site or arrange for their local authority to collect the equipment (this will be free with some local authorities).

It's easy to tell which products are covered by the WEEE regulations – just look out for the crossed-out wheeled-bin symbol (right). This means you must dispose of the item separately from other household rubbish.

Hazardous waste

Hazardous waste at home can include asbestos, some paints, oils, pesticides, fridges and freezers, fluorescent tubes, batteries and TVs. Your local council may collect this waste from your home, though they may charge for this service. Alternatively, take it to your local recycling centre where you can dispose of it free of charge.

A STEP-BY-STEP GUIDE TO COMPOSTING

Composting our kitchen and garden waste is an easy and natural way of cutting down on the amount of waste we send to landfill. Follow these simple steps to create your own quality compost for the garden

01

Buy a composting bin. These are available from most garden centres, though many local councils also sell them at a reduced price. It's always worth contacting your council as they sometimes provide them for free. Alternatively, build your own.

02

Put it on level soil in a well-drained and preferably sunny place. Being on soil allows in the microbes and insects that break down your waste, and is better for drainage and aeration. If you must place your bin on concrete, put a layer of rich soil in the bottom.

03

Your compost should be ready to use after about six or nine months. Finished compost is very dark brown and soil-like, with a spongy texture, and is full of nutrients. Use compost in your flowerbeds, pot plants and vegetable patches to enrich the soil and help keep moisture in.

Composting gadgets

The CompoSphere has a unique spherical design which means you can mix the contents of the 315l drum to accelerate the speed of composting. It also means you can roll it around the garden to where you need the compost. Made from 100% recycled, UV protected plastic and complete with a 5-year manufacturer's warranty. Available from www.originalorganics.co.uk, priced £97.82 excluding delivery.

The dos and don'ts of composting

☑ Do use...

- Vegetable plants
- Grass cuttings
- Cardboard
- Tea bags
- Crushed egg shells
- Old vegetable plants

☒ Don't use...

- Sick plants
- Meat
- Cooked food
- Young annual weeds
- Glass or metal
- Weeds that are making seed

Keep it green... and brown

For good compost you need the right ingredients, which are often put into two categories: green and brown. The secret lies in getting the right balance and ensuring your compost is aerated. Stick your hand in it and if it feels too wet, add more browns. If it's too dry, add some greens or some water. Mix the contents occasionally to air it.

Nitrogen-rich 'greens'

- Old vegetable plants
- Grass cuttings
- Vegetable peelings
- Pet manure from vegetarian animals (like rabbits and hamsters – not cats and dogs)
- Tea bags
- Coffee grounds

Carbon-rich 'browns'

- Shredded or crumpled paper
- Woody stems and twigs
- Fallen leaves
- Egg boxes
- Hay and straw
- Wood shavings

On seeing the bigger picture

THERE ARE MANY SOURCES OF ENERGY, BUT NOT ONE OF THEM IS THE SOLUTION.

THERE ARE MANY SOURCES OF ENERGY, AND THAT <u>IS</u> THE SOLUTION.

Affordable, reliable, low carbon energy

The perfect source of energy is affordable, reliable and low in carbon emissions. The problem is, it doesn't exist. No single source ticks all three boxes. This is not so much a dilemma, as a 'trilemma'. Nuclear is low carbon, but expensive. Fossil fuels are more economical, but will continue to produce carbon until we can perfect a way to capture and store most of it. Wind is carbon-free, but if it doesn't blow, the turbines don't turn. That's why we believe that the future lies in producing energy from a variety of sources – and why we continue to invest in them all. To have your say, visit our YouTube channel and get involved in the great energy debate.

We're on it

Join the conversation at youtube.com/talkingenergy

WHAT CAN

AEROSOLS

Accepted at recycling banks or kerbside collection schemes. Dispose of the lid and any other easily removable parts with the rest of your rubbish.

BATTERIES

Batteries are toxic. Some local recycling centres collect them, but if yours doesn't, dispose of them safely in your local recycling centre's hazardous-waste bins.

BICYCLES

If it's beyond repair, recycle the frame at your local recycling centre. But if it could be repaired and re-used, try The Bike Station (*www.thebikestation.org.uk*) and Re-Cycle (*www.re-cycle.org*).

BOOKS

Books cannot usually be recycled along with other paper recycling because of the glue used to bind them. Try selling them online instead or donate them to a charity shop.

BRICKS AND RUBBLE

If in good condition, bricks can be sold, donated or re-used. Try advertising in local papers, on community notice boards, or through online market places for building materials (try *www.bremap.co.uk* or *www.salvo.co.uk*).

CAR BATTERIES

Some recycling centres will take car batteries, though it is worth checking before lugging them there. If not, try your local garage or scrap-metal merchant.

CARDBOARD BOXES

Some local authority kerbside schemes and recycling banks will collect cardboard – but if yours doesn't you can take it to your local recycling centre.

CARPETS

If it is in a reasonable condition, you might be better off trying to sell it through your local papers or community notice boards, or giving it away on Freecycle. Otherwise try your local gardening group as carpets make good mulch.

CARRIER BAGS

Make sure you take some old bags with you when you go shopping. Some supermarkets offer in-store recycling banks for carrier bags.

CLOTHES

You can recycle clothes, shoes and other textiles at a number of recycling banks and centres. Alternatively, give clean and serviceable items to your local charity shop or door-to-door collection scheme.

I RECYCLE?

CDS/DVDS

There are a couple of companies that deal with CDs and DVDs including *www.keymood.co.uk,* while *www.recyclingcds.com* will turn them into clocks, coasters calendars and other handy items.

COMPUTERS

Turn to 'A word on WEEE' on page 19 for more on recycling electrical waste.

COOKING OIL

Only large amounts of cooking oil from restaurants or factories can be collected for recycling. Small amounts of cooking oil can be disposed of with the rest of your household rubbish once it's cooled. Don't pour down the drain as it causes problems when it solidifies.

DRINKS CARTONS

Cartons are now collected by more than 300 local authorities across the country. Visit *www.tetrapakrecycling .co.uk/locator.asp* to find out what's going on in your area.

DRINKS CANS

These can be recycled with local authority kerbside collections or at your nearest recycling bank. If you have lots you might be able to sell them to a local Cash for Cans organisation. *Visit www.thinkcans.net/cash-for-cans.*

ENGINE OIL

Your local recycling centre and some garages will take your engine oil for recycling. Visit *www.oilbankline.org.uk* to find your nearest oil bank.

ENVELOPES

Some local authorities will accept envelopes from kerbside collections and paper banks. Check with your local authority if in doubt.

FOOD WASTE

Some local authorities collect kitchen waste or provide containers at recycling centres so it can be composted. Ask your local council if they offer this service.

FURNITURE

If in decent condition, donate it to the Furniture Re-Use Network (*www.frn.org.uk*), a charitable organisation set up to redistribute old furniture. Otherwise check what your local recycling centre accepts before making the trip.

GARDEN WASTE

Some local authorities provide special bins for kerbside collection, otherwise you can recycle garden waste at your nearest recycling centre. If you have space in your garden consider establishing a compost tip.

WHAT CAN

GLASS

Many types of glass can be recycled with kerbside collection schemes, bottle banks or local recycling centres. Bottles and jars should be cleaned and any tops or corks removed. Dispose of window panes and glass ovenware carefully with your normal household waste.

GREETING CARDS

Either use your local authority kerbside scheme or recycling bank. Every January, The Woodland Trust teams up with Tesco and WHSmith to collect and recycle millions of Christmas cards from their stores.

KEYS

Like other metals, keys can be recycled in the mixed-metals recycling facility at most local recycling centres. If you have lots of them, try contacting a local scrap merchant to sell to.

LIGHT BULBS

Dispose of standard incandescent light bulbs in your normal household waste. Low-energy light bulbs contain small amounts of mercury and should be treated as hazardous waste (see p21) unless other recycling options are available. IKEA recycles low-energy bulbs in all of its stores.

MAGAZINES & NEWSPAPERS

These are normally covered by kerbside collections, or you can take them to your local recycling bank.

MOBILE PHONES

Sell, or give to any number of charities that refurbish and recycle (eg Fonebak, Action Aid, Oxfam, CRUMP, Scope and Fones4Schools). You could also re-home them through a website like Freecycle.

MUSICAL INSTRUMENTS

Some instruments have metal or plastic parts that can be removed for recycling, but consider giving instruments to charity shops or even putting them up for sale in local papers or community boards.

PAINT

Some recycling centres accept paint. Alternatively, donate to a local Community Repaint scheme (*www.communityrepaint.org.uk*).

PLASTERBOARD

A number of recycling centres recently took part in successful trials to work out the best way to collect plasterboard waste for recycling, and now many local authorities are looking to introduce a collection service.

PLASTIC BOTTLES

Most local authorities accept plastic bottles for recycling, either at kerbside collections, plastic bottle banks or recycling centres. If in doubt, give them a call. See page 19 for a guide to plastic recycling symbols.

I RECYCLE?

PRINTER CARTRIDGES

A number of organisations will refill or recycle them for you. Cartridge World has over 270 stores in the UK, where you can take your cartridges to be refilled and save up to 60% off the cost of a new cartridge.

SHOES

Most recycling centres and some recycling banks accept shoes. Otherwise donate them to a charity shop.

SHREDDED PAPER

If your council won't accept it try using it as packing material for sending fragile items by post, or put it in your compost.

SPECTACLES

Donate old pairs to Vision Aid Overseas' Second Sight Project (*www.secondsightproject.com*) where they will be re-used or recycled.

TELEVISIONS & MONITORS

See 'A word on WEEE' on page 19 for information on how to dispose of electrical goods.

TEXTILES

If you have clothes in a decent condition, take them to a local charity shop or put them on Freecycle. Otherwise, most recycling banks and centres accept different types of textiles.

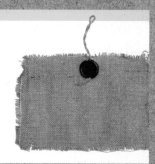

TIN FOIL

Tin foil is made of aluminium and will be accepted at your nearest recycling bank and some kerbside collection schemes as well as milk bottle tops, takeaway and barbeque trays and cigarette foil.

TOYS

Although your local authority is unlikely to accept toys for recycling, it may be possible to recycle plastic and metal parts. You can find a home for usable toys at your local toy library (*www.natll.org.uk*).

VIDEO CASSETTES

Try *www.keymood.co.uk*.

YOGHURT POTS

Check with your local authority as the plastics which can be included in your kerbside collection and plastic recycling banks vary from area to area. See page 19 for a guide to plastic recycling symbols.

Source: www.recyclenow.com

HEATING AND POWERING OUR HOMES ACCOUNTS FOR AROUND 28% OF ALL CARBON DIOXIDE EMISSIONS IN THE UK

HEAT & POWER

In the UK, two-thirds of our electricity comes from fossil fuels and most of the rest comes from nuclear power – not too good for the planet. Here we look at how small changes can save money and energy, and explore the options for generating your own domestic power

How energy-efficient is your house?

Whenever a house or flat is built in the UK it must be designed and made in compliance with strict building regulations. Every few years these regulations are updated, setting higher standards of construction for the industry – including in energy conservation.

What this means is that a huge percentage of the UK's older housing stock is losing heat left, right and centre because of inadequate insulation and outdated construction methods and materials. Not much can be done about the construction now, but you can do something about the insulation, and employ other energy-saving tactics.

Energy rating and the EPC

It is now a legal requirement for anyone selling or renting out a home to have an Energy Performance Certificate (EPC) made up for any potential buyer or tenant. This document is produced by a qualified assessor following an energy assessment of a home. It ranks the energy efficiency and estimated environmental impact of the building
on an easy-to-read A to G scale, where A is best and G is worst.

The most important aspect of the EPC is its list of recommendations for improvements which are tailored to that specific property and listed in order of cost effectiveness, ranging from installing low-energy light bulbs to solar panels.

DIY home energy-efficiency test

There are various DIY models of the above test available on the internet, which although not as accurate as an EPC can provide useful information on the best ways to improve a home's energy efficiency. Try the Energy Saving Trust's at *www.energysavingtrust.org*

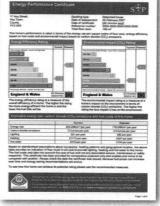

△ **Get tips on making your home more energy-efficient**

> " **The EPC lists recommendations for improvements tailored to each property in order of cost effectiveness** "

THERE'S NO PLACE LIKE HOME: SAVING ENERGY

The Government is very eager to quickly improve the energy efficiency of Britain's housing, and provides a wide range of financial support, incentive and offers of help to homeowners wanting to make improvements. The type and level of financial support will depend on your circumstances and where you live, but for some, improvements will be carried out for free.

Here we've illustrated some of the most common ways you can improve the energy-efficiency of your home. Once installed, energy-efficiency measures could not only cut your household's carbon footprint significantly, but should save you money on your fuel bills too. With the rising price of oil and gas, the lower running costs of an energy-efficient home should be an attractive proposition to prospective buyers and could potentially increase your property's market value.

Call your local Energy Saving Trust advice centre on 0800 512 012 for details of support available to you, and free and impartial advice on a range of energy-saving measures – from where to find professional installers to getting a free home-energy report.

The figures shown are approximate, based on a gas-heated semi-detached house with three bedrooms

Save Cash!

By making some of these simple DIY changes to your property, you could save £240 a year; make all the changes and save a whopping £1320 a year

Hot-water tank jacket
Annual saving £35
DIY cost £12
DIY payback less than 6 months
Annual CO2 saving 190kg

Internal wall insulation
Annual saving £380
Installed cost around £5,500 (but much lower if other work is being done simultaneously)
Installed payback over 15 years
Annual CO2 saving 2 tonnes

Primary pipe work insulation
Annual saving £10
DIY cost £10
DIY payback 1 year
Annual CO2 saving 60kg

Floor insulation
Annual saving £50
DIY cost £100
Installed payback 2 years
Annual CO2 saving 270kg

Illustration: Tim Ellis for Debut Art

Loft insulation (0-270mm)
Annual saving up to £150
Installed cost £250
Installed payback less than 2 years
DIY cost £250 to £350
DIY payback 2 to 3 years
Annual CO2 saving around 800kg

Cavity wall insulation
Annual saving £115
Installed cost £250
Installed payback 2 years
Annual CO2 saving 610kg

Getting into the habit: more energy-saving tips

☑ It sounds simple, but if you're cold put on a jumper before turning on the heating.

☑ If you have a programmer for your central heating system, use it – there is no point in having the heating on if nobody's at home.

☑ Turning down the thermostat by 1C can save you around £40 a year on your heating bills and around 325kg in carbon dioxide emissions.

☑ Don't cover radiator controls with curtains or furniture as this interferes with their thermostatic control. Turn off radiators in unused rooms.

☑ Use pot pourri instead of plug-in air fresheners.

☑ When choosing insulation consider natural, non-toxic materials that use less energy to produce, such as hemp, wool or recycled paper.

Filling gaps between skirting boards and floorboards
Annual saving £20
DIY cost £20
DIY payback 1 year
Annual CO2 saving 110kg

Double glazing
Annual saving £135
Installed cost varies
Installed payback varies
Annual CO2 saving 720kg

Draught proofing
Annual saving £25
Installed cost £200
Installed payback 8 years
DIY cost £90
DIY payback less than 4 years
Annual CO2 saving £130kg

External wall insulation
Annual saving £400
Installed cost £10,500
Installed payback over 20 years
Annual CO2 saving 2.1 tonnes

WIND POWER IS THE FASTEST GROWING ENERGY SOURCE IN THE WORLD

MICROGENERATION

Roof-top solar panels and miniature wind turbines are both examples of microgeneration. Although such technologies have been widely used in other parts of the world for several years, their uptake in Britain has been relatively slow. But there has been a recent increase prompted by growing awareness of climate change and its causes, rising fuel bills and a series of government grant schemes to promote the uptake of renewable energy sources.

WIND

The wind-energy industry is the fastest growing energy industry in the world. The UK is ideally placed to take full advantage of this renewable resource, having 40% of Europe's total wind energy potential. Wind turbines use the wind's lift forces to turn aerodynamic blades which turn a rotor to create electricity. Because wind power is proportional to the cube of the wind's speed, relatively minor increases in speed result in large changes in potential output.

While the biggest offshore turbines are generating upwards of 3 megawatts, a modest domestic system can still yield a respectable 2.5 to 6 kilowatts, depending on the location and size of the turbine.

Cost
A roof-mounted microwind system starts at about £1,500. Larger mast-mounted systems cost between £11,000 and £19,000, including installation. These provide enough electricity for lighting and appliances in a typical home.

Grants
Maximum of £1,000 per kW of installed capacity, subject to an overall maximum of £2,500 or 30% of the relevant eligible costs, whichever is the lower.

Savings
Recent monitoring of a range of small domestic wind systems has shown a well-sited, 2.5kW turbine could shave about £380 a year off electricity bills when some generation is exported, with a saving of around 2.6tonnes of carbon dioxide per year.

Maintenance
Checks are necessary every few years and a well-maintained turbine should last 20+ years. Battery storage life is between six and 10 years.

Is it suitable for me?
Wind speed increases with height so it's best to have the turbine high on a mast or tower. Generally speaking, the ideal site is a hill with clear exposure, free from excessive turbulence and obstructions such as trees or buildings.

While an understanding of local wind systems is critical to designing a wind-energy system and predicting output, planning issues such as visual impact, noise and conservation issues also have to be considered.

Small-scale building-integrated wind turbines suitable for urban locations are available to install in homes and other buildings, but there are no long-term studies of their benefits available.

Did you know...?
The UK is the windiest country in Europe. If we could harness this natural resource efficiently, we could power the whole country several times over.

"**Wind turbines can have a working life of over 20 years**"

How does it work?

Wind turbines use the wind to rotate aerodynamic blades (1) which turn a rotor (2). This rotor is connected to a main shaft, which spins a generator (3) to create electricity. Wind turbines can be connected to the national grid via a special inverter and controller (4) for widespread power distribution.

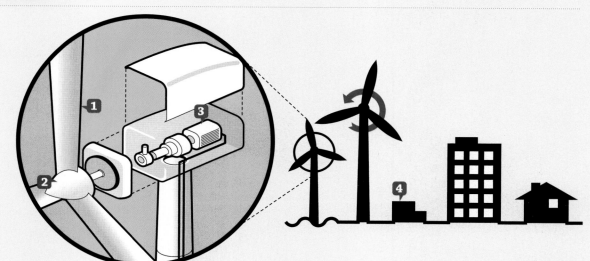

Main photo: PA Photos   Illustration: Infomen

GRANTS OF UP TO £2,500 ARE AVAILABLE FOR SOLAR PV PANELS

SOLAR PV

Photovoltaic (PV) cells use energy from the sun to create electricity to run appliances and lighting. The PV cell consists of one or two layers of a semi conducting material, usually silicon, which means that when light shines on it, it creates an electric field across the layers, causing electricity to flow. Although the cells do not need direct sunlight for power generation, the greater the intensity of the light, the greater the flow of electricity.

Technological breakthroughs in recent years have led to an ever-widening range of applications for the cells. For instance, you can now buy grey 'solar tiles' that look like ordinary roof tiles but actually generate electricity.

Costs

Prices of PV systems vary considerably depending on the type and size of the system to be installed, as well as the structure of the building on which the PV is to be mounted.

As a guide, a typical domestic system costs around £5,000 to £7,500 per kilowatt peak (kWp) installed. In general:
(1) the more electricity the system can generate, the more it costs, but the more it could save.
(2) solar tiles cost more than conventional panels
(3) panels built into a roof are more expensive. than those that sit on top.
(4) if you need major roof repairs, PV tiles can offset the cost of roof tiles.

Grants

Maximum of £2,000 per kW of installed capacity, subject to an overall maximum of £2,500 or 50% of the relevant eligible costs, whichever is the lower.

Savings

This depends on many different factors, but can be considerable – around 1.2 tonne of CO_2 a year and about £250 off your electricity bill. A 2.5 kWp system could provide 50% of a household's yearly electricity needs

Maintenance

Systems connected to the grid require very little maintenance but should be checked regularly by a qualified technician. Stand-alone systems need maintenance on other system components, such as batteries.

Is it for me?

You can use PV systems for a building with a roof or wall that faces within 90 degrees of south, as long as no other buildings or large trees overshadow it. If the roof surface is in shade for parts of the day, the output of the system decreases. PV systems are heavy so the roof must be strong enough to take their weight.

Did you know...?

Next year the government is expected to introduce a Feed-in Tariff to help promote solar power and other renewable energy sources. Under the system electricity companies will be obligated to buy renewable electricity at above market rates, providing long-term financial incentives for people to invest in microgeneration.

How does it work?

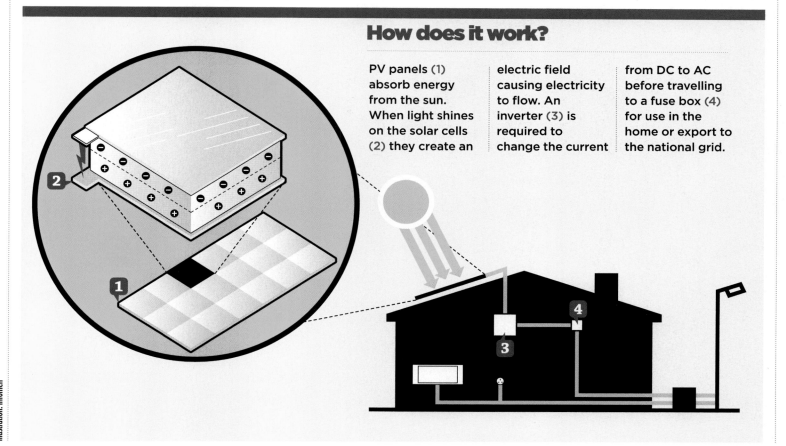

PV panels (1) absorb energy from the sun. When light shines on the solar cells (2) they create an electric field causing electricity to flow. An inverter (3) is required to change the current from DC to AC before travelling to a fuse box (4) for use in the home or export to the national grid.

5,950 GRANTS TOTALLING NEARLY £2.5M HAVE BEEN GIVEN TO HOMEOWNERS TO HELP PAY FOR SOLAR WATER-HEATING SYSTEMS

SOLAR WATER HEATING

Solar water-heating systems use heat from the sun to work with conventional water heaters, and are the most commonly used form of solar microgeneration in the UK. There are two main types of systems available: flat plate collectors and evacuated tube collectors. Both types operate in the same way: liquid (usually water mixed with anti-freeze) is circulated through the solar collectors absorbing heat from the sun's radiation. This liquid is then passed through the coil of a hot water storage cylinder to heat the water, which can be supplied directly or further heated by a conventional boiler.

Around the world

Flat-plate collectors for solar water heating first became popular in parts of Florida and Southern California in the 1920s.
Since then their popularity has spread across the globe; for example, it is estimated that at least 30 million Chinese households now benefit from solar water heating, and around 85% of Israeli homes have some form of solar thermal system installed.

Costs

Typical installation costs for a domestic system are between £3,000 and £5,000 depending on the size and type of system. A typical flat plate installation in the UK has a 3m² to 4m² solar panel and 150 litre to 200 litre storage tank, though this will depend on the amount of hot water used. Evacuated tubes take up approximately half the amount of roof space. DIY systems are also available and typically cost between £500 and £1,500.

Grants

Overall maximum of £400 or 30% of the relevant eligible costs, whichever is the lower. To be eligible for a grant you will need to use a certified installer and products.

Savings

A typical system can provide you with about a third of your hot water requirements over the year. They can reduce carbon dioxide emissions by up to 645kg a year and cut as much as £95 off your fuel bill, depending on the fuel replaced. Their output is naturally dependent on the season and in the summer a solar system should provide most, if not all, of the hot water you need at home. However, they will only make a small contribution in winter months.

Maintenance

Solar hot-water panels require very little maintenance during their lifespan. A yearly check by the householder and a more detailed check by a professional installer every three to five years should be sufficient.

Is it for me?

You will need between 3m² and 4m² of southeast- to southwest-facing roof receiving direct sunlight for the main part of the day. You'll also need the room to keep an additional water cylinder if required.

In most cases the cylinder part of the system will go inside the house

How does it work?

Solar panels (1) absorb the sun's radiation to heat water that is passed through the panel through a copper pipe (2). This heated water is then piped through the coils of a hot water cylinder (3) to heat the cylinder's water, which is then used in the home. Once the solar-heated water has passed through the cylinder it returns to the panel for reheating.

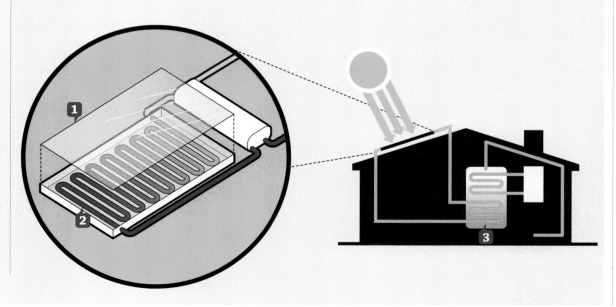

Illustration: Infomen

GRANTS OF UP TO £1,200 ARE AVAILABLE FOR GROUND-SOURCE HEAT PUMPS

GROUND-SOURCE HEAT PUMPS

Heat pumps transfer heat from the ground, air or water into a building to provide heating, and in some cases heat domestic hot water too. Fridges and air-conditioning units both use heat pumps to work

Costs

To install a typical 8 to 12kW system costs between £7,000 and £13,000 plus the price of connection to the distribution system – not an insignificant outlay by any stretch of the imagination, though this cost can be significantly reduced in new building developments when installation is combined with other building works.

Grants

You can get an overall maximum of £1,200 or 30% of the relevant eligible costs, whichever is the lower.

Savings

On average you can save between £350 and £1,000 on your heating bills and up to seven tonnes of CO_2 per year, dependent on the type of fuel being replaced.

Is it for me?

You need to have outdoor space for a borehole or horizontal system, and be above ground suitable for digging.

▲ **In the same way that your fridge uses refrigerant to extract heat from the inside, keeping your food cool, a ground source heat pump extracts heat from the ground, and uses it to heat your home**

AIR-AND WATER-SOURCE HEAT PUMPS

Unlike ground-source heat pumps, air- and water-source heat pumps do not rely on a collection system, but simply extract heat from the source at the point of use. Air-source heat pumps extract heat from the air outside to heat your home and hot water. One of the key benefits they have over ground-source heat pumps is that they don't need underground coils or bore holes and so take far less space and work to install. Water-source heat pumps are less common and work by extracting heat from rivers, streams and lakes for example to provide heating in homes.

The Government's grant scheme was extended this summer to include air-source heat pumps and now offers a maximum of £900 or 30% of the relevant eligible costs, whichever is lower.

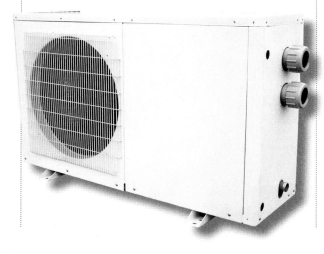

SMALL-SCALE HYDRO

Hydroelectric power systems use the kinetic energy of moving water to turn a turbine to produce electricity. Recent improvements in small turbine and generator technology mean that micro-hydro schemes are an attractive means of producing electricity and can even be employed on small streams to return useful amounts of power.

The amount of energy available in a given body of water depends on the water's flow rate and the distance (or head) that the water falls. The system's actual output will then depend on how efficiently it converts the power of the water into electrical power.

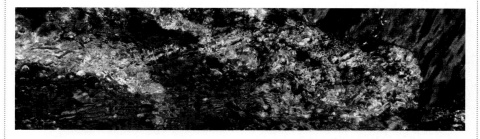

Cost

The costs of hydro power systems are high – as are the returns. Low head systems (not including the civil works) typically cost around £4,000 per kW installed up to about 10kW, but drop per kW for larger schemes.

For medium heads, there is a fixed cost of about £10,000 and then the cost is about £2,500 per kW up to around 10kW.

Grants

Maximum of £1,000 per kW of installed capacity, subject to an overall maximum of £2,500 or 30% of the relevant eligible costs, whichever is the lower.

Is it for me?

Probably not! For houses with no mains connection but with access to a micro-hydro site, a good hydro system can generate a steady, more reliable electricity supply than other renewable technologies at a lower cost. Total system costs can be high but often less than the cost of a grid connection and with no electricity bills to follow.

Anyone thinking of installing a turbine must be aware that the installation can have a seriously detrimental effect on the river's ecology so careful maintenance of the total flow diverted through the turbine is vital.

BIOMASS

Unlike fossil fuels which evolve over millions of years, biomass (also called bio-energy or biofuel) is organic matter which lived recently, and as a renewable energy source is likely to have an important role in tackling climate change. When biomass is burned to produce energy, the carbon dioxide emissions of that process are balanced by those that the plant absorbed while it was alive. As such, it is often referred to as 'carbon neutral' fuel. But the production of energy from biomass usually involves non carbon-neutral inputs such as fertilising the crop, harvesting it and transporting it to the plant.

Biomass is produced either directly from plants or indirectly from industrial, commercial, domestic or agricultural products. For small-scale domestic applications of biomass the fuel usually takes the form of wood pellets, wood chips and wood logs.

In the home, biomass can be used in a stand-alone stove or a woodburner or in a boiler connected to central heating and hot water systems. There are many domestic log, wood-chip and wood-pellet burning central heating boilers available. Log boilers must be loaded by hand and may be unsuitable for some homes and situations. Automatic pellet and wood-chip systems can be more expensive.

Costs

Stand-alone room heaters generally cost around £3,000 to be installed.

A typical 15kW pellet boiler, which is the average size required for a three-bedroom semi-detached house, costs from around £9,000 installed, including the cost of the flue and commissioning. A manual-feed system of the same size would be slightly cheaper.

Grants

Room heaters Overall maximum of £600 or 20% of the relevant eligible costs, whichever is the lower.
Wood-fuelled boiler systems Overall maximum of £1,500 or 30% of the relevant eligible costs, whichever is the lower.

Savings

Savings from a stand-alone room heater will depend on how much they are used and the fuel you are replacing. A biomass-powered boiler could save you around £470 a year on your household energy bills along with nearly 10 tonnes of CO2.

Unlike other forms of microgeneration featured here, biomass systems require fuel to work. Fuel costs generally depend on the distance between you and your supplier and will usually be more favourable if you live in an area that does not have a gas supply. It is most cost-effective when a local fuel source is used, which has the added benefit of local investment and employment.

Maintenance

Like all boilers, a biomass boiler will require regular servicing.

Is it for me?

You will need ample storage space for the fuel, appropriate access to the boiler for loading and a local fuel supplier. The installation must comply with all safety and building regulations. Wood can only be burned in exempted appliances, in compliance with the Clean Air Act 1993.

> **"It is most cost effective when a local fuel source is used, which has the added benefit of local investment and employment"**

▼ Like all boilers, a biomass boiler will require regular servicing

MICROGENERATION: Planning permission

Following changes made to planning laws last year, many microgeneration technologies – including solar-powered systems and ground-source heat pumps – no longer need planning permission in England, so long as they adhere to certain size criteria. Exceptions apply for listed buildings and buildings in conservation areas and World Heritage sites. Permission is necessary for the installation of wind turbines, small hydro and air- and water-source heat pumps.

GREEN TARIFFS

Nowadays most electricity companies offer what is called a 'green tariff', which gives customers the opportunity to buy electricity generated from sustainable sources. In theory, this is a great way of easing people's conscience over their electricity usage and creates greater demand for renewables. However, electricity can't be generated without at least some impact to the environment, so the measure of just exactly *how* green any particular green tariff is varies from supplier to supplier. Before going ahead and opting for your existing supplier's green tariff, it is worth taking a few minutes to compare its eco-credentials and prices with other companies' tariffs first. For more information and a comparison of the various green tariffs on offer by UK suppliers visit energy watchdog Energy Watch's website at *www.energywatch.org.uk* and click on Help and Advice/Green Tariffs.

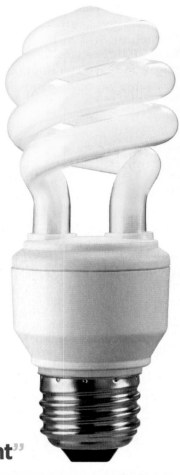

> ## "Electricity can't be generated without some impact on the environment"

To find out exactly what your carbon footprint is, go to the easy-to-use Act on CO2 Calculator at *http://actonco2 .direct.gov.uk/index.html.*

Good green buys

HY Mini wind turbine
The handheld HY Mini wind turbine offers a revolutionary way of capturing renewable power for your iPod, mobile phones, PDA, mp3, digital camera and more, by harnessing the power of the wind. Can be attached to bicycle handlebars, windows etc. Available from www. footprint-es.com, priced £44.99.

Power meter
The plug-in Power Meter from EcoSaver allows the energy conscious homeowner to easily and quickly measure precisely the amount of energy being consumed by individual appliances around the home. The plug and play device also calculates the cost of running each appliance. Available from www.footprint-es.com, priced £14.99.

Solar Gorilla
The Solar Gorilla represents the next generation of solar charger, capable of powering the most energy-sapping devices and gadgets on the move. Solar Gorilla's 24 volt and 5 volt USB socket make it the ultimate renewable power station for your notebook, cellphone, iPod and many more devices. Available from www.footprint-es.com, priced £139.95.

Radiator booster
This easy-to-use plug-in, low-energy device helps you get the most out of the energy you use. Put it on top of your radiator to fan warm air back into the room – and, in doing so, you'll reduce the time it takes to heat your room by up to 50%, thus reducing the demand for power on the boiler. Available from www.footprint-es.com, £14.99.

Radiator reflector panels
Such a simple idea, these reflective panels are stuck behind your radiators to reflect heat that would otherwise go into heating the wall back into the room. Helps reduce heat loss and cut your energy bills by up to 15%. Available from www.ecofirst.net, prices start from £21.50 for a twin-pack.

THE LOW CARBON BUILDINGS PROGRAMME

If you are thinking of installing a microgeneration system at your home, you may be eligible for a grant of up to £2,500 through the Government's Low Carbon Buildings Programme. Here's a summary of what's on offer and how to apply.

Phase one of the Low Carbon Buildings Programme was launched on April 1 2006 to provide people with grants for solar panels, wind turbines and other microgeneration systems.

The scheme aims to increase the use of emerging technologies and promote domestic energy generation as part of an holistic approach to reducing carbon emissions from buildings.

Householders can apply for grants of up to £2,500 per property towards the cost of installing a certified product by a certified installer. The level of grant depends on the type of system being installed (see pages 30 to 39 for details).

Since 2006, there have been more than 10,000 successful applications in the UK, totalling almost £13 million in funding. Nearly 6,000 of these were for solar water-heating systems and more than £7 million has been given for photovoltaic installations, which use energy from the sun to create electricity.

A second phase has been running concurrently with phase one and provides grants to community groups, as well as the public and non-profit sectors. Both programmes are managed by the Energy Saving Trust on behalf of the Department of Energy and Climate Change (DECC).

How do I apply?

(1) Complete the energy-efficiency measures required by the programme (see above), obtain planning permission for your installation if necessary and get a quote from an accredited installer.

(2) Make an application online at *www. lowcarbonbuildings.org.uk*. Claims are usually processed within 25 working days.

(3) After receiving a grant offer via email, order the equipment and begin installing the technology. The grant validity period ranges from three months to one year depending on the technology and whether it is being installed on a new or existing building.

(4) After completing the installation and paying the installer, submit the claim documents to the Energy Saving Trust.

(5) The claim will be checked and, if in order, the grant will be issued within 25 working days of receipt of all the documentation.

Applications are accepted on a rolling first-come-first-served basis. You can apply for funding for up to three different technologies on one building, with a maximum of three different buildings funded.

For more information about the scheme, including full details of conditions and a list of certified products and installers, visit *www.lowcarbonbuildings.org.uk*.

Am I eligible for a grant?

Grants are provided towards the cost of installing solar photovoltaics, wind turbines, small hydro, solar thermal hot water, ground source heat pumps and bio-energy. Renewable combined heat and power (CHP), MicroCHP and fuel cells will also qualify for funding once accredited installers and products become available.

Applicants must demonstrate their house meets certain criteria, including all of the following energy-efficiency measures:

- insulated loft (270mm of mineral wool loft insulation or suitable alternative)

- cavity wall insulation (if the house has cavity walls)

- low-energy lightbulbs in all appropriate light fittings

- basic controls for a heating system, including a room thermostat and a programmer or timer (note: you may be eligible for grants for energy-efficiency measures, see right for more details)

Applicants must also be UK residents and own the property (which must be in the UK, excluding the Isle of Man and the Channel Islands) for which the grant is wanted.

The property must also be a permanent building (mobile homes, caravans, houseboats etc. are not eligible) and have planning permission for the installation if required.

WHEN BUYING NEW HOUSEHOLD APPLIANCES, ASK THE RETAILER TO TAKE AWAY YOUR OLD ONES FOR RECYCLING

APPLIANCES

TVs, radios, laptops, DVD players, tumble dryers, games consoles, Hi-Fis, coffee machines, toasters, dishwashers.... The sheer number of electrical appliances we have in our homes is breathtaking, and our love for them comes at a huge price to the environment. Here we show you how to use your appliances more efficiently and with minimal impact on the planet

Choosing the right appliance

01 RESEARCH

Make sure you do your research before you buy. Compare different products and look out for those with the Energy Saving Recommended logo.

energy saving™
recommended

02 ASK FOR ADVICE

If you are not sure or want to know more about a specific product, then ask for advice. Sales staff are on hand to answer your technical enquires and should have a good working knowledge of the features and benefits of each product. Here are a few things you might want to check before you buy:

- Is it 'Energy Saving Recommended'?

- How much energy does the product use when on standby?

- Does the product have any special energy-efficient features, such as automatic standby or screen blanking (which allows you to listen to digital radio on your TV without using excess energy)?

- What is the expected lifespan of the product?

- AND REMEMBER - buy quality items that will last. If something is very cheap, there is normally a very good reason for it.

Did you know...?

The standby function on any particular device can use up to 80% of the energy that it needs to run properly, all of which is wasted, and each home in the UK has an average of 12 appliances on standby or charging. Switching your TV, DVD player and Sky box off every time (rather than leaving it on standby) can save up to £50 a year on your electricity bill.

WASHING MACHINES

Washing machines are one of the biggest symbols of household convenience around. The trouble with them is that they use a lot of power and water, yet getting rid of them in favour of more traditional methods is unlikely to ever win support with the masses. The good news is that there are a lot of models available now that use less energy and water than conventional models.

In fact, a new machine uses about half the water and energy of the average 10-year-old machine. Many efficient appliances use less than 50 litres of water per wash.

For the most energy-efficient machines check out the Energy Saving Trust website at *www.est.org.uk*. For a list of the most efficient machines ranked by water use visit *www.waterwise.org.uk*.

Keep it simple

STEP 1

Around 90% of the energy used to wash our clothes is used to heat the water. Washing at 40C uses half the amount of energy as it does to wash at 90C and is usually perfectly adequate for a decent wash. Better still, wash at 30C.

STEP 2

Don't wash clothes just because you have worn them once. This is particularly relevant to outer garments like jumpers which don't need to be washed after being worn just once – unless you are particularly stinky.

STEP 3

Fill the washer! It is an environmental crime to wash less than a full load of laundry as it needlessly wastes water and energy. But don't overfill the machine otherwise it won't clean effectively. If you must use the machine with only half a load, make sure you select the half-load option.

TUMBLE DRYERS

If you can't get by without a tumble dryer, make sure the one you buy is the most energy efficient available and preferably has in-built sensors to detect when the clothes are dry and switches the machine off accordingly. A lot of energy is wasted with dryers still going when everything inside is bone dry. Some newer models incorporate heat pumps which use waste heat to warm the air going in, making them more efficient.

Keep it simple

STEP 1
Whenever possible dry your clothes outside on a washing line or indoors on a clothes horse. If it is a warm, sunny day don't spin your clothes, let the sun do the work for you.

STEP 2
Use the spin on your washing machine to get rid of excess water before you dry them in a tumble dryer.

STEP 3
If you have a tumble dryer try to keep it in a warm place as it will help it work more efficiently.

DISHWASHERS

Dishwasher enthusiasts often cling to the claim that using a dishwasher uses less power and water than washing up by hand. And according to studies which have been carried out, they are right. Some researchers have found that some modern dishwashers, which use as little as 10 litres of water a wash, use up to six times less water to wash a full load than the average person uses to wash the same amount in the sink. However, this is as much to do with poor washing-up habits and practices than it is technological improvements. And don't forget that making a dishwasher takes a huge amount of energy and raw materials which can counteract potential benefits. For a list of the most energy efficient dishwashers check out the Energy Saving Trust website at *www.est.org.uk*. For a list of the most efficient machines ranked by water use visit *www.waterwise.org.uk*.

Keep it simple

STEP 1

Don't pre-wash your dishes before you put them in the dishwasher. Independent tests demonstrate that with modern dishwashers there is little difference in the final levels of cleaning between pre-washed and unwashed dishes. Just make sure you scrape off the bigger bits of excess food into the bin, and you'll save water.

However, if you have some really dirty dishes then don't put them in your dishwasher – it's probably best to wash these by hand.

STEP 2

Try to use eco-friendly dishwasher powder or liquid, as these won't contain phosphates or other chemicals that are harmful to the environment.

STEP 3

Set your temperature cycle to 'low'. If you live in a hard-water area, fill up with salt in your dishwasher's hard-water softener. This means any detergent you use is maximised in the softer water, and your dishwasher will last longer, needing fewer parts, and so have a smaller carbon footprint.

STEP 4

Make sure you regularly clean out your dishwasher filter. It helps your machine run at maximum efficiency, getting more dishes clean for less energy.

FRIDGES AND FREEZERS

We spend £1.8 billion as a nation cooling and freezing our food and drink in the home every year. However, some major technological advances in the design of home fridges and freezers has led to the best of today's models being in the region of 60% more energy efficient than many of the older versions. If you're looking to buy a new fridge or freezer – as with any new elecrical appliance at home – make sure it has the Energy Saving Recommended logo and you could save up to £36 a year in running costs and cut your carbon dioxide emissions by around 140kg for a fridge-freezer and £12 and 45kg for a fridge. Chest freezers tend to use less energy than upright freezers because the cold air does not fall out of them when they are opened. However, uprights are easier to organise so the door is not usually left open for so long.

energy saving
recommended

Save Cash!
Choosing the right fridge could save you £36 a year in running costs

Keep it simple

STEP 1
Defrosting food in the fridge helps the appliance do its job and reduces energy use.

STEP 2
A build up of ice reduces your freezer's efficiency so defrost regularly – but avoid frost-free appliances as they use more energy.

STEP 3
Wait for hot food to cool down completely before putting it in the fridge or freezer.

STEP 4
Position your fridge and freezer away from cookers, radiators, washing machines and other sources of heat, such as direct sunlight.

STEP 5
Try to keep your fridge and freezer full – it saves energy.

STEP 6
It is important to keep the black metal coils at the back of your fridge clean and dust free and far enough away from the wall to allow air to circulate.

IRONS

Only iron what you really need to, like shirts and skirts. If you are in the habit of ironing underwear, sheets and napkins, get out of it! We need to get serious about cutting our carbon footprint and having an ironed pillowcase is not going to help.

For clothes you must iron, make sure you fold them when you take them off the line or out of the tumble dryer. This will make it far quicker and easier to iron than scrunched up clothing.

Iron shirts when they are still very slightly damp. This makes ironing easier, reduces drying time and removes the need to use a steam iron.

De-calcify your iron by pouring a mixture of white vinegar and water into the steam cavity. Turn the iron on hot and let it steam for five minutes then pour the solution away and rinse.

ELECTRO-MADNESS

For almost every task in the kitchen there is now an electric-powered solution, whether it be a tin opener, carving knife or even mechanical bin lids!

These appliances may not all be the most energy-intensive products in the home, but when you add up all the energy and materials needed to manufacture and distribute them, you have to decide whether they are worth it. Choosing traditional hand-operated devices over electrical alternatives cost nothing to run, are usually cheaper to buy and less prone to breaking.

OVENS

Gas cookers and stoves typically use around half the amount of energy as electric ones. Where gas is not an option, ceramic hobs are better than rings, and induction rings are best of all. Slow-cookers operate at a far lower temperature and use less energy to cook a meal than a normal oven. Fan-assisted ovens are preferable too as they speed up cooking.

Digital damage

Energy Saving Recommended DAB radios use around 75% less electricity than a standard radio. If the next 6.8 million DAB radios bought in the UK are all Energy Saving Recommended we would save enough electricity to run the street lighting of the entire UK for a month.

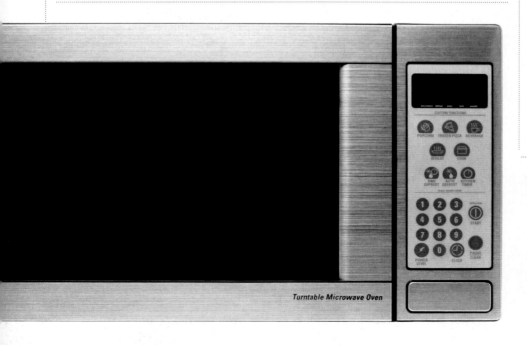

Turntable Microwave Oven

MICROWAVES

Microwaves use less energy to cook and are far quicker than ovens. The trouble with microwaves, however, is that they tend to increase consumption of ready-meals, which are a major source of packaging waste and have questionable health benefits.

TV AND HOME ENTERTAINMENT

The key to buying new home-entertainment appliances is to do some serious research before you go shopping. There are many energy-efficient options across every category available, but there are also plenty that use more energy than ever. New large flat-screen TVs, for example, can cost up to three times as much to run as traditional TVs – and have been the cause of much shock and dismay up and down the country when opening up the latest electricity bill.

The UK's DVDs and VCRs consume over £200 million in electricity each year, mainly because they are continuously left on standby.

Take a look at *www.gooshing.co.uk* for a wide range of consumer electronic goods ranked by their ethical credentials, including energy efficiency.

Save Cash!
You could save up to £50 a year simply by switching off your appliances rather than leaving them on standby

Keep it simple

STEP 1

Don't leave appliances on standby. The average household wastes £50 a year – or a tenth of their electricity bill – powering appliances on standby. Across the UK this is equivalent to the annual output of two power stations.

STEP 2

Choose integrated appliances. Fewer products means less electricity, so buying an integrated digital television, which combines a TV with a digital receiver, is good not only for your wallet but for the environment too.

APPLIANCES: WHAT TO LOOK OUT FOR

Here's a guide to the cash savings that can be made by changing to energy-efficient products, but we're not saying you should chuck out your old appliances to buy new ones – use them until they die. Savings listed assume replacing an average appliance purchased new in 1998 with an Energy Saving Recommended model of similar size, and an electricity cost of 12.96p/kWh.

APPLIANCE	EU ENERGY RATING	SAVING PER YEAR (UP TO)	CO2 SAVING PER YEAR (UP TO)
FRIDGE FREEZER	A+ OR A++	£36	140kg
UPRIGHT/CHEST FREEZER	A+ OR A++	£22	80kg
REFRIGERATOR	A+ OR A++	£12	45kg
WASHING MACHINE	A	£8	42kg
DISHWASHER	A	£12	48kg
INTEGRATED DIGITAL TV	A	£7	24kg

Savings for A++ cold appliances are on average £6/yr greater. Source: EST

Save Cash! Choosing the best rated products could save you up to £99 a year in running costs.

Energy Saving Recommended logo

Whenever you buy a new domestic appliance make sure it sports this. The idea is that whatever the product, and whichever the labelling system, all the consumer needs to do is look for the Energy Saving Recommended logo. It's your guarantee that the product has the highest level of energy efficiency in its category, and so will cost less to run and help prevent climate change. The EST works with the price-comparison site PriceRunner.co.uk so you can search and compare the energy-efficiency ratings and prices of different models at the Energy Saving Trust website at *www.est.org.uk*.

EU energy label

By law, this label must be shown on all refrigeration appliances, electric tumble dryers, washing machines, washer dryers, dishwashers, electric ovens, lamps, air conditioners and light bulbs. The labels shows levels of energy consumption and average annual running costs, as well as additional useful information depending on the category. Products are rated from A to G, where A is most efficient and G is least efficient. The only exceptions are refrigeration products which range from A** to G. Laundry and dishwashing labels also have A to G ratings for washing, spin and/or drying performance.

SEDBUK rating

SEDBUK stands for the seasonal efficiency of domestic boilers in the UK and provides a basis for fair comparison of different boiler models by arranging boilers into bands according to their efficiency. SEDBUK rates boilers on a scale of A to G, where band A is the most efficient and band G the least. Old domestic boilers have a typical seasonal efficiency of between 55% and 65% (band G on the SEDBUK ranking system), whilst modern gas condensing boilers are usually 90% efficient or better, putting them in band A. For more information on energy efficient boilers see the Heating and Insulation section on page 27 or visit *www.boilers.org.uk*.

BRFC window ratings

Under the British Fenestration Rating Council (BFRS) Domestic Window Energy Rating scheme, windows are assessed for their efficiency at retaining heat. They are ranked on a similar looking A-to-G rating as the EU label and assess the performance of the whole window, including frame and glass. Because this is a voluntary scheme used by the glazing industry not all windows currently carry the logo. For more information go to *www.bfrc.org*.

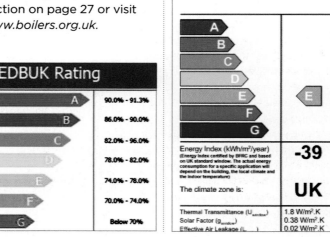

Energy
Manufacturer
Model

Washing machine

More efficient
A
B → **B**
C
D
E
F
G

Less efficient

Energy consumption kWh/cycle **1.75**
(Based on standard test results for 60°C)

SEDBUK Rating

A	90.0% - 91.3%
B	86.0% - 90.0%
C	82.0% - 96.0%
D	78.0% - 82.0%
E	74.0% - 78.0%
F	70.0% - 74.0%
G	Below 70%

Energy Window

A
B
C
D
E → E
F
G

Energy Index (kWh/m²/year)
(Energy Index certified by BFRC and based on UK standard window. The actual energy consumption for a specific application will depend on the building, the local climate and the indoor temperature.)
-39

The climate zone is: **UK**

Thermal Transmittance (U_window)	1.8 W/m².K
Solar Factor (g_window)	0.38 W/m².K
Effective Air Leakage (L)	0.02 W/m².K

GADGETS: ECO-TECHNOLOGY TO SAVE ENERGY

While buying more gadgets for your house is not good for the planet, if you need to replace any of those standard appliances, there are plenty of energy-efficient options available. Here are some of our favourites this year...

ENERGY MONITORS

Real-time home energy monitors show how much electricity you are using, how much it is costing you and how many kilograms of carbon dioxide you are producing. The user can quickly learn which appliances cost the most money to run and use the most energy by watching the data changes on the display. You'll find a good range available at *www.footprint-es.com*. Prices range from £44.99 for the Efergy Elite to £99.99 for the designer Wattson.

SLOW COOKERS

Slow cookers use far less energy than conventional ovens because of their very low wattage. The Morphy Richards Ecolectric slow cooker (pictured) uses up to 44% less energy compared to standard slow cookers, without compromising on performance, thanks to its ultra low wattage and unique insulated lid. Available from www. goodenergyshop.co.uk, priced £34.25.

STANDBY SAVER

It is well known that the amount of devices left on standby wastes an astonishing amount of energy in the UK. To address this issue several manufacturers have come up with devices that make it easier for us to turn things off properly.

The Bye Bye Standby (pictured), for example, uses a remote control and socket system to turn appliances off at the wall. Perfect for when sockets are difficult to reach or when you are watching TV in bed and don't want to get out and turn it off because you're warm and snug. To see a range of standby savers, visit *www.footprint-es.com*.

ENERGY SENSE KETTLE

This attractive see-through kettle from Kenwood has been fitted with a technologically advanced element to give up to 35% energy savings over standard design kettles. Available at www.houseoffraser.co.uk, priced from £44.99.

90% OF THE ELECTRICITY WE USE TO LIGHT CONVENTIONAL LIGHT BULBS IS WASTED IN THE FORM OF HEAT. ENERGY-SAVING ALTERNATIVES CAN SIGNIFICANTLY REDUCE YOUR ENERGY BILLS AND YOUR HOME'S CO2 EMISSIONS

LIGHTING

The Energy Saving Trust says that if every house in the UK fitted just three low-energy compact fluorescent light bulbs (CFL), we could power every street light in the UK with the energy saved. Here we've got some more useful figures to help you see the light

Save £££s
Simply changing to energy-saving lightbulbs could save you £128.42 over the bulb's life

ENERGY-SAVING BULBS

Energy-saving bulbs can use as little as a fifth of the energy that a standard bulb uses. Check this conversion table to find the equivalent energy saving in wattage.

ENERGY-SAVING EQUIVALENT
5-7W
25W

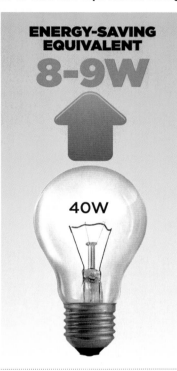

ENERGY-SAVING EQUIVALENT
8-9W
40W

ENERGY-SAVING EQUIVALENT
11-14W
60W

ENERGY-SAVING EQUIVALENT
20-23W
100W

LIFETIME COSTS

Comparing compact fluorescent lamps (CFLs) with general lighting service (GLS) lamps. Based on an electricity price of 12.96p/kWh. Note: Figures do not take into account the heat replacement effect.

	100W TUNGSTEN FILAMENT OR INCANDESCENT LAMP	20W CFL
COST	50p	£2.00
LAMP LIFE (IN HOURS)	1,000	12,000
TOTAL BULB COST (OVER LIFE OF 1 CFL)	£6.00	£2.00
TOTAL ELECTRICITY COST (OVER LIFE OF 1 CFL)	£155.52	£31.10
TOTAL COSTS	£161.52	£33.10
SAVINGS	N/A	£128.42

IT IS ESTIMATED THAT AROUND 70,000 CHEMICALS ARE USED IN CLEANING PRODUCTS AND TOILETRIES AND YET LESS THAN A QUARTER OF THESE HAVE BEEN FULLY TESTED FOR SAFETY

HOUSEHOLD CLEANING

Bleach, limescale busters, antibacterial sprays, drain unblockers, foaming oven cleaners, multi-purpose wipes – the cleaning products market is huge and feeds on our fear of germs and infection. But how safe are the products, and what are they doing to the planet when we flush them down the drain? Read on to find out...

KEEP IT CLEAN: the truth on products

We might think that keeping our homes clean is one way of avoiding illness, but what if the chemicals we clean our homes with actually damage our health and the planet?

When it comes to cynical marketing there is perhaps no worse a culprit than the producers of home-cleaning products who manipulate our fear of disease and infection with ruthless ability.

It is common sense that a dirty home acts as a breeding ground for germs and harmful bacteria. But most detergent companies will have us believe (through their various multi million-pound advertising campaigns and promotions) that if our homes are anything less than spotless and sterile, we are taking perilous risks for ourselves and our children. At best this is misleading and unhelpful, at worst it is hugely irresponsible.

The truth is that you don't need to obliterate every bit of grease and grime in order to have a healthy home, and many of the products on display go far and beyond the call of duty, and there are concerns that they can actually pose a risk in themselves.

Ever since synthetic detergents started to appear in the 1940s our obsession with absolute cleanliness and sterilisation has been encouraged and nurtured. Unfortunately, research into the safety of these synthetics has been far less developed, and there are serious fears attached to the potential effects many of these chemicals are having on people and the wider environment.

Synthetics, which are commonly made with petrochemicals, can have a bad effect on skin and do not biodegrade efficiently,

A clean bill of health?

A study of more than 3,500 people at the Municipal Institute of Medical Research in Barcelona found that the incidence of doctor-diagnosed asthma was significantly higher among people using cleaning sprays at least four days a week.

leading to an excess of pollutants for the waterways to cope with.

Worse still is the link between the massive increase in chemicals and respiratory problems, such as asthma, and an increasing number of scientific studies are bearing this out. According to a study by the Municipal Institute of Medical Research in Barcelona, using household cleaning sprays and air fresheners regulary can increase the risk of asthma by 30 to 50%.

It is largely down to the consumer to make sure they are buying home-cleaning products that are not potentially damaging to them. The good news is that are plenty of alternative products available on the market that are both natural and effective.

Air fresheners

Air fresheners and other aerosols such as polish, spray deodorant and hairspray have been linked with diarrhoea and earache in infants and headaches and depression in mothers. Plug in fresheners are even worse since not only do they require electricity to run but have been linked with respiratory problems.

Try using: an orange studded with cloves and rolled in cinnamon

Anti-bacterial cleaners

Overuse of these products runs the risk of leading to super-resilient bacteria, in the same way that many doctors are concerned by the over-prescription of antibiotics.

Try using: a few drops of tea tree oil – a natural antiseptic and disinfectant – mixed with a couple of cups of water and use a spray bottle to administer. Leave for 30 mins and then wipe away with warm water.

Floor Cleaners

The NHS warns that floor cleaners are a common trigger for asthma attacks because of the fumes given off by solvents and other chemicals. Selecting the right type of floor cleaner will be especially important for parents of young children who are likely to be crawling all over it.

Try using: Ecover's Floor Soap which uses natural ingredients for its cleaning power

Multi-surface cleaners

These are made of a concoction of detergents, grease cutting agents, solvents and disinfectants. Among them is butyl cellosolve, a neurotoxin that represses the nervous system and has been linked to reproductive problems. ethylene glycol, which is a neurotoxin and a nasal irritant.

Try using: brands from Bio-D, Botanic Gold or Ecover

Oven cleaners

These contain sodium hydroxide and sulphuric acid which are both extremely hazardous and corrosive substances to humans. They also cause untold damage to ecosystems and prevent good bacteria in your septic tank from working properly.

Try using: vinegar for baked-on deposits. For microwaves, place few slices of lemon in a bowl of cold water and turn the machine on for a few minutes

Window Cleaners

Most window cleaners are made up principally of water with added ammonia to cut through the grease. Ammonia is corrosive and can cause burns and irritations.

Try using: E-Cloth's glass polishing cloth, an effective glass cleaner requiring no detergent. Otherwise use white vinegar with newspapers

Washing-up liquids

Since washing-up liquids come into regular contact with the skin they do not contain the same level of toxic chemicals that most household detergents have.

Try using: Ecover's Washing-Up liquid or Citra Dish, which use only natural ingredients

Laundry Detergents

As well as corrosive substances like sodium hydrochlorite and calcium hypochlorite many detergents incorporate bleaching agents and artificial musks.

Try using: EcoBalls, which use no detergent, at all (see p59)

Toilet Cleaners

A typical toilet cleaner will contain sodium hypochlorite, which is known to irritate and corrode the mucous membranes.

Try using: Bio-D Toilet Cleaner. For a deep clean, use a dessert spoon's worth of Ecover's non-chlorine bleach, swirl it around and leave overnight

Limescale Removers

Many of these contain sulfamic acid, which is toxic to lungs and mucous membranes. Skin contact with this acid is corrosive and causes irritation, dryness and burning.

Try using: Ecover's citrus-based limescale remover. To prevent limescale build-up, try a Magnoball

EASY STEP-BY-STEP WORKSHOPS

2010 EDITION

BUILD A BETTER WEBSITE

YOUR COMPLETE GUIDE TO WEB DESIGN

BUILD A SITE IN **30** MINUTES

MAGBOOK

FROM THE EXPERTS AT
COMPUTER SHOPPER
MacUser
PC PRO

...th images

Limiting your content

Making money from your website

How to... Use Amazon Associates schema

Finding inspiration

View your **FREE** sample at **www.computershopperbooks.co.uk**

TOXIC SHOCK: Man-made chemical nasties

All the bottles of bleaches and cleaners we've grown up with are so commonplace we rarely think about what might be in them, or what they are doing to us or our environment

A cause of concern with many household cleaning products is that they contain a high level of man-made toxic chemicals that could have dangerous implications for both our health and the wider environment. These can be broadly categorised into two main types: **persistent organic pollutants (POPs)** and **endocrine-disrupting chemicals (EDCs)**.

POPs are chemical-based and primarily the products and by-products of heavy industry and chemical manufacturing. POPs are bio-accumulative, which means they can be stored in body fat and passed on to foetuses and into the food chain, and they are persistent, meaning they are hard to break down and remain in the environment for decades.

They can travel long distances by air and water, thus giving them global reach. POPs can cause cancer and affect the nervous, reproductive and immune systems of both people and animals.

EDC is the term for any chemical that interferes with the endocrine system, which controls the body's growth and functions. EDCs can cause mutation and other adverse effects in both humans and animals during growth, development and reproduction. This makes babies and children most at risk. Unfortunately, under existing labelling laws consumers are rarely provided with the detailed information they need to make the safest choices.

Top tips: change your cleaning habits

• **Don't tip toxic household waste down the drain. Things like paint, car oil and battery fluid should be taken to your local recycling centre for proper and safe disposal**

• Remove strong odours from the fridge by putting half a lemon inside and leaving it overnight

• **Open windows regularly to air rooms**

• You don't need to use a different cleaner for every single task. A good multi-surface cleaner can be used on pretty much any washable surface

• **You don't need to use 'kill all' chemicals. Baking soda is a very effective cleaning agent and can be used for many jobs around the house, from scrubbing sinks and bath tubs to cleaning the stove and fridges**

• A dirty roasting tin can be cleaned simply and effectively by adding a splash of washing up liquid into about a centimetre of cold water, then simmering on the stove for a while before rinsing and cleaning

• **Before loading the dishwasher scrape off any excess food.**

• Use cuts of old clothes, towels and sheets to clean

• **Read the label! Avoid harsh chemicals like chlorine and try to buy products that will biodegrade quickly and completely in the waterways. Many conventional products leave toxic residues behind.**

• For really stubborn pots and pans, scrub them lightly with a cream cleaner and leave them to soak overnight.

In focus: E-cloths

With 'Perfect Cleaning Without Water' as its strapline, you might think that the manufacturers of E-Cloths have found some kind of wonder product. And in many ways they have.

E-Cloths contain no chemicals and do not require chemicals to clean. True to the claims of makers Enviroproducts, the cloths really do work using just water and in light of this won this year's Good Housekeeping Green Living Award.

The secret to their success are the millions of wedge-shaped fibres in each cloth, which measure 1/100th the width of a human hair. It is these specially designed fibres that give the cloths their remarkable cleaning capability and their high absorbency. Unlike conventional cloths, as you draw an E-cloth across a surface, the fibres clean by breaking up, trapping and absorbing dirt and grease into the material.

E-cloths can be washed and reused at least 300 times. The original cloths were designed for all hard surfaces but are especially effective on glass, chrome and stainless steel. The range now includes dusters, towels, face cloths and more. Thanks to their lack of chemicals, E-Cloths are also ideal for use in homes and offices where there are allergy sufferers; an achievement that has earned them a Consumer Award by Allergy UK.

Ecover

Ecover is the world's largest producer of ecological detergents and cleansing products and sells in more than 20 countries. The company now boasts more than 30 products in its portfolio, ranging from laundry detergents and floor cleaners to hand washes and car wash and wax. Widely available in all supermarkets and most convenience stores.

Ecover is the world's largest producer of ecological detergents

ECOLOGICAL
SQUIRT ECO
ALL PURPOSE CLEANER
ECOVER
NATURALLY POWERFUL
for people who care

LOGICAL
REAM CLEANER
ON-SCRATCH
COVER
FFECTIVE CLEANING WITH
ATURAL POWER
for people who care

Good green buys

Ecoballs
Ecozone Ecoballs are a detergent-free, environmentally friendly alternative to traditional washing liquid or powder. They work by ionising the water, allowing it to get deep into clothes and lift the dirt away, and are fully hypoallergenic – good news for people sensitive to phosphates and optical brighteners. www.footprint-es.com, £34.95.

Ecoballs get your clothes clean with no washing powder

Toilet Descaler
Simply drop one of these ingenious Magnoloo descaler rings into the cistern to keep your toilet free from a build up of deposits for up to five years. This chemical-free magnetic ring will polarize the calcium preventing unsightly stains and lime scale build up. www.ecozone.co.uk, £14.99 for a pack of two.

Toilet Smell Killer
Effective, ecological and long-lasting, the Toilet Smell Killer from Ecozone overcomes even the most persistent odours. Hung in the toilet bowl, it works by the known reaction of high grade steel combined with water and cleaning the air of all unpleasant smells without chemicals. Guaranteed for life. Size: 5cm (diameter). www.footprint-es.com, £16.99.

RATHER THAN THROWING UNWANTED FURNITURE AWAY, WHY NOT DONATE IT TO A CHARITY THAT HELPS THE UNEMPLOYED, SINGLE PARENTS, THE ELDERLY, DISABLED AND FAMILIES ON LOW INCOMES?

FURNISHING

We all like to live in a comfortable and beautiful home, and decorating it to our individual tastes and styles is a joyous process – but, with chemical-laden paints, irresponsibly sourced timber and energy-intensive furniture manufacturing, it can be an eco-minefield. Here's the lowdown on decking out a green home

When DIY-mania hammered into Britain in the 1980s it captured the nation's imagination – and wallets – like no other pastime had before. From worktops and tables to windows and loft conversions, it seemed there was nothing that stood beyond the self-perceived capabilities of the do-it-yourself enthusiast.

Since then, barely a home has been spared, as this army of home improvers continues unabated to devote its free time to destruction, design and redevelopment.

But while our annual spend on DIY and home furnishings has topped £23 billion, it is the environmental cost of this love-affair that is starting to make the headlines. Far from making our ideal homes we are making them hotbeds for harmful chemicals and toxins, while stripping the earth of valuable resources in the name of what's questionably titled 'home improvement'.

Here we take a look at the most common materials used in home renovation, the impact they have on ourselves and the wider environment, and what we can do about it.

▼ **Annual spend on DIY and home furnishings recently topped £23 billion**

Did you know...?

- **A WHO report found painters and decorators were 40% more likely to develop lung cancer because of the toxic content of paints and supplies.**
- **Every year around two million pieces of furniture are re-homed through the Furniture Re-Use Network, leading to 85,000 tonnes of waste being diverted from landfill.**

Freecycle: save piles of cash, reduce waste and furnish your house for free

Freecycle is an online community, broken into geographical groups, where people can turn trash into treasure without exchanging a penny.

The grassroots movement is the brainchild of American Deron Beal who started out by sending an email to about 30 or 40 friends inviting them to take part in his scheme.

Since that first email in 2003 the concept has achieved worldwide recognition with thousands of local groups and more than seven million members in 75 countries as far flung as Mexico, Nepal and Romania.

The way it works is that people join their local group and then advertise online what they are trying to get rid

of, whether it be an old bed, a set of golf clubs or even a pile of rubble. Different rules apply to different groups, but generally once you have given something away once you can then take from other members.

Freecycle's aim is to build a 'worldwide gifting movement that

reduces waste, saves precious resources and eases the burden on our landfills while enabling our members to benefit from the strength of a larger community.'

So far it's doing well. It is estimated that more than 300 tonnes of would-be waste is being kept out of landfill sites every day thanks to the Freecycle Network.

To find your nearest group, go to *www.freecycle.org*, enter the name of your nearest town or city in the search box and click 'Go'. Once you have found your nearest group, click on the name and you will be taken to the group website. From there follow the onscreen instructions to join up.

PAINTS

The lead and other toxic components of older paints have been replaced with titanium oxide (TiO2). However, the compound has its own far-reaching environmental implications, using a large amount of energy in its manufacture. Modern-day synthetic paints are made from petrochemicals, use huge amounts of energy in their production and create a lot of toxic waste. Most paints – particularly gloss paints – also contain volatile organic compounds (VOCs) which can cause headaches, allergic reaction, nausea and other health problems.

Try using...

... Natural paints made from biodegradable materials. They are usually either water- or alcohol-based, making them far more benign. Check the tin closely though as even these can contain harmful additives such as synthetic alkyds and white spirit. Paints that avoid harsh chemicals altogether are best.

PAINT STRIPPERS

Anyone who has ever tried removing paint with sandpaper will know that it is no mean feat. So much so that manufacturers had to delve deep into the store of toxic substances to come up with an easy-to-use solution.

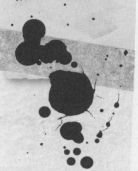

Try using...

... New effective water-based strippers that are now available. Visit *www.ecosolutions.co.uk* for a range of eco-friendly alternatives to the chemical-rich products on the market.

TIMBER

The UK is one of the world's largest timber consumers with annual imports equivalent to six million hectares of forest. But, our insatiable demand for it to build homes, make furnishings and furniture and turn into paper comes at a heavy environmental price. Much of the wood sold in the UK is not from sustainable sources, meaning that precious natural habitats and carbon stores are being lost.

Try using...

... Reclaimed and salvaged wood when possible. If you need to buy new wood make sure it's certified as being legitimately sourced from sustainable forests by the Forestry Stewardship Council. Avoid exotic woods from ancient forests, such as mahogany and teak, and, if possible, buy wood from sustainable UK forests.

PVC WINDOWS

PVC is an unplasticised polyvinyl chloride described by Greenpeace as an 'environmental poison throughout its lifecycle'. Once welcomed as the next-to-no-maintenance alternative to timber and widely used in buildings since, time has shown that PVC degrades over time as wood does.

Try using...

... Timber framed windows, although you should expect to be paying far more than you would for PVC.

CURTAINS & TEXTILES

European law dictates, quite wisely, that the fabrics used in upholstery must be flame retardant. The trouble with this is that many retardants are brominated flame retardants (BFRs), which have been linked with liver, hormone and reproduction problems.

Good wood

If you are buying new wood, make sure it has the FSC (Forestry Stewardship Council) logo. It's your guarantee that you are not contributing to global forest destruction or the unethical displacement of forest communities. Go to www.fsc-uk.org.

Try using...

... Products protected with Borax. It's made from naturally occurring mineral salts, borates, and has long been recognised as an effective flame retardant due to its capability to prevent smouldering. But because they're water-soluble, borates are not suitable for clothing or materials that have to be washed regularly.

COTTON

Cotton uses more synthetic fertilisers than any other crop in the world, and accounts for around of 25% of all pesticide use.

CARPETS & FLOORING

A Greenpeace study noted the presence of organotins, permethrin and brominated flame retardants in new carpets as 'particularly undesirable given their hazardous properties, a matter which therefore demands urgent attention'.

Try using...

... Organic cotton. In the UK, Marks and Spencer is just one of a number of high-street retailers boosting their eco-credentials by incorporating more organic cotton into their brands. Organic cotton offers a toxin-free alternative to conventional types and should be the preferred choice wherever possible.

Try using...

... Carpets made from 100% natural materials. Otherwise try sustainably sourced flooring from natural materials, such as wood, linoleum, cork and ceramic. Use carpets without synthetic latex backings. These backings are non-biodegradable and contain a cocktail of chemicals, including styrene, a possible carcinogen.

ARTIFICIAL FERTILISERS CAN CONTAMINATE SOIL AND WATER IN YOUR GARDEN AND CAN GET INTO THE FOOD CHAIN

GARDEN

Until a few years after WWII, most gardens were used to grow food using hard graft, some knowledge of nature and a real need to put food on the kitchen table. Since then, vegetable patches have been turned to flower beds and decking, and greenhouses replaced with garden sheds full of mowers, weedkillers and slug pellets. Here are the facts to get you back to nature, and help you make the most of your garden without damaging the planet

Not all doom and gloom

Things are definitely improving. Organic produce is one of the fastest-growing sectors in food and drink shopping, and our desire to revert to sustainable practices is being seen across all areas of our lives.

While many modern gardening practices may be out of kilter with nature, there are signs that traditional methods are making a comeback. Home composting, for example, is on the increase, water butts sell out each summer and media attention is encouraging us all back to natural ways of doing things.

But there is still more to do. By choosing natural and sustainable gardening methods it is not just the soil, vegetation and wildlife in our back gardens that benefit, but the wider environment too, by indirectly reducing the pressure on natural resources and lowering greenhouse gas emissions.

Patio heaters

If there is any one image that reflects the monumental challenge we have in tackling climate change today, it is that of a group of people huddling around a patio heater outside on a cold autumn or winter evening. These resource-guzzling monstrosities require huge amounts of energy to run and almost all of it is wasted. Yet despite this, patio heaters have become one of the top selling additions to our gardens in recent years.

"These resource-guzzling monstrosities require huge amounts of energy"

Room for change: lawns

Lawns may be as integral to the British garden as the English rose, but the fact is they require huge amounts of water and energy to grow and be maintained. Many gardeners also add fertilisers and herbicides to keep their lawns weed-free and green. One of the best things you can do if you have a big lawn is to let most of it return to nature or turn it into a flowerbed. By letting a patch of grass grow wild you will not only have to spend less time and money maintaining it, but it will encourage more wildlife into your garden too.

CHANGING HABITS
Create an eco-friendly garden

☒ Dont use artificial fertilisers and agrochemicals. These products use lots of energy and natural resources in their production, contaminate soil and water in your garden and can get into the food chain.

☑ Deter aphids with a fine spray of water from your washing-up.

☑ Grow your own food (see Food and Drink on page 92 for more information).

☑ Create a compost heap or a wormery for your organic waste (see page 20 for tips on how to make compost or visit www.bubblehouseworms.co.uk).

☑ Plant a hedgerow instead of a wall or fence – it is not only a valuable wildlife habitat but it absorbs carbon dioxide and costs less to maintain.

☑ If you are buying garden furniture or timber for sheds and decking, make sure it comes from a sustainable source. Look for the Forest Stewardship Council (FSC) logo or re-use timber from your local reclamation yard.

FSC

☒ Never use peat.

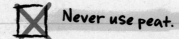

☑ Plastic bottles cut in half make ideal cloches for individual seedlings needing protection. Alternatively turn them upside down and put them in the ground by growing shrubs and trees to help you water directly to the roots. Use plastic take-away trays for growing seedlings.

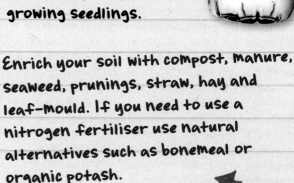

☑ Enrich your soil with compost, manure, seaweed, prunings, straw, hay and leaf-mould. If you need to use a nitrogen fertiliser use natural alternatives such as bonemeal or organic potash.

☒ Don't use weedkillers – use a hoe instead.

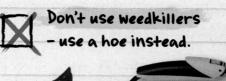

BEES

One in three UK bee colonies have been lost over the past two years and a similar story is being reported in other parts of the world.

A third of our food production relies on bees for pollination, and the scale of these recent deaths have sent shockwaves through the agricultural, scientific and political arenas.

With such reliance on the workings of the honey bee, it is feared its mass decline – and possible extinction – could result in many crops failing, leading to widespread hunger.

There are several theories about why bee populations are falling, but the growing consensus within the scientific and beekeeping communities is that the problem is multi-factorial. In February, the New Scientist reported that infections, lack of food, pesticides and breeding were having a synergistic effect, pushing bee survival to a 'lethal tipping point'. Saving the insects will depend on us appreciating this complexity and taking a multi-faceted response.

To stay alive, bees need to forage from February to October, and have beekeepers to look after them, space for hives and a vigilant public, which will tell experts when a swarm of bees needs collecting.

Swarms that have access to a continuous supply of pollen and nectar throughout the summer form strong colonies by autumn and are more likely to resist pests and disease, and so survive winter.

Earlier this year, the British Beekeepers' Association (BBKA) launched a campaign calling for the nation's gardeners to 'dig deep' to help our honey bees.

Philippa O'Brien, who designed the BBKA's bee garden at this year's Chelsea Flower Show, said: 'One of the best ways to help the honey bee is to plant a succession of flowering trees. Five or six large trees can provide as much forage for bees as an acre of wild flower meadow. They also provide a single source of nectar that bees find easy to harvest. Gardeners are tuned into the seasons: they know when there is likely to be a shortage of flowering plants locally –

and this is the time to plant pollen-rich annuals or hardy perennials.'

Tim Lovett, president of the BBKA, said: 'It doesn't matter whether you are planting acres or an allotment, a garden or a window box, or are responsible for landscaping roadsides or urban centres, creating a green environment with nectar- and pollen-rich flowers, trees and vegetables is best for bees, best for beekeepers and the best way to ensure we can all have a healthy and varied diet, thanks to honey-bee pollination.'

While gardeners are encouraged to do their bit to save the honey bee, the Government has announced £10 million of funding for research into pollinator decline. However, this pledge has come under fire by bee experts, who believe more money should be spent on bee health.

The BBKA raised 142,000 signatures in support of its £8 million programme for honey-bee health and received the support of the Women's Institute, which voted for a resolution urging the Government to provide funding for honey-bee health. The Public Accounts Committee has also expressed concern for the health of honey bees in light of their contribution to the agricultural economy and Defra's (Department for Environment, Food and Rural Affairs) failure to provide the funding needed for research and provision of solutions to the problems facing the insect.

The Soil Association is petitioning for a ban on the use of neonicotinoids in agriculture, pointing to strong evidence that the chemicals – a class of pesticide – are involved in bee deaths.

The UK's leading organic organisation is concerned that the cumulative impact of small doses of neonicotinoids on thousands of bees over time is affecting individual bee's ability to work and communicate effectively as part of a colony. Neonicotinoids have already been banned or suspended in France, Germany, Italy and Slovenia.

To find out more about the petition and how buying organic produce can help the plight of the bee, visit www.soilassociation.org and click on Why Organic?

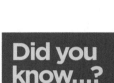

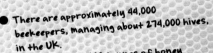

- There are approximately 44,000 beekeepers, managing about 274,000 hives, in the UK.
- They produce 6,000 tonnes of honey per year.
- Pollination contributes £200 million annually to the economy, making each hive's contribution about £700.
- The UK produces only 20% of the honey it consumes – the rest is imported.
- To collect a pound of honey, a bee might have to fly a distance equivalent to twice around the world. This is likely to involve more than 10,000 flower visits on, perhaps, 500 foraging trips.
- A queen bee can lay up to 2,000 eggs per day.
- In the summer, there are about 50,000 bees in a colony. This reduces to about 20,000 in winter.

IN PRACTICE:

RuralZed

The technologies inside may represent dreams of the future, but everything about the ruralZED zero carbon house is practical and affordable today.

This ground-breaking eco home took centre stage at the annual Eco Build exhibition at Earl's Court and is being hailed as the UK's first commercially viable and affordable house to achieve Level 6 under the Code for Sustainable Homes.

And what's more, it's ready to purchase as a kit of parts complete with solar panels, pellet boiler, bathrooms and kitchen for a mere £136,000 for a three bedroom house, less the price of the land and connection to street services and hard landscaping. This price includes for the installation of shortbore minipile foundations which work well for most sites, and includes for frame erection by specialists. With the heavy duty specialist work done, you can then finish the home as a self build or find a local building team.

The house was designed by ZEDfactory, a consortium of architects and specialist green manufacturers, and is delivered as a flat-pack kit in two secure shipping containers which can be erected in just three weeks, and the containers sent back to the factory for reuse.

Chief architect Bill Dunster claims the draughtproofed superinsulated home hardly needs space heating at all, and is capable of generating all of its annual electric demands from the grid-connected and highly durable monocrystalline solar electric panels. It can also generates half of its annual hot water demand from evacuated tube solar hot water collectors – with the remaining heat topped up by a small automated biomass woodpellet boiler. The house frames are built from WWF-certified FSC-sourced laminated timber similar to a medieval post and beam barn, and are designed to be strong enough to take the extra weight of terracotta, polished eco-concrete or stone floors, walls and ceilings – providing the essential thermal mass that prevents most timber frames from overheating as climate

▲ You can finish the home as a self build or get your local builder to complete the internals.

change accelerates. The walls contain around three times the amount of insulation as found in a normal home, keeping its residents warm in winter and cool in summer.

Electricity use in the house is kept to minimum thanks to its ultra-efficient domestic appliances and low energy lighting throughout.

Interior touches include worktops and tables made from recycled glass and a grey-water recycling system to conserve water.

The flexible design and construction of the kit means ruralZED can be built as detached, semi-detached or terraced houses with a range of different internal layouts and external appearances.

It is also possible to order an optional car port with enough extra solar electric panels to meet around 8,000 miles/year of electric car use.

The first terrace of six homes to receive the coveted government Code 6 as built certification has just been completed at Upton in Northampton, with another detached home completed in Dunkirk. And with around 70 units currently in the planning process, the designs are finding an enthusiastic welcome from local authorities wishing to demonstrate the viability of the zero carbon specification. With 70% of the UK's housing stock being built at densities of 50 homes per hectare, around three million new homes planned over the next ten years, the ruralZED system provides a solution that stops these new homes from further contributing to the national carbon footprint. ∎

"The house frames are built from WWF-certified FSC-sourced laminated timber"

CHANGING HABITS
Water-saving tips for the garden

☑ Water your garden in the cool of the early morning or evening. This will reduce the amount of water lost to evaporation.

☒ Dont overwater. If you water plants and shrubs too often their roots will remain shallow, weakening the plant. Leave them alone until they show signs of wilting.

☑ Regularly weed and hoe your garden, to ensure that watering helps plants and not weeds.

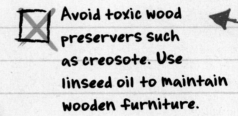

☑ Plant flowers and shrubs that thrive in hot and dry conditions such as thyme, evening primrose, rock rose, Californian poppy, pinks, lavender and buddleia.

☑ Collect rainwater in water-butts and use a watering can instead of a hose. Most local authorities offer discounted butts from around £20. For a wider range, check out www.crocus.co.uk, or visit the Centre for Alternative Technology's website (www.cat.org.uk) for ex-industrial food barrels. You may want to consider installing a rainwater harvesting system (see page 10).

☑ If you use a hosepipe, fit a trigger nozzle to control the flow. These are available from most gardening shops.

☒ Avoid toxic wood preservers such as creosote. Use linseed oil to maintain wooden furniture.

☑ If you're buying plastic garden furniture, make sure it's recycled plastic.

☑ Use water from washing-up and baths in the garden – but not water that has been exposed to strong detergents.

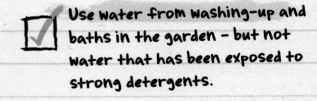

☑ Mulches such as wood chips, bark and gravel help to prevent water evaporation and also suppress weed growth, saving both water and time spent weeding. Your local garden centre should have a range on offer.

☑ Lawns can survive long periods of dry weather if the grass is not cut too short, so try to maintain it at least 4cm during summer. Even if the grass turns brown, it will quickly recover after a few days of rain.

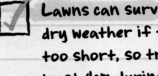

CHAPTER 2
FAMILY & CHILDREN

Where to look

FAMILY & CHILDREN

We all want the best for our children; to be able to provide them with a loving home, treat them to wonderful holidays and toys and save for their future. In this chapter there's loads of great advice on keeping your kids happy and healthy right now, while still safeguarding the future of their planet

Decisions decisions...

Every day parents make choices for their children: what food to feed them, what clothes to dress them in, what toys to buy them, which method of transport to use to get them to school: the list goes on and on. With every choice comes a consequence. If we choose to drive our kids to school in a gas guzzler because we want to know they have every chance of arriving safely, we are also emitting higher levels carbon dioxide into the air, which contributes to climate change.

In choosing to use chemical-rich disposable nappies for our babies, we may be taking advantage of a labour-saving convenience, but we're filling up landfill sites.

Of course, making the right decision is not always easy. It can often be very difficult to find the best solution and can be more expensive than other less environmentally friendly options.

A numbers game

One parent is not going to make any real difference, except perhaps to their own conscience. It takes numbers to affect change. The more parents who convert to a more sustainable lifestyle, the more pressure they will put on their peers and on others to do the same; on governments to do more to support them; and on manufacturers to work harder to develop greener alternatives.

Just say 'no'

As any parent will testify, saying no to a child is not always easy. When a child wants something enough, there is no amount of nagging they will not employ in order to get it. Aside from that, we also want our children to be happy, and if that means giving in to them occasionally, then so be it.

Sometimes saying 'no' is easy because the consequences are so clear to see. 'Can I pour some petrol on the fire to really get it going, Mum?' is not a request likely to be accepted, for example.

But saying no because of climate change or the environment is different, because the consequences of our actions are not always immediately apparent. If you tell your son he can't have the latest gadget because you can't afford it, he might accept that. If you refuse because it's made of metal and plastic, requires batteries and was made in a Chinese sweatshop, he'll probably think you've gone crazy. Having strength in your convictions and looking out for their long-term future may be all the support you have in sticking to your decisions.

➤ **Get the right information, and keep your child happy with a clear eco-conscience**

Kid's stuff

In 2008 a Roper poll found that people identified having a child as their primary motivation to 'go green'; 91% said the most important reason to recycle was the impact it would have on the child's future

SCHOOL

When it comes to addressing climate change, school can play just as important a role for children as home. It's the perfect place to engage young people and show them the crucial role they have to play in the future of their planet. Here are some tips to ensure they get the most out of the 'best days of their lives'...

Walking the walk...

The school run has become an increasingly contentious issue in recent years with growing concerns over localised pollution and climate change, as well as the associated traffic problems. The wealthy mother doing a one-mile round trip to drop off the kids in the 'Chelsea tractor' is the bane of any bus driver's morning, trying to get commuters to work on time – and other school children to school.

The debate has prompted many schools up and down the country to work with parents to devise more community-friendly alternatives. One of the most successful schemes is the walking bus, which not only helps to cut down on congestion and pollution, but also helps keep children fit and healthy – a real concern now, with 'childhood obesity' a commonly heard phrase.

Under the scheme, children make their way to and from school on foot and in the safety of a supervised group. The size of the walking bus ranges from just a few kids taking part in an informal scheme run by a small group of neighbours, to school-wide initiatives involving dozens of children. Larger schemes operate with official pick up points – although children can usually join en route as well – and strict rotas for adult supervisors. Some even have coloured tops or bands for the children to wear for easy identification.

... and talking the talk

Arrange an appointment with a senior member of staff at your child's school to discuss the options, and talk to other parents who might be willing to act as supervisors. Alternatively, you may find a number of parents who live nearby who are interested in co-founding a smaller bus.

Once it's up and running, get in touch with your local paper to see if they'll write a story on it – a walking bus in action provides a great photo opportunity and the concept has a strong community feel about it. You can also see if a local business is interested in sponsoring the bus and providing free high-visibility tops for the children to wear, and you can even hand out leaflets to parents who drive their kids to school – it may be just what they're looking for.

Shocking, but true...

In Denmark, 50% of all children cycle to school. n the UK it is just 2%..

◄ **Keep your child fit and healthy *and* save the planet**

Get to school the green way

School-run.org
(www.school-run.org)
This great site helps parents to pool school-run resources saving both time and the environment.

Sustrans' Safe Routes to Schools
(www.sustrans.org.uk)
Visit this site for great tips and advice from the UK's leading sustainable-transport charity.

Is your child's school an Eco-School?
If not, why not ask a senior member of staff whether they'd consider signing up? Visit www.eco-schools.net for all the information you'll need to register your school.

A pupil at Ellingham Primary School in Norfolk checks the output from the wind turbine installed at the school. The school has been awarded Green Flag Status as an Eco-School

Get educated

Eco-Schools is an international award programme set up to help schools become sustainable. Through the programme, schools work towards achieving one of three awards and the children take the driving seat. The bronze and silver awards are both self-accredited, while the most ambitious schools aiming for the prestigious Green Flag award are externally assessed by the programme administrator.

Participating schools elect an action team – or 'eco-committee' – made up of at least one representative from each year group and a member of staff. Parents, governors, head teachers, non-teaching staff and even members of the community are also encouraged to join.

The action team then carries out an environmental review of the school to give a realistic picture of its current environmental performance, highlighting existing good practice as well as areas for improvement and change. This review should cover the nine key topics of the programme; water, biodiversity, energy, global perspectives, healthy living, litter, school grounds, transport and waste.

The action team consults with the rest of the school and the community about which themes they want to address. It may be that a school wants to boost the level of recycling across all departments and clamp down on litter. Another school may want to focus on water conservation and transportation issues. Ultimately it's the children who have the final say in how they want to take things forward.

The environmental review then forms the basis of the school's action plan helping to prioritise the key issues needing attention. The plan must be communicated to everyone involved with the school so that everyone knows what is being done and why. The Eco-Schools programme operates in 46 countries worldwide and has been adopted by more than 40,000 schools, nurseries and children's centres. Participating schools from across the globe can pool ideas and explore ways of working together to help one another become more sustainable.

The programme is run internationally by the Foundation for Environmental Education (FEE). It is administered in England by Keep Britain Tidy; in Scotland by Keep Scotland Beautiful; in Wales by Keep Wales Tidy; and in Northern Ireland by Tidy Northern Ireland.

"Ultimately it's the children who have the final say in how they want to take things forward"

Did you know...?

○ **Grants of up to £5,000 can be awarded to schools through the 'Switched On Communities' grant scheme.**

○ **You can order the Eco-Schools promotional leaflet by emailing eco-schools@ encams.org. You should provide your name and full address.**

BABY CARE

Having a baby is a life-changing experience in every way. There's the joy of a new arrival, swiftly followed by the endless dirty nappies and lack of sleep. But it is also a time when we no longer have to think only about our own future, but our child's as well. This section explores some of the most pertinent issues for new parents

NAPPIES: The lowdown

Disposables: the facts

Standard disposable nappies are made up of paper pulp, super-absorbent chemicals, plastics and adhesives. Around three billion nappies are thrown away in the UK every year – that's more than eight million a day. The vast majority of these end up in landfill and take hundreds of years to fully decompose.

The annual cost to each local authority in disposing of these nappies runs into hundreds of thousands of pounds, and this is expected to spiral upwards as tighter EU-led restrictions on the use of landfill start coming into force in 2010. Not surprisingly, many local authorities are keenly pushing nappy schemes in their waste strategies. In March 2007, the Local Government Association called for manufacturers to contribute to the £67m cost of dealing with nappy waste going to landfill.

Cost The average cost of a disposable nappy is around 12p, and the average baby gets through between 4,000 and 6,000 before they're potty trained, at an overall cost of £480 to £720.

Did you know...?

Disposable nappies make up on average between 2% and 4% of an average household's rubbish – which means a shocking 400,000 tonnes clogging up landfill sites every single year.

Reusables: the facts

Luckily, nappy design has come a very long way since the days of soaking and boiling terries, origami-like folding techniques and fiddley safety pins. Today, they come in all types of different shapes and sizes, the old-fashioned nappy pin has been replaced with far more user-friendly poppers or Velcro, and the fabrics are soft and absorbent and can even be washed at a low temperature.

There are three types of real nappies: flat nappies, shaped nappies and all-in-ones. To get started you need the nappies themselves – the inner liners to catch solids and help keep moisture away from your baby's skin – and the wraps, and then you're good to go!

Cost The cost of reusable nappies ranges from around £5 to £15 each. An average baby will typically need about 24 reusable nappies from birth to potty.

According to a study by parenting website Cuddlebabes, the cost of buying and home washing real nappies from birth to potty trained ranged from £269.55 to £422.55 depending on nappy type and based on 5,475 washes.

Further savings can be made by using the same nappies for your second child.

Where to buy them Supermarkets and high-street retailers now stock various real-nappy brands, including Tesco, Sainsbury, Waitrose and Boots. Alternatively, visit Go Real's website at www.goreal.org.uk/retailers for an extensive list of retailers.

Save Cash! You could save up to £387 per child by opting for reusable nappies.

Airing your dirty laundry...

If you don't fancy washing your nappies at home, you can pay a local nappy laundry service to do it for you. Schemes typically offer weekly services that collect used nappies and provide a fresh supply of clean nappies for the next seven days. You will be given a deodorised bin to store the used nappies in. Prices range from around £6 to £11 per week, though you may be required to pay a joining fee.

To find your nearest local nappy laundry contact Go Real at advice@goreal.org.uk. Make sure the laundry service works to PAS106, the British Standards Institute's specification for laundry services.

Top Tips Using real nappies:

☑ **Wash soiled nappies at 60C. Wet nappies and waterproof wraps should be washed at lower temperatures with the rest of your laundry**

☒ **Do not tumble dry or iron**

☑ **Wash nappies a couple of times before the first use as this helps to improve absorbency**

☒ **Don't use fabric conditioners as this reduces absorbency**

☑ **Use washable liners.**

Happy old nappies: The future of reycycling nappy waste

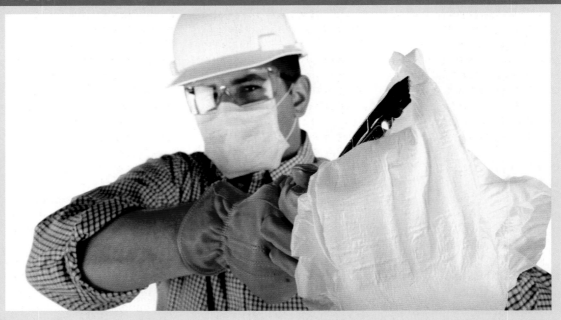

A dirty disposable nappy is not pleasant, so it's understandable that when a parent dumps it in the bin that's the last time they will ever want to see it. But all of that is set to change with the introduction of Britain's first disposable-nappy recycling plant, which will convert them into plastic cladding and roof tiles.

This revolutionary facility will bring new life to 36,000 tonnes of nappies – or around 4% of Britain's total nappy waste each year. Knowaste, the Canadian company behind the scheme, hopes the £12 million plant, earmarked for Tyseley, Birmingham, will eventually recycle up to 13% of nappies.

Initially, the plant will only process nappies, bed liners and incontinence products from commercial sources such as hospitals and nurseries, but plans eventually to target the domestic market.

Purée and simple

A realistic alternative to buying packaged baby food is to invest in a purée machine or hand blender to process organic vegetables for your baby. This way you can control exactly what your baby is eating, you don't have to worry about all the additives that go into most non-organic food produce and you'll be cutting down on lots of unnecessary packaging at the same time. Since this method takes more time than preparing food from a jar, try making the food in large batches and freezing it in ice-cube trays or other containers for later use. For more on feeding the family, see Food and Drink on page 92.

Useful links

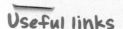

www.goreal.org.uk
Provides information and advice

www.nappyvalley.co.uk
Buy and sell high-quality baby items online

www.wen.org.uk
Women's Environmental Network

"Try making food in large batches and freezing it in ice-cube trays for later use"

Growing pains

Babies develop very quickly, outgrowing their clothes within months. With the global population increasing at a rate of around 210,000 a day, there's an ever-increasing demand on the resources available to make and distribute clothes for our infants.

In the UK, most baby clothes are only worn a few times and then binned, despite still having plenty of life left in them. Many parents might turn blue at the thought of putting their child in anything other than something brand spanking new, but using second-hand clothes is a very positive environmental choice, as well as being far cheaper than buying all new gear. If you really can't stomach the idea of your child wearing a stranger's old clothes (even a sweet and innocent three-month-old's!), see if you can get hold of some from your family and friends – at least that way you know where they've come from.

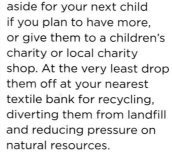

Once your child has outgrown their clothes, don't throw them away. Instead keep them aside for your next child if you plan to have more, or give them to a children's charity or local charity shop. At the very least drop them off at your nearest textile bank for recycling, diverting them from landfill and reducing pressure on natural resources.

Most maternity units are very grateful for any donations of baby clothes to give to those parents who rush to hospital without their painstakingly prepared 'hospital bag'.

If you do buy new clothes, consider those made from organic cotton – they are far more environmentally friendly than standard cotton and most other types of fabric (see below and page 179 for more information).

see below and page 179 for more information

Useful links

www.welovefrugi.com
Sells organic cotton baby clothes to fit over big cloth nappies, as well as breast-feeding tops and clothes for young children

www.baby-o.co.uk
Blankets, clothes, skincare, toys, bibs and more

www.ecobaby.co.uk
Natural mother and baby products

www.greenbaby.co.uk
An extensive range of products for bringing up a green baby

▼ **Non-organic cotton farming puts workers' health at risk, takes up a huge amount of natural resources and affects rural communities**

Why buy organic cotton?

• **Conventional cotton farming accounts for 25% of global pesticide use, damaging local environments and eco-systems.**

• **Seven of the 15 pesticides used on cotton are considered 'possible', 'likely', 'probable', or 'known' human carcinogens according to the US Environmental Protection Agency, putting workers at huge risk.**

• **Cotton uses massive amounts of land, water and fertiliser, which can cause many social and economic problems in more rural farming areas.**

For more information on these and other issues concerning cotton farming turn to page 179, and check out the Soil Association's website at *www.soilassociation.org* for a comprehensive list of UK retailers selling certified organic clothes.

turn to page 179

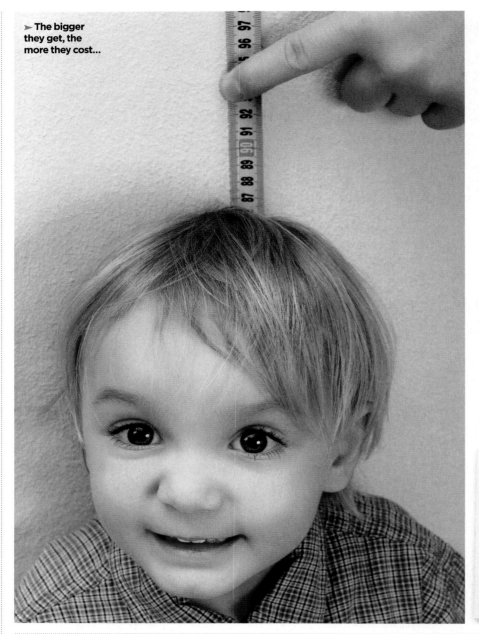

➤ The bigger they get, the more they cost...

The first year of a child's life can be extremely expensive, with the average child clocking up an outlay of somewhere in the region of £14,000 on nappies, clothes, food and equipment and child care. As the child gets older, the costs mount up. One reason for this is that babies outgrow things so quickly, whether it be their clothes, toys or whatever. Another reason is that marketing departments are good at convincing new parents that they need things they don't, and that the more something costs the better it will be for their child!

The best way of keeping costs down, and reducing the pressure on our natural resources, is to buy second-hand items where you can or to borrow from friends and family. Old baby equipment takes up a lot of space in cupboards so most other parents will probably be delighted to see it out of the house.

If your friends and family can't help, try the National Childbirth Trust's clothes sales, jumble sales and charity shops. You will be amazed at the quality and cost of some of the unwanted items on offer. Alternatively, try online at free exchange websites like *www.freecycle.com* (see page 61).

Useful links

www.mumsnet.com
Reviews, tips and advice for parents by parents

www.freecycle.org
A free exchange of all kinds of unwanted items

www.greenboardgames.com
Family board games, puzzles, jigsaws, card games and more

Plastic: not fantastic

Last year, serious concerns were raised over the safety of chemical bisphenol A (BPA), which is widely used in plastic baby bottles, water bottles and food containers.

The US Government's National Toxicology Program said there was genuine cause for concern about physiological changes that occur in people when they ingest BPA that has leached from plastics into their food.

As well as switching baby bottles to BPA-free alternatives, another way to lower exposure to the chemical is to avoid heating foods and liquids in plastic containers that contain the compound. It is thought that the amount of BPA that leaches out may depend more on the temperature of the liquid, food, or container itself than on the age of the plastic bottle or dish.

• BornFree specialises in producing smart and safe baby products, and have developed a range of baby bottles, cups and accessories that are totally free of BPA, phthalates and PVC.
www.babybornfree.co.uk

• Green to Grow is a family company that make bisphenol A-free and phthalate-free baby bottles.
www.greentogrow.com

• Babisil makes the Silbottle, the award-winning bisphenol A-free and phthalate-free baby bottle made out of medical-quality silicone.
www.babisil.co.uk

IN PRACTICE:

Sheep & Chandeliers

Hidden among myriad online and high street toy stores selling cheap, plastic products, is an environmental and ethical treasure just waiting to be discovered

Jeremy Lewis-Phillips and his girlfriend Paulina Krzywosinska were working in dead-end jobs that were taking them nowhere. They would come home each night, watch the news and go to bed saddened and frustrated by what was happening to the environment, and the social injustices they saw linked to that.

Then, in June of last year, the couple decided they could no longer sit back and do nothing. They liked the idea of online, ethical retail and so united their mutual passion for traditional children's toys and clothing with fair-trade principles.

'Quality wooden toys are hard to come by,' said Canadian-born Jeremy, 27. 'When our customers visit Sheep & Chandeliers, they know they will find toys that are exciting, fun and natural, and which stimulate children's imaginations. They also promote and sustain a decent way of life for the makers.'

All of the children's products on sale through Sheep & Chandeliers are selected on their ethical and environmental merits.

Wooden toys are FSC (Forest Stewardship Council) approved or made from rubber trees in Thailand that have come to the end of their useful lives and are chopped down to allow other trees to be planted in their place. Glues are non-toxic, as are the water-based paints.

'When customers make a purchase from us, they are directly helping to maintain a sustainable environment in communities all over the world, while giving their child a long-lasting smile,' said Jeremy.

'Each product on our website directly contributes to the success and fair pay of others, and to essential elements – such as shelter, water, clothes and pencils for schools – for the artisans and their families.'

Jeremy finds the continuing demand on the high street for cheap-and-cheerful plastic toys disheartening.

'Maybe people think traditional gifts are not as fun to play with, or that they cost a lot of money,' he said.

'Our products offer great value for money,

➤ **Customers love the simplicity and handcrafted feel of Sheep & Chandeliers' toys, such as this sorting boat.**

but what our customers really love are the simple movements, the handcrafted feel and the fact the toys are so unusual.'

Sheep & Chandeliers sells predominantly through its website, but also via a stall in Brighton's North Laines and at fairs and promotional events. Jeremy and Paulina hope to establish a permanent presence in Brighton.

'For now, though, we are focused on building our website and making it the best online toy store in the UK,' said Jeremy.

Visit www.sheepandchandeliersecostore.co.uk

All in a name

Co-founders Jeremy Lewis-Phillips and Paulina Krzywosinska wanted a name for their business that had a 'local, organic feel with a touch of class and style'. 'Sheep being the cosy, natural, organic side and Chandelier being the wonderfully elegant, yet efficient, light that is often a symbol of homes' hallways, bedrooms and living rooms,' explained Jeremy.

TOYS

With the average UK child getting around £250's worth of toys each Christmas – most of which are destined for landfill – keeping offspring entertained can be an eco-nightmare. If you know where to look, though, it's easier than you'd think...

A LITTLE BIT OF GIVE AND TAKE

Before chucking toys out, check if there's a local children's hospital or hospice where you might be about to rehome them, or donate them to a children's charity (like Barnardo's) or a local charity shop. Toy libraries are a great resource, saving parents money and offering a huge range of toys. There are more than 1,000 toy libraries throughout the UK, serving approximately 250,000 children. For details on your nearest library contact the National Association of Toy and Leisure Libraries on 020 7428 2288 or visit their website at *www.natll.org.uk* for more information. Visit *www.greengiving.org.uk* where you can give and take children's clothes, toys, books, furniture and equipment for free. It's available to parents, carers and organisations working with children. Freecycle's website at *www.freecycle.org* is worth looking at too. Or why not host a toy-swap party at your home, inviting other parents and their kids to bring and exchange unwanted toys.

> **"Toy libraries are a great resource, saving parents money and offering a huge range of toys"**

▼ **Why not host a toy-swap party with other parents and their kids?**

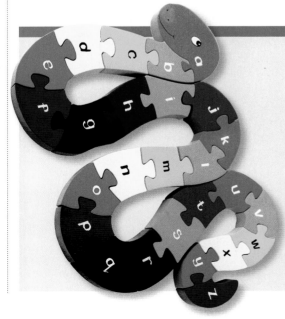

Toy story

In 2005, the European Parliament voted to permanently ban the use of phthalates (a group of chemicals used to soften PVC) in toys after they were linked to damage to the reproductive system and an increased risk of asthma and cancer. Although this is good news for the future, what does this say about all the other PVC toys that already fill our children's nurseries and playpens? Today wooden toys are enjoying something of a revival. More ethically sourced wooden toys are making their way onto gift-shop shelves and online outlets as parents seek safe and sustainable playthings. Wood Like to Play is a family-run business making handcrafted toys, and Bournemouth-based Escor Toys recently won *Ethical Consumer* magazine's new Best Buy butterfly label due to its sustainable sourcing policies and the fact it employs people with disabilities.

AEROPLANES USE EIGHT TIMES AS MUCH OIL-BASED FUELS AS TRAINS

OUTINGS & HOLIDAYS

Growth in international tourism has come at a heavy cost to the environment. Local eco-systems are under pressure as natural habitats have made way for hotels, airports and golf courses; local amenities have been stretched far beyond their limit; not to mention the carbon footprint of the aircraft themselves – but there are alternatives. In this chapter we take you exploring...

BE AN ECO DAY-TRIPPER

The UK is blessed with some of the most beautiful scenery on earth, which is part of the reason why millions of people across the globe holiday here each year. But, being British, it can be easy to take this for granted and overlook some of the wonderful tourist destinations this land has to offer – as the Aussies say: 'You never explore your own back yard'. Below is a selection of top eco-attractions for the family in the UK, but you can find out more on the Earth Centre Network's website at *www.earthcentrenetwork.org.uk*. This useful resource gives details of around 50 attractions in the UK that place great emphasis on the principles and practice of sustainable living. Alternatively, visit the National Trust's website at *www.nationaltrust.org.uk* for details of their Big Green Day Out events around the country.

Holiday-makers stay in the UK

The number of visits abroad by UK residents decreased by 8% from 70.6 to 64.6 million in the 12-month period to May 2009, compared with the previous 12 months.

Centre for Alternative Technology

Established in 1973, the Centre for Alternative Technology (CAT) has been on the front line of pioneering green technology for decades. Set in the stunning hillsides of Southern Snowdonia, the seven-acre attraction provides a fun-packed day out for all the family, where you can learn about all aspects of sustainable living in a hands-on and genuinely exhilarating way. To reach the main site, for example, visitors ascend the centre's famous cliff railway. It's powered entirely by 'water-balancing' – the two carriages are connected by cable via a winding-drum at the top; water is run into a tank beneath the upper carriage until it is just heavier than the lower carriage and its passengers; then the parking brakes are released and gravity does the rest. Once at the top they can explore the interactive displays that demonstrate the incredible power of wind, water and sun and visit the working examples of environmentally responsible buildings, energy conservation, organic growing and waste management. There's also plenty of hiking, bike rides and country walks nearby.

CAT's visitor centre is open seven days a week all year, except for two short winter breaks.

Admission charges: Peak season (1 April to 1 November): Adults, £8.40; children, £4.20; under-fives, free. To support sustainable transport, the centre offers half-price admission for all visitors on production of a valid train ticket to Machynlleth. Arrive by bus, foot or bike and get £1 off. Visit *www.cat.org.uk* or call 01654 705950 for opening times and more information.

Plane and simple

In 2004, aviation accounted for 5.5% of the UK's carbon emissions and that figure is rising fast. If we are to reduce carbon emissions by 80% – which experts say is needed to combat climate change – and aviation is not included in the cuts, that 5.5% rises to 27.5%. So, we will have to make huge cuts across other sectors or heavily restrict our flying.

The Eden Project

The world-famous and undeniably stunning Eden Project in Cornwall is described as 'a living theatre of plants and people that unites visitors with the plants we use everyday for food, shelter, clothing and fuel'. Since it opened to the public in 2001, it has become one the UK's most popular tourist attractions, drawing more than 1.2 million visitors from across the globe each year.

Built in a former clay pit, the Eden Project houses the world's largest conservatory – named the Rainforest Biome – and is surrounded by 35 acres of gardens made up of plants from all around the world.

The newly opened Core is an impressive hi-tech education centre with exhibitions, interactive displays and dedicated space for workshops, which further enhances the centre's excellent reputation as an educational facility. It is owned by the Eden Trust, an educational charity, and hosts exhibitions, events and workshops. All money raised goes to further the aims of the Trust.

Admission charges: £16 for adults, £11 for over-60s, £5 for children and free for under-fives. **Visit *www.edenproject.com*** or call 01726 811911 for opening times and more information.

> A view of the spectacular 'Biomes' that house plants from all around the world at the Eden Project

Nature's World

Nature's World is a thriving eco-experience for the whole family to enjoy. Brimming with fun and exciting attractions and demonstrations, the site near Middlesbrough will appeal to any parent or child wanting to learn more about the world of sustainable living in a fun and absorbing way. Its mission is to provide information, education, ideas and inspiration for looking after the environment.

One of the key focal points is the earth-sheltered 'hydroponicum', an indoor rainforest heated using geo-thermal bore holes. Nature's World recently benefited from a £500,000 refurbishment project, and now boasts a new range of eco-attractions such as its solar-powered talking posts, giant bank-side slide and an interactive sustainability challenge.

Admission charges: Adults, £5.30; children, £2.75; family tickets, £13.20. **Visit *www.naturesworld.org.uk*** or call 01642 594895 for opening times and more information.

Living Coasts

Living Coasts is a coastal zoo and conservation charity, where visitors can see plants and animals from around the world living in specially designed, naturalistic habitats.

Like all good zoos, the Torquay-based attraction places great emphasis and resources on education and conservation, rather than simply entertainment for visitors. The centre is part of the Whitley Wildlife Conservation Trust and supports many conservation projects in the UK and around the world.

Living Coasts recently won the Green Tourism Business Scheme's Gold Award because of its staff's commitment to a wealth of eco practices on the site, including waste management, recycling and the use of environmentally friendly materials and produce. It was one of the first retail outlets in the UK to ban plastic bags in its gift shop and carries out regular events to promote environmental awareness among its visitors.

Admission charges: Adults, £9.20; children, £6.90 (under-3s free). **Visit *www.livingcoasts. org.uk*** or call 01803 202470 for opening times and other information.

Eco-House

This internationally renowned environmental show home is a demonstration of hundreds of environmental features and ideas, making it a great attraction for the eco-conscious family.

Built in Leicester, Britain's first Environment City, the Eco-House seeks to inspire and encourage visitors to make green choices in their own lives, and in the way they keep their homes and gardens, by providing information, advice and practical help.

Admission charges: Adults, £2.50; children and concs, £1.50; under-3s, free. Visit *www.gwll.org.uk/ecohouse* or call 0116 254 5489 for opening times and more information.

Deep Sea World

Get up close and personal with some of the 44,000 species that live off Scotland's coast at the spectacular Deep Sea World Underwater Safari in Fife.

It boasts the UK's longest underwater viewing tunnel, so visitors will be well placed to spot all sorts of marine life, including 12ft-long Sand Tiger sharks. Elsewhere, there are coral reefs to study, a seal sanctuary to enjoy and the chance to dive with sharks.

Deep Sea World is a Gold Award winner through the Green Tourism Business Scheme and actively participates in conservation projects, including the Angel Shark Breeding Project and Coral Farming Conservation.

Deep Sea World is open every day except Christmas Day and New Year's Day. For more information on times and prices, call 01383 411880 or *visit www.deepseaworld.co.uk*

Garden Organic

Garden Organic is the UK's leading organic growing charity and has been at the forefront of the organic horticulture movement for half a century. The charity, which has HRH The Prince of Wales as its patron, exists to research and promote organic gardening, farming and food and has two demonstration gardens run in conjunction with English Heritage at Ryton in Coventry and Audley End in Essex. It provides great advice for any budding organic gardeners, too.

Admission charges: Prices vary between sites. Visit *www.gardenorganic.org.uk* or call 024 7630 3517 for Ryton and 01799 522148 for Audley for opening times and more information.

Look out for...

...the Blue Flag, a voluntary eco-label working towards sustainable development at beaches and marinas through strict criteria dealing with water quality, environmental education and management, safety and other services.

Green Wood Centre

This innovative interpretation centre, near historic Ironbridge, in Shropshire, teaches visitors about sustainable living through a wood-based economy.

The centre runs courses on woodland management, coppicing, sustainable building and other technologies, as well as making landscape furniture from local FSC (Forest Stewardship Council) approved timber.

The site has one of the UK's most energy efficient timber buildings and is now a national centre of excellence for crafts and coppicing.

Green Wood is also home to the Ironbridge Woodland Experience, which includes a woodland hall, vegetarian cafe, retail outlet for coppice products and woodland walks around the Ironbridge Gorge World Heritage Site.

For more information on courses, events and opening times visit *www.greenwoodcentre. org.uk* or call 01952 432769

Green Tourism Business Scheme

The Green Tourism Business Scheme is a comprehensive and invaluable resource for the eco-friendly holiday maker, providing a simple certification system of more than 1,400 places to stay and visitor attractions across the UK. Businesses opting to join the scheme are assessed against a rigorous set of criteria, covering areas including energy and water efficiency, waste management, biodiversity, social involvement and communication and natural and cultural heritage. Those that meet the required standard receive a Bronze, Silver, or Gold award based on their level of achievement. Below is a selection that are on offer in the UK.

Go to www.green-business.co.uk and click on the tabs to the right of the screen to find places to visit and things to do in all areas of the UK. You can then rank the listings according to area, award status and type.

Birdworld

With penguin feeding, safari rides, an owl prowl and an underwater world, there is enough at Birdworld, in Surrey, for all ages to enjoy. Set in 26 acres of landscaped parkland gardens, the popular visitor attraction boasts one of the largest collections of birds in the UK that includes many endangered and conservation species. There are lots of seating and picnic areas around the park, or you can enjoy a meal in the restaurant, which serves healthy, organic and Fair Trade options.

Admission charges: Adults, £13.95; children, £11.95; family ticket, £45. **Visit www.birdworld.co.uk or call 01420 221140 for opening times and more information.**

Wish you were here

According to Visit Britain, the top 10 British tourist destinations currently are Liverpool, London, Bath, Scottish Highlands, Cornwall, Cardiff, Stratford-upon-Avon, Manchester, Cambridge and Birmingham.

B&Bing near Chichester

Nestled in an Area of Outstanding Natural Beauty, a short hop from the historic city of Chichester, Englewood Bed & Breakfast provides an ideal retreat for the active eco tourist. Kingley Vale National Nature Reserve, the picturesque harbour of Bosham and, of course, Chichester are all within a few miles, and the B&B is perfectly placed for country-side walks.

Englewood is a Green Tourism Business Scheme Gold Award winner thanks to owners John and Sylvia Jones' continuous commit-ment to sustainability. The bungalow's cavity walls and loft are well insulated, the windows are all double glazed, every light bulb is low energy and all appliances are A-rated.

A re-use and recycling policy is rigorously adhered to by the Joneses and the provision of recycling bins for paper, cans, card, glass and plastics in all bedrooms encourages guests to do their bit.

Breakfasts are made using local produce and free-range eggs and meats, with many of the herbs and vegetables taken straight from the garden, where uncooked vegetable kitchen waste is composted.

Visit www.SmoothHound.co.uk/hotels/englewood.html

Canal boating

Once the lifeblood of Industrial Revolution, Britain's intricate network of canals have been given a new lease of life as beautiful settings for environmentally friendly holidays. UK Boat Hire offers boat travel holidays from 11 locations around England and Scotland lasting from three days to several weeks.

Admission charges: Prices range to suit most budgets. **Visit www.ukboathire.com /green_holidays.htm or call 0845 126 4098 for more information.**

Forest wood cabins

Want to get away from the hustle and bustle of modern life? There is little to top spending a few nights in a wood cabin in Britain's amazing woodlands. Set within some of Britain's best forests, these retreats are the perfect base for exploring the countryside and getting close to nature, with hidden glades, babbling streams, dramatic mountains, breathtaking scenery and rippling lakes all on your doorstep. Forest Holidays have built wood cabins in Forestry Commission-maintained woodlands in Scotland, Yorkshire and Cornwall. Depending on the location, you can go walking, cycling, rambling, fishing, pony trekking, exploring, have a barbecue or simply relax and enjoy the scenery.

Admission charges: Prices range to suit most budgets. **Visit www.forestholidays.co.uk or call 0845 130 8225 for more information.**

10 green travel tips (source: Visit Britain)

☑ Travel responsibly – Use Britain's public transport system to travel easily between destinations and within cities. Try to incorporate 'car-free' days into your holiday and remember cycling is also a great environmentally friendly way to get around. And if you're travelling within a city, why not see if it's walking distance? Nothing beats seeing a city on foot and it also keeps you fit!

☑ Reduce energy use in your hotel room - Simple things like using your towels more than once, turning down the heating and switching off appliances can make a big difference, so make sure you think about these things during your trip.

☑ Stay in green accommodation - More and more accommodation providers are becoming conscious of their negative effects on the environment and making efforts to counteract them. See the panel on Green Tourism Business Scheme for more information.

☑ Reduce waste - The miniature toiletries you find in hotels contribute to thousands of bags of waste every year, so bring your favourite toiletries from home to reduce waste. It's also a good idea to bring a reusable water bottle and pack your own cloth bag to carry any purchases rather than using plastic bags. And don't forget rechargeable batteries for your camera and other gadgets.

☑ Take Eurostar - Did you know you can take connecting Eurostar trains from hundreds of European destinations direct to London's new 'destination station' Kings Cross St Pancras? If you have to fly, you could consider offsetting the carbon emissions of your flight.

☑ Buy local products - Support local business and independent shops where the products are more likely to be less energy-intensive in their production. Sample regional food specialities and don't miss the local farmers' markets where you can discover delicious selections of locally sourced meats, cheeses, and organic produce.

☑ Recycle guide books - Once you've finished your trip, pass on your brochures and guidebooks to a friend or second-hand bookshop. Or why not leave them at your hotel for another guest to use – that way you'll have less to carry back too.

☑ Try volunteer travel - On a volunteer break you can work alongside experts and other volunteers on a special project. Whether you're interested in conservation, wildlife or organising special events, there's a volunteer break for you in Britain.

☑ Talk to a local - Don't miss out of the best sights and activities near to where you are staying. Ask for recommendations about local things to see and do, what's typical for the area and enjoy things that are locally traditional such as festivals and attractions.

☑ Respect the area and above all have fun.

IN PRACTICE:

It's not just the planet that benefits when a school develops its eco-credentials. Pupils' educational performance can also improve, as one innovative headteacher discovered...

Brabin's Endowed School

Ten years ago, Brabin's Endowed School, in Lancashire, was in deep trouble. Standards were slipping, morale was low and there was a danger of it being placed in special measures by Ofsted inspectors.

The small, rural primary school needed a lifeline and it came in the form of new assistant headteacher Glynis Goldsbrough. With her hands-on approach to nurturing an appreciation of nature and the outdoors, she has developed in her pupils a passion for their environment and made them want to become agents for change.

Today, Brabin's, in Chipping, near Preston, is a five-time Eco-Schools Green Flag holder, enjoys Healthy Schools status, is an International School Award holder and was recently given the highest level of commendation by Ofsted inspectors.

It has also been chosen by the National College For School Leadership as one of just 56 ambassadors for sustainability. The school now actively shares best practice with its local community and neighbouring schools, and, last year, hosted a children's eco-sustainability conference. More than 200 children, heads, governors, teachers and parents from across Lancashire took part in workshops about the Eco-Schools scheme and the National Framework for Sustainable Schools.

'Working close to nature and the outdoors teaches children so much about geography, science, citizenship and much more,' said Mrs Goldsbrough, who is now the full-time head.

'It has raised the children's self-esteem by making them proud of what they and the school have achieved, which has a knock-on effect on how they perform in the classroom. They are very articulate and confident.'

One of the first things the school did was to turn a non-descript playing field into a wildlife haven teeming with bugs, birds, bats and 'mini-beasts', as Mrs Goldsbrough likes to call them. The children have planted trees and hedges, dug a bog garden, and have eight composters, two food digesters, a wormery and a paper skip for waste.

The school recently secured nearly £10,000 from the Big Lottery Fund to put towards a community-led project to grow fruit and vegetables, thereby promoting understanding and awareness of the link between eating and a healthy lifestyle.

The school has invested some of the money in a large greenhouse and the children grow all manner of vegetables to sell to parents and community members, with the aim of putting the cash back into the project to make it self-sustaining. They also have 11 hens and a chicken run.

At Brabin's, the children are encouraged to act in an environmentally friendly manner in everything they do. Energy saving is a key concern and ensuring all lights and equipment are turned off when not in use is becoming second nature. The school is also halfway to securing funding to install photovoltaic panels on the roof to generate electricity and solar-thermal panels to heat water. It already harvests rain by way of water butts located around the site and there are plans to install a greywater system to further cut water usage.

In July, Mrs Goldsbrough was one of five national winners of an Eco-Hero Award at the Eco-Schools Annual Exhibition, in recognition of her commitment to the programme.

> ## "Working close to nature has raised the children's self-esteem, which has a knock-on effect in the classroom"

▼ **Pupils at Brabin's learn about healthy eating – and business – by growing fruit and veg, and selling it to the local community**

Main photo: Eastern Daily Press

Their parents and grandparents may share responsibility for the world's environmental mess, but pupils at one eco-school are now leading the fight against global warming...

Long Eaton School

They may not have been intended to prick the consciences of an older generation, but the 1,355 footprint-shaped eco pledges that adorn the walls of Long Eaton Secondary School have had that effect.

As awareness of climate change increases, so too does the understanding that we adults are largely responsible for the environmental mess the world is in. So it is with ironic pertinence that pupils at Long Eaton have each made a pledge to lessen their carbon footprint. While many adults are still not willing to make changes to their lives, these children are doing all they can to sort out their futures.

In fairness, Long Eaton is no ordinary secondary. It has been an Eco-School for 10 years, is one of 56 selected by the National College For School Leadership to promote sustainable leadership to other schools and is holder of a coveted International Eco Award.

Nevertheless, its pupils reflect the determination of many young people in the UK to battle climate change. They are not looking to blame anyone; they are looking for a way out.

'As adults, we talk with so much doom and despair, but it's not so bad for us because we're halfway through our lives,' said Barbara James, the school's bursar and eco co-ordinator. 'What must it be like for children who have their whole lives ahead of them? We need to give them hope and inspiration that they can find solutions to the problems we have made.

'The children here have that hope and want to do everything they can to lessen their own impact on the world.'

In 1999, Long Eaton became the first Derbyshire school to win an Eco-Schools Green Flag. Until then, the specialist science and applied learning school had been making modest progress through resource management and buying recycled products.

'Eco-Schools emphasised the fact we were on the right track,' said Mrs James. 'It was also encouraging that there were so many like-minded schools out there, doing the same things we were.'

At the time, the school's eco committee was looking at ways to reduce water use in the boys' toilet block, where the urinals flushed all

▼ **Children at Long Eaton have pledged to reduce their carbon footprints, knowing small steps now can have a big impact later**

day, every day. The committee calculated the amount of water being wasted and then asked for a sensor to be installed so the urinal only flushed when necessary. The study was enough to earn the school its first Green Flag.

Long Eaton has since taken huge strides forward. When the dilapidated school building was bulldozed to make way for a new one, the committee was asked for its input – and, on the children's instruction, a fully integrated rainwater harvesting system was installed.

They also negotiated provision of a sensory garden, pond, allotment – the school has its own gardening club – orchard and wetland area. Bike stands have also been installed for the 150 children who cycle to school each day.

Long Eaton is committed to using its experience to help others and, in recent years, teams of pupils, led by Mrs James, have attended the United Nations' Children's Conferences on the Environment in Canada, the USA, Japan and Norway.

'What opened our eyes at these conferences was hearing hundreds of children from all over the world talking about the same problems we are – landfill, litter, the world's limited resources, plastic bags,' said Mrs James. 'No matter where they were from, they were all saying the same things.'

To honour the achievements of everyone at Long Eaton, 1,780 trees and shrubs were recently planted in the grounds to represent all of the students, staff and governors. The final tree was planted by Paralympic gold medallist Ellie Simmonds to commemorate Green Britain Day.

> **"We need to give them hope that they can find solutions to the problems we have made"**

CHAPTER 3
FOOD & DRINK

OUR DEMAND FOR CHEAP MEAT HAS A SERIOUS ENVIRONMENTAL EFFECT AS WELL AS A SOCIAL ONE

FOOD & DRINK

When global grain shortages and increased food prices reached their peak last year, it led to violent uprisings as millions struggled to feed themselves and their families – and there are fears that the worse is yet to come. Ensuring food production is sustainable and secure for all is not just important to people in poor and vulnerable countries, it is important for us all

FOOD: reality bites

Environmentally speaking the damage caused by the world's food production is clear-cut: it's huge and out of control.

There are currently around 6.7 billion people on the planet and this figure is rising fast. This level of population, and the voracious appetite of the Western world, has only been made possible with the development of intensive farming practices seen since the Second World War. But it has come at a huge environmental cost.

Our oceans are so over-fished and polluted that some species of fish are on the brink of extinction and many eco-systems are in tatters; our rainforests and woodlands have been cut down to make way for agriculture with such reckless abandon that we have deprived the world of one of its most important carbon sinks and rich sources of wildlife; our soil has been polluted with agrichemicals and other synthetic chemicals, which are seeping into rivers and seas causing yet more damage to vulnerable eco-systems. We use so much land and water rearing livestock that many natural habitats have been starved out of existence, and communities are facing severe water shortages. The sheer number of farmed animals is so great (around 60 billion are reared around the world each year) that their flatulence has become a significant contributor to climate change adding to all the fossil fuel emissions associated with modern farming methods, the production of agrichemicals and 'food miles'. The list goes on and on and on...

It is easy to blame the Western world for the state we are in because, by and large, we are the culprits. Much of this environmental devastation in developing parts of the world is caused by our 'needs'. We may not be the ones, for example, who are physically chopping down ancient woodlands in the heart of the Amazonian jungle to make way for soya fields, but it is our demand for the cattle that is reared on this crop that has led to deforestation in the first place.

Sadly, this massive exploitation of the land is often coupled with an equal exploitation of the workforce. Millions of farmers all around the world live and work in unacceptable conditions and are exposed to dangerous agrichemicals every day. Our demand for cheap meat – and lots of it – and the constant year-round supply of all fruits and vegetables does not just have a serious environmental effect, but a social one too.

What's the answer?

As a consumer in the UK there are many ways we can limit our impact on the environment while ensuring a better deal for farmers, both at home and abroad. Some of these, such as 'going organic', cost more money and may not be achievable with everyone's budgets. But attempting to minimise your waste and growing your own vegetables could actually save you money.

The following sections look in detail at organic farming and why it is important to buy local and seasonal foods, as well as addressing the benefits of buying Fairtrade products, the importance of animal welfare and what is involved in growing your own fruit and veg.

Did you know...?

People will have to be rationed to four portions of meat and one litre of milk a week if the world is to avoid run-away climate change, a new report warns. The study by the Food Climate Research Network also says overall food consumption should be reduced.

> "**Much of this environmental devastation is caused by our 'needs'**"

ORGANIC FARMERS FERTILISE THEIR FIELDS BY ROTATING CROPS, USING COMPOSTED MANURE, AND PLANTING CROPS THAT FEED THE SOIL WITH NITROGEN

ORGANIC

The hundreds of chemical pesticides used by non-organic farmers not only damage the land they're laid on, but also the farm workers who come into contact with them. Meanwhile some experts believe the drugs and antibiotics given to animals reared for meat can lead to superbugs in humans. In this chapter, we show you that getting back to nature is the way forward

Organic farming and the environment

The widespread use of chemical pesticides in non-organic farming not only damages wildlife and the environment, but also unprotected farm workers that come into contact with them. But, the level of impact depends largely on the type of farming practised. According to a recent government study, organic farms use half the energy that non-organic farms use to produce the same amount of food.

This is partly thanks to the fact that artificial fertilisers are banned in organic farming. Man-made fertilisers contribute to climate change in a number of ways. Producing them is a very energy-intensive process using fossil fuels as a raw material, and resulting in huge greenhouse gas emissions. When they are added to the land they release nitrous oxide and suppress soil micro-organisms that help prevent methane from escaping into the atmosphere. Furthermore, artificial fertiliser makes the soil more acidic, and this is counter-balanced by adding lime to the soil, producing carbon dioxide. It's a vicious circle.

Organic farmers fertilise their fields by rotating their crops, using composted manure, and planting crops which naturally feed nitrogen to the soil.

In this sense organic farming is a reversion to traditional farming methods which worked in harmony with nature to produce the best results. However, today's organic farmers also make best use of the latest technologies and practices that are in keeping with the organic ethos and are required for large scale farming. It is this successful combination of the old and the new that has made organic farming such a winning industry in recent years.

Organic farming enhances biodiversity in terms of crops and livestock, as well as flora and fauna. Trees, hedges and wide un-farmed field edges are an important feature on organic farms, providing habitats for natural predators such as beetles, spiders and birds which control pests. Surveys have shown organic farms to have 44% more birds in the fields and five times the number of wild plants.

The use of genetically modified (GM) crops is forbidden and the use of pesticides is limited to just seven of the 450 or so different types, and only these can be used as a last resort following an infestation or outbreak of disease. This restrictive use of pesticides is not only better for the environment but also the farm workers who would otherwise be exposed to these harsh chemicals as they are on conventional farms. In the UK, farmers on mainstream farms wear adequate protection when in contact with pesticides, but in many poorer countries protective garments are luxuries not often afforded to workers.

Organically reared animals are done so without the routine use of drugs, antibiotics and wormers common in intensive livestock farming. This has particular relevance to increasing concerns over the presence of residual antibiotics used to suppress infectious diseases and artificially promote growth in conventionally farmed food. Some health experts fear this is leading to superbugs and antibiotic resistance in humans.

Animal health is protected by regularly moving the animals to fresh pastures and using a mix of other preventative methods, including the highest standards in animal welfare which lead to healthier, happier livestock.

Did you know...?

Approximately 32.2 million hectares worldwide are now farmed organically, representing approximately 0.8 percent of total world farmland. Organically managed land now accounts for 4% of the UK's total agricultural land

▼ **Organic farms have 44% more birds than their non-organic counterparts**

Organic sales rocked by recession

The increase in sales of organic products in Britain slowed to just 1.7% in 2008 as the recession forced consumers to rein in their spend. The figure, which was released in April by the Soil Association, falls a long way short of the 26% average annual growth that the industry had been enjoying over the last decade.

Supermarket giant Tesco reportedly saw like-for-like volume sales of organic produce fall a whopping 29% at the end of last year. However, in July this year the retailer reported that sales of organic produce where starting to stabilise as it prepared to launch an Organic Produce week to help bolster the sector.

During 2006, direct sales of organic food through box schemes, farmers' markets and farm shops grew by 54% to £146 million, with total organic sales in the UK rising to just under £2 billion. Sales of organic products sold through supermarkets increased by 21%.

Seven years ago less than a third of all organic produce sold in the supermarkets was grown in the UK. By 2007 this had more than doubled to 66% as more and more farmers staked their claim in one of the fastest growing food sectors.

How to spot organic food

Certified organic food will be clearly labelled as such on packaging and usually comes with a price premium to cover the greater associated costs with farming organically. Produce also has a unique UK code for each of the different certifying bodies. The Soil Association, for example, has the code UK5.

If you are at a farmers' market or farm shop and you are not sure whether the produce is organic, it is perfectly reasonable to ask the farmer for proof of accreditation.

Is organic food better for your health?

The question of whether organic food is healthier than conventionally farmed produce is a cause of controversy. Whilst many people choose to buy organic food on health grounds, the Food Standards Agency does not support claims that eating organic food is better for you.

Organic food contains far lower amounts of pesticide and antibiotic residues than non-organic food; however, even in conventionally farmed foods these residues are in such minute quantities that they do not pose an immediate risk of poisoning to the consumer.

What proponents of organic food claim, however, is that there is so little research into the long-term health risks of these residues that no-one really understands the potential dangers they pose. By eating organically reared meat you are erring on the side of caution.

➤ There's very little research into the potential long-term health risks of chemically treated food

⋏ Events all over the country celebrate the best of the nation's produce during British Food Fortnight

British Food Fortnight

Every year thousand of activities take place as part of British Food Fortnight, including food and drink festivals, promotions, tastings and special menus in pubs, restaurants and shops. For more information and a list of events in your area go to www.britishfoodfortnight.co.uk.

ORGANIC ON A BUDGET TOP 10 TIPS

01
JOIN AN ORGANIC BOX SCHEME
Get local, seasonal and organic fruit and veg delivered straight to your doorstep, and get excellent value for money while you're at it.

02
COOK FRESH FRUIT AND VEG FROM SCRATCH
Avoiding over packaged convenience foods is usually both healthier and cheaper.

03
TRY OTHER CUTS OF MEAT
Eat less meat, and when you do eat it then try lower cost cuts such as belly of pork or neck of lamb. Offal too can provide tasty nutritious meals. Get friendly with your local butcher for advice on cuts.

04
COOK IN BULK
Make meals in larger batches, use herbs and spices, and cheaper ingredients like tinned tomatoes or beans and pulses to bulk things out, and then freeze left over portions.

05
CREATE A BUYING GROUP
Bulk-buy your store cupboard staples with a group of friends at wholesale prices. The Soil Association is working to encourage more buying groups around the country.

06
JOIN A CSA SCHEME
Community Supported Agriculture is a partnership between farmers and the public where you make an annual investment for a share of the harvest, and it can prove great value for money.

07
WRITE A SHOPPING LIST
As a nation we throw away nearly seven million tonnes of food every year. By planning meals in advance, buying what you need and not what you fancy, and using left-overs, you should be able avoid the need to throw away any food at all, and save up to £50 a month.

08
CHICKEN OR EGG?
Keep your own chickens and enjoy a great house pet and super fresh eggs every day. You can learn more about chicken keeping, and range of other courses on growing and cooking, through a Soil Association Organic Farm School Course.

09
GROWING VEG IS FUN !
Grow your own for the freshest, most local food you can get, right on your doorstep - and free.

10
TAKE A WALK ON THE WILD SIDE
There's plenty of free wild food available, and identifying and picking it is a great way of having fun outdoors. Visit www.soilassociation.org for advice on foraging from forager Fergus Drennan.

Source: Soil Association

KNOW YOUR LABELS

DOLPHIN SAFE

Means no dolphins were intentionally chased or encircled with deadly tuna nets, nor were any dolphins killed or seriously injured.

RAINFOREST ALLIANCE

Means the product has been grown or made sustainably. Affiliated companies meet rigorous standards to conserve biodiversity and provide sustainable livelihoods.

FAIRTRADE

Enables the sustainable development and empowerment of disadvantaged producers and workers in developing countries.

SOIL ASSOCIATION

One of the most stringent organic-certification schemes both in the UK and internationally. Applies to farmers, growers, food processors and packers, retailers, caterers, textile producers, health and beauty manufacturers and importers.

FAIR TRADE ORGANISATION MARK (FTO MARK)

Issued by the International Fair Trade Association (IFAT) to identify organisations that practice fair trade.

WHOLESOME FOOD ASSOCIATION

The WFA local symbol scheme is a low-cost, grassroots alternative to organic certification for people who are growing or producing food for sale in their local region. The association also campaigns to promote small-scale, sustainable food production.

FRIEND OF THE SEA

Approved fisheries only target stocks which are not overexploited; use fishing methods which don't impact the seabed; and generate fewer discards than normal fishing practices.

RED TRACTOR LOGO

This is your guarantee that the produce has come from farms assessed to standards concerned with food safety, animal welfare and environmental regulations.

GOOD SHOPPING GUIDE: ETHICAL COMPANY

UK-certified scheme covering issues of environment, animal welfare and human rights across a number of categories, including food and drink.

RSPCA FREEDOM FOODS

The only farm assurance and food labelling scheme dedicated to improving farm-animal welfare in the UK. Food bearing this logo shows the animal was reared on a farm meeting the scheme's strict higher welfare standards covering every stage of the animal's life.

MARINE STEWARDSHIP COUNCIL (MSC)

This environmental standard for sustainable fishing demonstrates the product has not contributed to over-fishing. Any seafood displaying this is from a fishery that has met these standards in independent tests.

VEGETARIAN SOCIETY APPROVED

Products carrying this logo must fulfil certain requirements laid down by the Vegetarian Society. The Suitable for Vegetarians logo is not regulated, however it is illegal for labelling to include anything misleading or false.

▼ Some pesticides were originally developed as nerve poisons for military use

Pesticides

Pesticides are designed to kill or damage living organisms in the environment. They are used extensively in conventional farming to control insects, weeds and plant diseases and to prevent fungicides from rotting harvested crops during transportation. Their application also extends to a wide variety of other uses, ranging from domestic pest control and gardening to head-lice treatments and bacterial soaps.

In 2005, more than 31 million tonnes of pesticides were applied to crops in the UK alone, and around 30% of food bought here contains pesticide residues.

But despite the scale of their use, pesticides have a bad record when it comes to their damaging effect on the environment and human health: some were originally developed as nerve poisons for military use.

The world's eyes were opened to the devastating effects of DDT in 1962 with the publication of Rachel Carson's Silent Spring, which revealed with startling alarm how the pesticide was killing off birds in great numbers. Although DDT was banned in the UK more than 20 years ago, traces of it can be found in most humans today due to the fact that it breaks down so slowly and builds up in the fatty tissues of all animals.

Pesticides and health

There are around 1,000 different pesticides in use globally today. While many are not thought to be harmful to us, some are immediately poisonous, while others have a more subtle, long-term effect.

The herbicide paraquat, for example, is a highly toxic compound, which according to Pesticide Action Network UK (PAN UK) is responsible for thousands of human poisonings every year. PAN UK also claims that of the millions who experience acute pesticide poisoning every year, most are inadequately protected farm workers in developing countries. The World Health Organisation estimates that there are around 200,000 pesticide-related deaths every year.

But it is the long-term consequences of exposure to different pesticides which are believed to be of most concern to us in the UK, since there is very little understanding among scientists of the 'cocktail effect' of the different chemicals.

According to PAN UK, many chemicals in pesticides can lead to serious physical and psychological health problems including cancer, Parkinson's disease, infertility, low birth weight in babies, depression and lower IQ.

Pesticides and the environment

The effect of pesticides on wildlife and the wider environment makes for equally unsettling reading. The increased use of pesticides has led to a significant, and well documented decline in many native species of birds, either by direct poisoning or by eating other animals and insects that have been killed by the pesticides.

In 2001, about half a pint of the insecticide chlorpyrifos was accidentally spilt into the Sussex River Ouse. Although the concentration was less than 0.001mg (parts per million) per litre it wreaked havoc on the river's aquatic life for 20km downstream, killing as much as 80% of fish in affected areas.

It is estimated, some say conservatively, that, through water rates, taxpayers pay at least £120 million a year cleaning agricultural pollutants – including pesticides – from our water supplies. The Soil Association is campaigning for a pesticide tax to reflect this hidden cost.

For more information on pesticides and how to avoid them you can download Pesticide Action Network UK's Pesticides on a Plate: A consumer guide to pesticide issues in the food chain at *www.pan-uk.org/Poap.html*.

The worst 10 foods for containing pesticide residues

- Flour
- Potatoes
- Bread
- Apples
- Pears
- Grapes
- Strawberries
- Green Beans
- Tomatoes
- Cucumbers

Source: Pesticide Action Network UK

Genetic modification

The genetic modification (GM) of food is a fairly new technology widely used in the US, Canada, China and Argentina, and is a highly contentious issue. Supporters claim GM is the answer to alleviating world hunger and disease by increasing crop yields and bringing down prices. Sceptics are worried about the effects of what is a largely untested method of farming on broader ecosystems, the economy and our health. We've rounded up a few opinions for you to help you make your own mind up.

'I'm no friend of big biotech. I think GM has created a dangerous power shift in agriculture in favour of multinational corporations. So I'm cautious about GM foods, but they seem safe overall. If there's something new and frightening, then I want to see it published, in full, so we can all sit down and get frightened by it together, on the basis of well conducted research that we can see and read. Before that, I'm not sure anyone's very well served by scare headlines.'
Ben Goldacre, writer, broadcaster, and medical doctor

'GM chemical companies constantly claim they have the answer to world hunger while selling products which have never led to overall increases in production, and which have sometimes decreased yields or even led to crop failures. As oil becomes scarcer and more expensive, we need to move away from oil dependent GM crops to producing food sustainably, using renewable energy, as is the case with organic farming.'
Peter Melchett, Soil Association policy director

'To label GM crops as either good or bad for the environment completely misses the point. GM is just one of a range of methods used to produce novel crops, and it is how that new crop is managed that will determine its environmental impact. The scientific evidence shows that some GM crops – for example, those resistant to insect pests – can actually bring environmental benefits, by reducing the application of synthetic pesticides. We should maintain an open mind and assess all options if we want to develop sustainable agriculture.'
Prof Rosie Hails, ecologist at the Centre For Ecology And Hydrology

If you want to avoid GM ingredients:

- Buy organic food. GM is strictly forbidden in the production of organic produce
- Don't buy processed food like ready meals unless you can be certain that they are GM-free
- Buy locally produced foods directly from the producer (such as farmers' markets and farm shops) where you can ask how the food was produced.

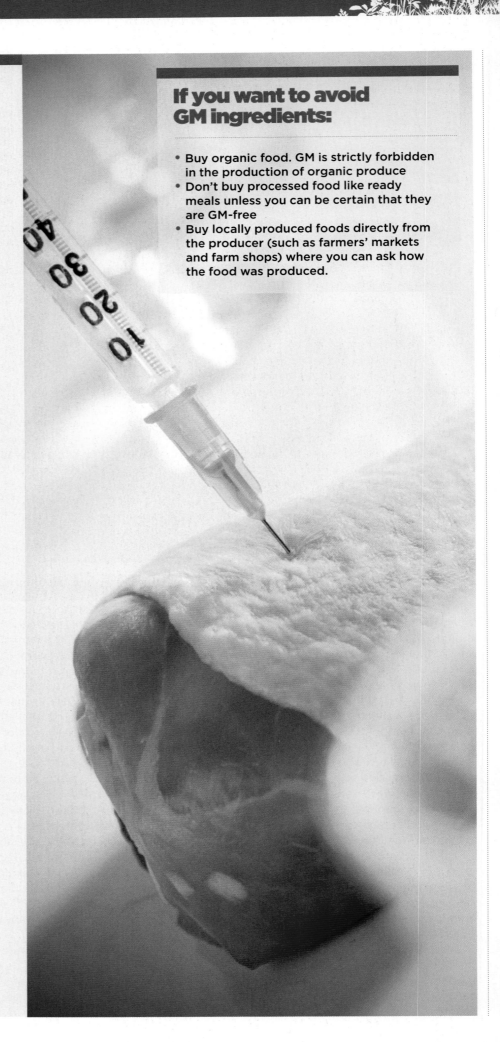

IN PRACTICE:

Sedlescombe Vineyard

When Roy Cook was given an opportunity to escape the rat race, he seized it with both hands. Within a few years, ambition got the better of him and he created Britain's first organic vineyard. This is his story.

Back in the 1970s, a heart-warming television series captured the imagination of millions of viewers by offering a nostalgic glimpse of what it meant to 'live off the land'.

For some, The Good Life even helped spur a complete change of life, as couples and individuals sought to follow in the footsteps of Tom and Barbara by turning their backs on modern convention and returning to the self-sufficient lifestyle of yesterday. Among them were Roy Cook and his wife Irma.

Their big break came when Roy inherited a 10-acre plot of land a few miles inland from Hastings in East Sussex close to the picturesque village of Sedlescombe. Roy decided to pack in his career as a salesman and follow the couple's dream of leading a low impact life living in a caravan and growing all their own fruit and veg. Surplus food would be sold to locals to raise a little cash for life's other necessities.

Within a few years Roy got a yearning to do more with his inherited plot and for a while considered venturing into organic tomato farming.

"Then I discovered I had all the right conditions for growing vines," he said. "It was a warm site, well sheltered from northerly and easterly winds and had a southerly aspect which meant it got plenty of sunshine.

"In my attempt to become self-sufficient I had developed a successful organic vegetable garden and realised that it was quite possible, against the prevailing wisdom of the time, to grow successfully without using the array of chemical fertilizers, weedkillers and disease control sprays that most growers assumed were necessary."

In 1979, with just 2,000 plants spread over 1.5 acres of his most fertile land, Roy became Britain's first organic wine producer using a traditional technique he discovered in a German Gothic textbook written by Dr Julius Nessler in 1885.

Today the business is flourishing and Roy has extended his Soil Association-accredited plantation to around 23 acres spread over five plots of land in the local area.

Annual yields vary enormously. In 2006, for example, the vineyards produced almost 30,000 bottles, but in 2007 there were just 5,000 bottles and last year, 8,000 bottles. So far the signs are looking good for 2009.

Over the last three decades, Sedlescombe Organic Vineyard has won a number of notable awards and commendation and in 2008 Roy was nominated an Eco Hero by The Telegraph in recognition of his contribution towards saving the environment.

As an industry, things are looking bright for English and Welsh winemakers. There have been many new plantings in recent years which will be starting to mature soon, and existing wines are already winning awards in international competitions and gaining credibility.

"These facts, together with increased consumer awareness of the carbon footprint of products and consumers desire to buy local wherever possible means demand should increase," said Roy.

But even with his optimism for the industry, Roy remains firmly committed to his organic roots and is particularly hopeful for his niche sector.

"Despite the recent decrease in demand for organic products due to the recession, it is likely that this is only a blip and that rates of increase in demand will revert to pre-recession levels once the recession ends," he said.

"As I see it, it is only organic farming principles which can regain the health of the countryside and wild-life habitats, and reduce pollution."

Find out more about Sedlescombe Organic Vineyard and where to buy its wines at **www.englishorganicwine.co.uk.** ■

> **"Even with his optimism for the industry, Roy remains firmly committed to his organic roots and is particularly hopeful for his niche sector"**

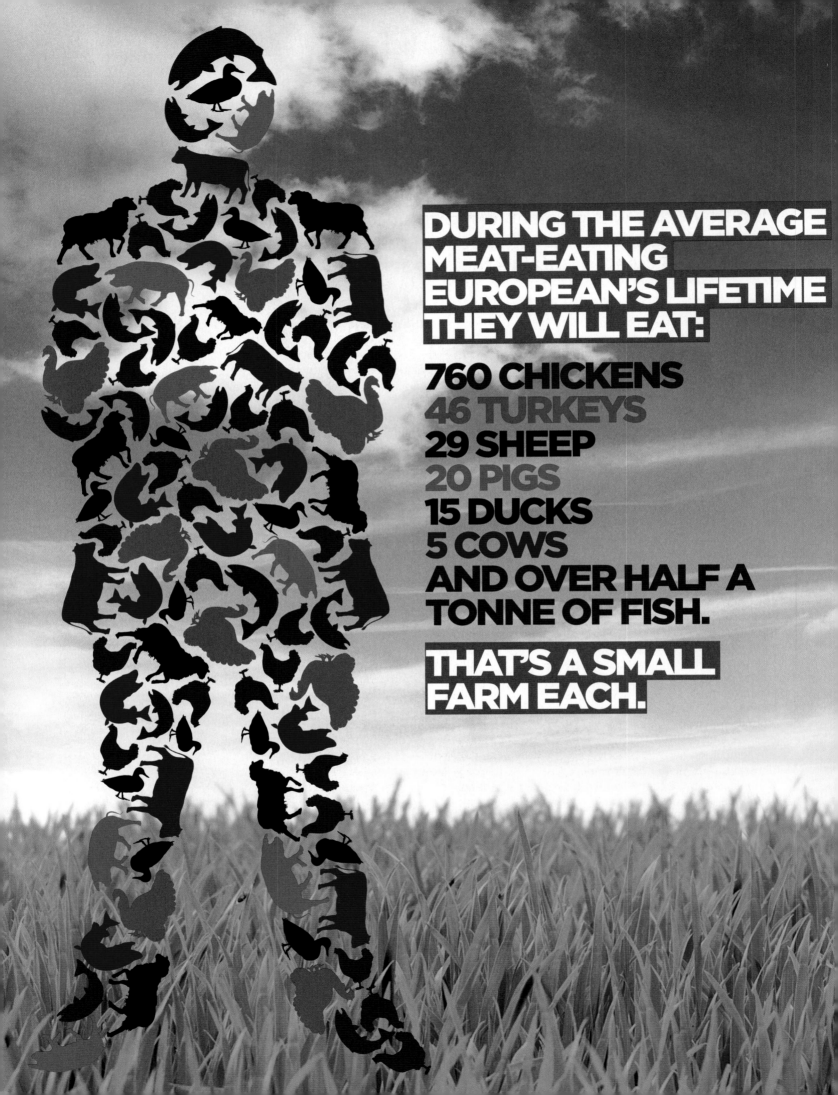

FOOD IN FOCUS

Free-range, fairtrade, locally sourced, organic – when it comes to buying our food, the choice and responsibility we face as consumers is dizzying. Here we've broken down all the facts and figures to help you make the best choices for you and your family

MEAT

Livestock production is a major cause of global warming, land degradation, air and water pollution and loss of biodiversity. Every year human beings slaughter nearly 60 billion animals for food – not including fish. That's nearly 10 animals per person. The UN's Food and Agriculture Organisation (FAO) predicts that by 2050 global meat consumption will be twice that of 2001 levels and milk consumption will nearly double. This expected rise will put a huge extra strain on the environment and will mean many millions more farm animals will suffer through intensive farming.

In the Western world we eat vast amounts of meat. Where once it was a treat, today meat and two veg has more or less become our staple diet. As well as being damaging to the environment, eating too much meat can be bad for your health, increasing the risk of coronary heart disease and obesity. **Here are some steps you can take to make a difference:**

• Compassion in World Farming (CIWF), the international farm animal welfare group, is campaigning to achieve a global reduction in meat production and consumption. We can all play our part by actively choosing to cut back on our own meat consumption and use vegetarian options in more meals.

• Expect to pay more for free-range and organic produce and remember that the low cost of meat in our supermarkets is artificial and unethical.

• Make the most of the animal produce you do buy. A chicken carcass, for example, will make an excellent stock when boiled, just as many other bones form the basis of delicious soups.

DAIRY PRODUCTS

Modern dairy practices bring new meaning to the term intensive farming. The average cow produces around 6,770 litres of milk a year, which is more than double the amount of 50 years ago.

To lactate, cows have to give birth first and are often given fertility drugs to help them become pregnant. They never usually get a chance to suckle their young because it makes no economic sense for farmers to let them do so. Instead the male calves are killed within a few weeks or carted off to be reared as veal. The mothers are milked up to three times a day until the milk runs dry, by which time they have usually been pregnant (via artificial insemination) for several months, ready to start the cycle again after a short rest from milking. Most dairy cows give birth three or four times before being slaughtered for meat at the age of around seven. **Here's how you can make a difference:**

• Buying organic milk ensures a far higher standard of animal welfare as well as avoiding antibiotic residues.

• Try never to buy milk or dairy products from outside of the EU, and preferably not from outside the UK; the EU has banned the commonly used cow growth hormone bovine somatotrophin (BST), which has been linked to colon and breast cancer, diabetes and hypertension.

> **"Buying organic milk ensures a far higher standard of animal welfare"**

Did you know?

The word organic describes food that has been grown or reared without the reliance on artificial fertilisers or pesticides and in a way that emphasises crop rotation, making the most of natural fertilisers and ensuring that the life of the soil is maintained. There are several organic accreditation bodies in the UK, which can makes things a little confusing for the consumer. Different bodies have slightly different standards for what constitutes something as organic. It is illegal to market something as organic unless it has been approved by at least one of these bodies.

FISH

Years of over-fishing has left many species perilously close to extinction and many others in serious decline. The Food and Agriculture Organisation (FAO) reports that over 70% of the world's fish stocks are now fully fished, over-fished or depleted. In the North Sea, for example, many once-common species such as cod, skate and plaice have been fished to such an extent that cod stocks are close to commercial collapse, whilst common skate is virtually extinct.

When buying fish look for the Marine Stewardship Council (MSC) or Friends of the Sea logos (see page 100) which means the fish is from a well managed, sustainable fishery.

Nearly 70% of the world's fish stocks are over-fished

FISH TO AVOID

- ATLANTIC COD
- ATLANTIC HALIBUT
- ATLANTIC SALMON (WILD-CAUGHT)
- BRILL
- CONGER EEL
- EUROPEAN HAKE
- LING
- MARLIN
- ORANGE ROUGHY
- PLAICE
- RED OR BLACKSPOT SEABREAM
- SEABASS (TRAWL-CAUGHT ONLY)
- SHARK
- SNAPPER
- STURGEON
- SWORDFISH
- TIGER PRAWN
- TUNA (EXCEPT DOLPHIN-FRIENDLY, POLE-AND LINE-CAUGHT YELLOW FIN, SKIPJACK AND ALBACORE)
- TURBOT (FROM NORTH SEA)
- TUSK

FISH TO EAT

- BLACK BREAM
- BROWN CRAB (POT-CAUGHT OFF SOUTH DEVON COAST)
- CLAM (SUSTAINABLY HARVESTED)
- COCKLE (MSC CERTIFIED)
- ATLANTIC COD (ORGANICALLY FARMED)
- PACIFIC COD (SUSTAINABLY HARVESTED)
- DOVER SOLE (MSC CERTIFIED)
- FLOUNDER
- PACIFIC HALIBUT (MSC CERTIFIED)
- HERRING OR SILD
- LEMON SOLE
- WESTERN AUSTRALIAN ROCK LOBSTER (MSC CERTIFIED)
- LYTHE OR POLLACK (LINE-CAUGHT AND TAGGED FROM CORNWALL)
- MACKEREL (MSC CERTIFIED)
- MUSSEL (SUSTAINABLY HARVESTED)
- OYSTER (SUSTAINABLY HARVESTED)
- PILCHARD AND SARDINE
- ATLANTIC SALMON (ORGANICALLY FARMED)

For a full list visit www.fishonline.org. The MSC prints a free guide of what fish to eat and avoid for easy reference when shopping or eating out. The Good Fish Pocket Guide is available from MCS on receipt of a SAE to Marine Conservation Society, Unit 3 Wolf Business Park, Alton Road, Ross-on-Wye, HR9 5NB

EGGS

Every year the UK gets through around 10 billion eggs. Most of these are laid by battery hens confined to small cages stacked one on top of the other. Their food and water is supplied – and dropping and eggs removed – via automated machines. The cages are so small and cramped that the birds do not have enough room to exhibit natural behaviours and often suffer from broken bones and other physical harm. In 1999, after years of campaigning by Compassion in World Farming and its supporters, the EU passed the Laying Hens Directive which required complete phasing out of the use of battery cages by 2012. However, this ban is under threat with certain EU member states and members of the egg industry calling for the ban to be delayed or even dropped completely because they think it will be economically damaging.

One step up from battery hens are barn systems, a less intensive alternative which allows birds to perch, lay eggs in nest boxes and have room to dust themselves. However, the conditions are still very cramped and a far cry from a hen's natural outdoor environment.

Free-range eggs means that the birds have been given access to the outdoors and have more space to roam, flap their wings and scratch the ground. However, flocks can still be very large.

Organically reared hens fair the best of all farmed chickens, with stringent standards requiring the highest levels of animal welfare.

Eggs are stamped with a numbering system to tell you how the hens were kept, the country they originated from and the farm they came from. The first number relates to the way they were kept: '0' is organic, '1' is free-range, '2' is barn and '3' is caged.

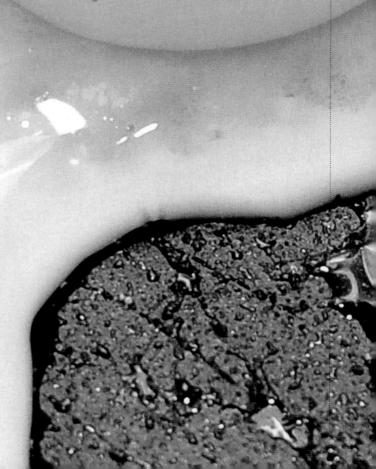

A GUARDIAN STUDY CALCULATED THE COMBINED DISTANCE TRAVELLED BY 20 FRESH FOOD ITEMS BEFORE ARRIVING AT THE SUPERMARKET: IT AMOUNTED TO AN ASTONISHING 100,943 MILES!

BUYING LOCAL

The distance that our food travels can be shocking – and it's not just imports that are a cause for concern. Many locally produced products can travel miles around the country from farm to warehouse to supermarket. This section shows you how to cut down on food miles, get the freshest produce and help your local economy in the process

Farmers' Market

A farmers' market is a market where people can buy well presented local produce directly from the farmers and growers who produced them. Different markets have slightly different rules, but generally all the goods on sale must come from within a 25 to 30 mile radius ensuring very low food miles and freshness. As well as selling meats, fruits and vegetables a number of stallholders will typically sell prepared foods and drinks all made with local ingredients.

The idea is that all products on offer at a farmers' market should be grown, reared, caught, brewed, pickled, baked, smoked or processed by the stallholder, or one of their colleagues or member of family. That way the consumer can ask anything they like about the produce, such as where it comes from, how it was grown or reared, whether it is organic or pesticide free, and so on.

There are more than 500 farmers' markets in the UK; about half of which are FARMA Certified, which means they have been independently assessed to ensure they meet the necessary criteria.
Visit *www.farmersmarkets.net* to find your nearest farmers' market.

Farm Shops

Another great way to cut down on food miles and get the freshest seasonal produce is to buy directly from farm shops. Farm shops sell food and drink that has been grown, picked, reared or produced locally, and usually on the farm where the farm shop is located.
Visit *www.farmshopping.net* to find your nearest farm shop.

Pick Your Own

When it comes to getting your hands on the freshest fruit and veg there is no better way than to pick it yourself. If you don't have the space or inclination to grow your own food, the good news is that there are a number of farms and nurseries sprinkled around the countryside which allow paying members of the public directly onto their fields to do just that. Picking your own fruit and veg can be a great trip out for the family as well as for individuals, and gives you the opportunity to select only the ripest and juiciest of foods while keeping food miles limited to just the journey home. Ask the farmer for his advice on how to know what's ripe and also the best way to pick the produce to ensure longevity and freshness.
To find Pick Your Own farms and nurseries near you, visit *www.yell.com* and search for 'Pick your own fruit vegetables'.

Did you know...?

Air-freighting is by far the worst form of food transport. A 2007 study found that green beans flown in from Kenya were 20 to 26 times more greenhouse gas intensive than those grown in season at home in the UK.

Useful links

www.farmersmarkets.net
Lists FARMA-certified farmers' markets by area

www.farmshopping.net
Lists FARMA-approved shops by area

Box fresh

Getting fresh fruit and vegetables delivered straight to your door from the local farm has never been easier. The number of these so-called 'box schemes' has risen steadily in recent years, meaning that – more likely than not – there will be a farm in your area offering the service.

Different box schemes work in different ways, but generally involve the weekly delivery of fresh, locally grown and in-season fruit and veg directly to the customer's home. The level of choice and control of what goes into the box will depend on the scheme operators, though customers can usually opt out of things they don't like. Some box schemes also offer meat and dairy products, while some offer a nationwide service, often with food bought in from co-operatives and wholesalers.

For a scheme to be organic the produce must have been certified as such by a government-approved body, such as the Soil Association (see p100). A number of schemes only offer non-organic food.

Some box schemes offer an online recipe service covering all of the products you are likely to find in your box. Grow Wild's website, for example, has a page dedicated to recipes using all the vegetables they supply. This can be a great resource for finding ways to get rid of leftovers.

To find organic box schemes in your area try doing an internet search. Alternatively, ask your local farm shop if they will deliver to your home.

Fruits of your labour

Why not encourage uptake of box schemes at your place of work? You could specify a fruit-only box that everyone can tuck into.

Grow Wild

Wild about organic.

How convenient? Ready meals under the microscope

Part of the trouble with ready meals is that they are cooked twice, which means they waste lots of energy and lose much of their nutritional value before they are eaten. They also contain lots of packaging – normally a plastic tray with a plastic film covered with a cardboard sleeve.

The ingredients are usually the cheapest available, which means they are the result of intensive farming using all manner of fertilisers, pesticides and other agrichemicals.

Some farm shops and farmers' market stallholders have started to make their own ready meals for sale using local ingredients. These are a huge step above your average processed ready meal found in the supermarket, though they are still cooked twice and use loads of packaging. If you don't have time to cook try stocking up your freezer with a few of these locally made alternatives to the supermarket ready meal. They taste far superior, are more healthy and you may even be surprised at how reasonably priced they are.

▼ Ready meals are usually made with the cheapest ingredients available

10 REASONS TO GO TO A FARMERS' MARKET

ORGANIC

01
LESS FOOD MILES
Since all of the produce is local, farmers' markets cut food miles down to a minimum which is good for the environment as well as keeping producers' costs down

06
CUSTOMER SERVICE
Consumers can ask the producers questions directly about the food, so they can be sure of how it is produced and where it comes from

02
LESS WASTE
Most produce is loose and unpackaged, which means overall packaging is reduced significantly

07
LOCAL BUSINESS
By buying from a farmers' market you are helping the local economy by supporting local businesses as well as increasing employment

03
FRESH GOODS
Meat and veg at farmers' market is among the freshest you are ever likely to buy, unless you rear the animals and grow vegetables yourself

08
SUPPORTING PRODUCERS
Farmers' markets cut out the middleman allowing the producers increased financial returns.

04
BETTER PRACTICE
Farmers' markets encourage more sustainable production practices, such as organic farming or pesticide-free

09
TRADITION
Farmers' markets restore a sense of traditional life back into towns and cities which may have come alienated from country ways and farming

TOMATO

05
GET MORE
Farmers' markets have a reputation for offering a rich variety of produce not commonly found in supermarkets, which is great for the consumer as well as biodiversity through farm diversification

10
COMMUNITY
The relaxed, community feel of a farmers' market make them popular social occasions, as well as opportunities to buy fresh, local produce

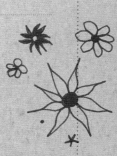

FARM

BUYING IN SEASON

JANUARY

VEGETABLES
- Artichokes (Jerusalem)
- Brussels sprouts
- Celery
- Chard
- Beetroot
- Leeks
- Parsnips
- Salsify
- Spinach
- Swede

FRUIT & NUTS
- Last of the English apples
- Nuts

FEBRUARY

VEGETABLES
- Brussels Sprouts
- Leeks
- Parsnips
- Shallots
- Spinach
- Swede

MARCH

VEGETABLES
- Calabrese
- Purple-sprouting broccoli
- Spring greens
- Spring onions
- Winter cauliflower

FRUIT
- Rhubarb

JULY

VEGETABLES
- Artichokes (Globe)
- Beetroot
- Broad beans
- Carrots
- Summer cauliflower
- Cucumbers
- Parsnips
- French beans

FRUIT
- Bilberries
- Blackcurrants
- Blueberries
- Cherries
- Gooseberries
- Raspberries
- Redcurrants

AUGUST

VEGETABLES
- Artichokes (Globe)
- Aubergine
- Beetroot
- Broad beans
- Broccoli
- Carrots
- Courgettes
- Cucumber
- Fresh beans

FRUIT
- Apples
- Apricots
- Cherries
- Loganberries
- Melons
- Plums

SEPTEMBER

VEGETABLES
- Artichokes (Globe)
- Aubergine
- Beetroot
- Broccoli
- Autumn cabbages
- Carrots
- Cauliflower
- Cucumber
- Fresh beans

FRUIT
- Apples
- Blackberries
- Elderberries
- Figs
- Grapes

Buying in-season produce saves food miles and CO2 emissions, but many of us have become out of touch with the growing cycles of our fruits and veg. Check our calendar for an easy guide to what's in season and when...

APRIL

VEGETABLES
- New potatoes
- Leeks
- Spring cabbages
- Lettuces and other salad leaves

FRUIT
- Rhubarb

MAY

VEGETABLES
- Asparagus
- Broad beans
- Some cabbages
- New potatoes
- Spinach
- Radishes

FRUIT
- Rhubarb

JUNE

VEGETABLES
- Artichokes
- Asparagus
- Courgettes
- New potatoes
- Salad leaves
- Watercress
- Radish

FRUIT
- Cherries
- Gooseberries
- Rhubarb
- Strawberries

OCTOBER

VEGETABLES
- Broccoli
- Carrots
- Autumn cauliflowers
- Celeriac
- Celery
- Autumn cabbages
- Kohlrabi
- Lettuces and salad leaves

FRUIT & NUTS
- Crab apples
- Hazelnuts
- Pears
- Quince
- Sweet chestnuts

NOVEMBER

VEGETABLES
- Artichoke (Jerusalem)
- Beetroot
- Brussels sprouts
- Autumn cauliflowers
- Cabbages
- Carrots
- Winter Cauliflowers
- Celeriac
- Celery

FRUIT & NUTS
- Crab apples
- Hazelnuts
- Pears
- Quince
- Sweet chestnuts

DECEMBER

VEGETABLES
- Artichoke (Jerusalem)
- Brussels sprouts
- Celery
- Chard
- Curly kale
- Garlic
- Leeks
- Parsnips
- Pumpkin
- Salsify
- Spinach
- Swedes
- Turnips

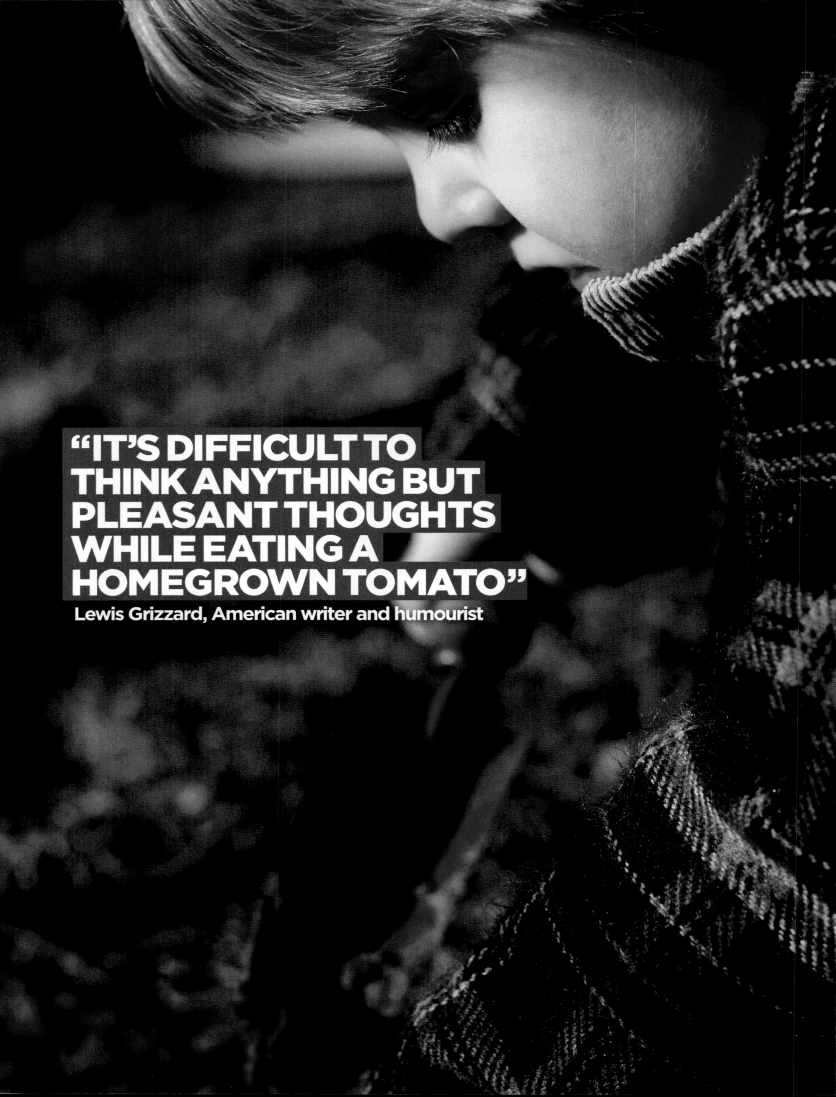

"IT'S DIFFICULT TO THINK ANYTHING BUT PLEASANT THOUGHTS WHILE EATING A HOMEGROWN TOMATO"

Lewis Grizzard, American writer and humourist

GROW YOUR OWN

During the Second World War 'growing your own' was common, but the end of rationing and the birth of modern farming techniques saw this need fade away as the cost of food fell. But now it's coming back in favour, and we have all the info you need to do it yourself!

Better for you, better for everyone!

There are loads of benefits of growing your own vegetables, not just for the environment and health, but also as a physical activity which offers rich rewards and modest savings. Environmentally speaking, growing your own vegetables is great news for a number of different reasons:

- No or very few food miles
- No packaging
- No preservatives
- No or limited pesticide use
- Good for wildlife and biodiversity.

Many home growers are organic from the outset, whilst many others adopt the practice once they've got up and running and want to reap the most benefits from their smallholding.

When it comes to health, growing organic fruit and veg is good news – it avoids the use of pesticides and artificial fertilisers, which are suspected of causing long-term health problems, as well as negative effects on the wider environment. As a grower you have a level of control over what goes into making your food, which you cannot get when you buy from someone else. And, of course, when you come to eat it you know that the taste is exactly as nature intended.

Growing your own can also be a good way to get exercise and fresh air, as well as being hugely psychologically beneficial. If you ask almost any home grower why they do it, chances are that the feeling of satisfaction in seeing something grow and nurturing it until it's ready for the table will be high up on their list. For many, this feel-good factor extends to simply spending time outdoors and seeing nature in action.

Then of course there's the eating! Popping into the garden to dig some potatoes, cut a vine of tomatoes and grab a bunch of lettuce for your supper is a delight only bettered by the eating itself.

In terms of cost and savings, growing your own vegetables and fruit is not likely to yield large returns. However, certain produce costs more than others, so if you are looking to start growing as a means to saving money it is best to grow things which will offer the greater rewards (such as butternut squash or strawberries). And if you grow organically then the savings are likely to be greater still.

Save Cash! With the average allotment yielding a ton of vegetables a year, the average family could save in the region of £950.

GROWING YOUR OWN: get started

If you are growing a single vegetable in a pot on the windowsill you will only need a pot, some soil and a seed. For more ambitious projects you may want to invest in some of these items:

- ☑ SPADE AND FORK
- ☑ HOE
- ☑ WATERING CAN
- ☑ TROWEL
- ☑ GLOVES
- ☑ MAT
- ☑ DIBBER

- ☑ STRING
- ☑ RAKE
- ☑ COMPOST
- ☑ MANURE & ORGANIC
- FERTILISER
- ☑ NETTING / RABBIT FENCING

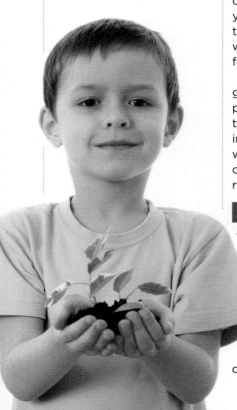

When you're starting up, it may be better to pick crops that are quite easy to grow

Where to grow

Whether it be in the garden, on an allotment or just a few pots on the windowsill, nearly everyone will have access to somewhere they can start growing. Of course the more space you have the greater the scope for big returns, though keeping it small and simple is a great way to start, and often the most preferred way for a lot of experienced growers.

You will need to prepare the ground for growing by digging up any weeds, grass and plants and turning the soil. You can improve the quality of your soil at this stage by adding organic compost and manure to enrich it with extra nutrition. Add an organic fertiliser a couple of weeks before planting or sowing to ready the bed.

Sowing

A key thing to keep in mind when you're starting is to choose the right crops and not to do too much at once. Some vegetables are a lot easier to grow than others, so it may be best selecting those that will have the greatest chance of success. This will not only be good for your confidence but it will also give you a good idea of how much work is involved in growing your own produce. When you get ready to sow the

> "The more space you have, the greater the scope for big returns, though keeping it small and simple is a great way to start"

following year you will have a lot of experience under your belt, making you better placed to try things a little more tricky and unpredictable.

Once you've made up your mind on what you're going to plant and have bought all your seeds, you will need to sow them either into the ground or into small pots to be transplanted later. Different plants grow in different ways so it is always important to check the growing instructions on your seed packets for the manufacturer's advice on when and how to sow.

Remember that planting and growing should be a continual process throughout the year. If you time things well you can have seedlings ready to put in the ground just as another crop is coming to an end. Being a good grower is about keeping on top of your vegetable patch so that you are always getting the most out of the ground.

Keep it fresh!

For a user friendly guide to storing and preserving your garden produce so you can eat home-grown vegetables all year round, read How to Store Your Garden Produce...The Key to Self Sufficiency, by Piers Warren, priced £7.95

Planting on

Once seedlings are big enough to handle they need to be transplanted to the ground, grow bags or large pots, depending on what and where you are growing. Seedlings will need thinning out so that they are appropriately spaced to allow them to grow into full plants. Give your new plants plenty of water and for best results, feed them with an organic fertiliser such as seaweed or fish, blood and bone.

Maintenance

Once the seedlings are in the ground, make sure they have enough nutrients and water and are protected from pests and disease. Some plants will need even more attention, so it's important to check the individual requirements for each crop in advance.

Harvesting

Consult your seed packet for the manufacturer's advice on the best time to harvest, though a close inspection of the crop should usually tell you when it is ready to eat.

Storage

Unless you are planning to eat your entire harvest within a few of days you are going to have to spare thought as to how and where you are going to store it, or else all that work and dedication could quickly end up as rotting waste. Certain fruits and vegetables last much longer than others. Apples and potatoes can keep for months in a cool, dark place, but herbs need to be eaten fresh unless they are dried or frozen. Many crops can be cooked and made into sauces, preserves and pickles.

Crop Rotation

It is important to rotate the vegetables you plant in a bed from year to year to help prevent the build up of pests and diseases. New crops can benefit from the nutrients left by the previous crops. Usually, the rotation cycle is three years, but if you're growing potatoes it is better to have a four-year rotation.

Pest control: natural ways to keep pests at bay

As a grower you have to accept the fact that you are going to lose some produce to insects, birds and diseases. However, there are lots of things you can do to stop these unwanted intruders from wreaking havoc on your vegetable patch without having to turn to the pesticide spray or slug pellets.

- **KILL PESTS BY HAND** Done regularly, killing insects such as lily beetles and greenfly yourself can be a very effective method of pest control.

- **BE DIVERSE** Grow a variety of vegetables to spread the risk of losing all your crops. Different pests and diseases attack different plants, so by growing a range of species you would have to be extremely unlucky to lose more than a few.

- **USE NATURAL PEST DETERRENTS** Put up wire fences and netting to keep larger pests like rabbits and birds out of your vegetable patch and use crushed egg shells to deter slugs and snails.

- **MAKING FRIENDS** Encourage wildlife to do the hard work for you: many creatures feast on the pests you are trying to get rid of, so lure them to your garden by installing special insect boxes available from garden shops.

- **PLANT PEST-RESISTANT VARIETIES** Ask at your local garden centre for advice.

- **TRY COMPANION PLANTING:** This is a system where two or more plants are grown together to benefit each other, whether it be as a decoy for pests and diseases or to improve growth and flavour. It is usually aromatic foliage or flowers of the companion plant that deters the pest or draws it away.

▼ There are plenty of natual ways to deter pests

Finding an allotment

There a tens of thousands of allotments in the UK, but it is not always easy to find the ones closest to you. Visit the National Society for Allotment and Leisure Gardeners' website at *www.nsalg.org.uk* for handy hints on finding your nearest allotment or call them on 01536 266576.

Finding an allotment close to home can be difficult, but the NSALG can help

Did you know...?

By law, councils have to provide an allotment to any group of six or more adults over the age of 18 and registered on the Electoral Roll that request one.

GYO Books

Dr D. G. Hessayan's The Vegetable & Herb Expert is the world's best-selling book on vegetables and herbs and at £7.99 is well worth a try. If you want to get your kids involved at an early stage, try Growing Vegetables is Fun (www.growingisfun. co.uk), which comes with 4 free packs of seeds to get you started.

GROWING VEGETABLES IS FUN!

CHECKLIST

Keep it simple: the top 10 easy vegetables to try growing first

- ☑ Herbs
- ☑ Tomatoes
- ☑ Lettuce
- ☑ Spring onions
- ☑ Potatoes
- ☑ Broad beans
- ☑ Runner beans
- ☑ Onions
- ☑ Leeks
- ☑ Courgettes

Rear your own: smallholding for the average Joe

Like vegetable growing, rearing livestock at home has also seen a resurgence in recent years, thanks in no small part to the likes of Hugh Fearnley-Whittingstall and Dick Strawbridge, who have tempted the public with their honest, no-nonsense and ethical attitudes to smallholding. It may not to be to everyone's tastes, but for those with a passion for it, rearing animals for meat and dairy products offers huge rewards and a closeness to nature that most people have never experienced.

Getting into keeping livestock is not a decision to be taken lightly. It involves time, money, knowledge and a lot of commitment.

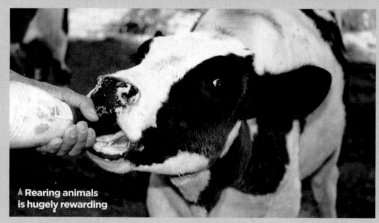

▲ Rearing animals is hugely rewarding

"**Rearing animals offers a closeness to nature that most people have never experienced**"

Many people therefore start off small and grow their smallholding as their confidence and practical knowledge improves.

Keeping chickens for eggs, for example, is a great way to get things off the ground with limited start-up costs (see panel).

Feeling clucky?

Eglu chicken houses

If you are thinking about keeping chickens for the first time, then the Eglu could be just what you are looking for. These easy-to-clean and safe contraptions have been designed by animal experts to be an ideal habitat for chickens as well as a colourful addition to your garden. All Eglus come with slide out dropping trays, hose clean surfaces, twin walled insulation and 'No Foxes Allowed' protection. Prices range from £360 for an original Eglu to £695 plus delivery for an Eglu Cube complete with 3m fox-proof run and big enough for 10 chickens. For more information visit *www.omlet .co.uk* or call 0845 450 2056.

A fair deal for farmers

As consumers, refusing to buy goods produced by exploiting workers gives us real power in the market. Look out for the Fairtrade mark as a guarantee of outstanding practice

FAIRTRADE

The aim of fair trade is to ensure the world's poorest farmers and workers get a fair deal for their products so that they can progress sustainably and avoid the exploitation the poorest producers have already suffered.

Today there are a number internationally recognised fair trade organisations in operation, though in the UK it is the Fairtrade Foundation that is most widely recognised.

There are now more than 3,000 Fairtrade products on sale in the UK covering a wide range of commodities from coffee and tea to bananas and coconuts, as well as a number of non-food products such as cotton, cut flowers, ornamental plants and even sports balls.

Supporting change

When you buy a Fairtrade product in the UK, part of the price goes directly towards the producers' investment in economic, social and environmental products of their own choice. This enables farmers to invest in the technologies and practices that will lead them to fully sustainable farming procedures in the future.

Tea workers in India, for example, have used their Fairtrade premium to replace traditional wood-burning heating with a solar-panelled system. Costa Rican coffee farmers have planted trees to prevent soil erosion and invested in environmentally friendly ovens, fuelled by recycled coffee hulls and dried macadamia shells.

Although, Fairtrade produce is not necessarily organic, Fairtrade premiums are often used for training in sustainable and organic techniques like composting and using recycled materials, which can help producers make progress in organic conversion in the

future. The Fairtrade system's environmental standards and guidelines currently forbid the use of GM seeds by farmers, and encourage active monitoring in nearby fields.

Finding products

Fairtrade products are widely available in the UK. Look for outlets that are part of BAFTS (British Association of Fair Trade Shops).

Tough decisions

A pertinent moral dilemma facing the conscientious shopper is whether to buy local produce to reduce food miles, or to support the world's poorest farmers despite their products being flown thousands of miles.

The Fairtrade Foundation's stance is that since many Fairtrade products cannot be grown in the UK, such as coffee and bananas, or products that cannot be produced in sufficient quantities to meet demand, such as honey and grapes, the two are not in competition with one another and purchases do not have to be mutually exclusive:

'Ultimately, it is up to each person to do what they see as being in the interests of people and the planet. What is important is that we all try to make informed choices wherever possible.'

Did you know...?

People around the world spent £1.6 billion on Fairtrade certified products in 2007. This was a 47% increase on the previous year and directly benefitted over 7 million people - farmers, workers and their families - in 58 developing countries.

LISA: "DO WE HAVE ANY FOOD THAT WASN'T BRUTALLY SLAUGHTERED?"
HOMER: "I THINK THE VEAL DIED OF LONELINESS."

MATT GROENING, THE SIMPSONS

ANIMAL WELFARE

For many, factory farming is so horrific they dissociate what they put in their mouths from what goes on in the sheds. This section lays out the reality of animal farming, gives advice on learning how your meat has been reared, and alternative ways to shop for and eat it

Meat as a treat

Fifty years ago eating meat was considered a luxury. Today meat features in most people's daily diets and access to cheap chicken and other meats has come to be seen as a right. As well as being bad news for animals, there are a number of health concerns linked to eating too much meat, and livestock farming worldwide is causing devastating environmental damage and contributing to climate change. By eating less meat and choosing more ethically sound options consumers can make bold environmental and social statements, whilst acting in the interests of their long-term health.

RSPCA Freedom Foods

The RSPCA's Freedom Foods is the only farm assurance and food labelling scheme dedicated to improving farm-animal welfare in the UK. When you see the Freedom Food logo on a product, it means the produce was reared on a farm that has met – and continues to meet – the scheme's strict higher welfare standards. These standards are based on scientific research, veterinary advice and practical farming experience; they cover each stage of the animal's life including food and water, environment, health, transport and slaughter.

Chickens, for example, are required to have bright lighting to encourage more activity and improve health, as well as periods of darkness when they can rest. Conventionally-farmed chickens often receive inadequate lighting and as little as an hour of darkness to rest a day.

Freedom Food produce does not necessarily mean that the animal was free-range, but it does guarantee that the farming system satisfies an animal's key welfare requirements. The scheme currently covers nine commonly farmed animals: beef cattle, dairy cattle, chickens, laying hens, ducks, pigs, sheep, turkey and salmon.

Free-range

For meat or eggs to be classed as free-range they must have been produced to standards laid down by EU law. In essence, a free-range animal is one that has been allowed to roam freely instead of being constrained in cages or crates. Animals should be allowed as much freedom as possible to live out their instinctual behaviours in a reasonably natural way.

Free-range food costs more than non-free-range Freedom Food and is available in most supermarkets and butchers. The term is most commonly applied to poultry, meat and eggs.

Be careful about misleading labelling such as 'barn eggs', 'farm fresh' and 'country fresh' which do not mean free-range.

Organically reared livestock

A happy animal is a healthy animal, and so the highest standards of animal welfare are at the heart of organic farming. Although different certification schemes set different criteria for producers, welfare standards are set to ensure all of the animal's needs, behavioural and physical, are satisfied and usually far surpass the standards set for free-range animals. Organically reared animals must be able to range freely in fields (when weather and ground conditions permit) and have plenty of space, which reduces stress and the chance of disease.

An organic hen will have about four times as much space to roam outdoors as a free-range hen and will spend as much as two-thirds of its life with access to the outdoors. Organic birds are kept in smaller flocks and have better access to fresh grass and air.

If you want the very best in animal husbandry, the Soil Association sets some of the most stringent standards around.

> **"Watch out for labelling like 'barn eggs' and 'farm fresh', they do not mean 'free-range'"**

▼ **Organic chickens have far more freedon than free-range chickens**

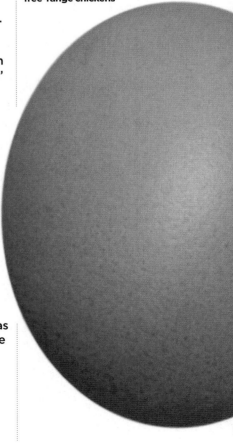

CIWF COMPASSIONATE SUPERMARKET AWARDS

Every couple of years, Compassion in World Farming (CIWF) carries out a detailed survey of UK supermarkets' performance on farm animal welfare to help consumers understand what matters to farm animals and how they can make a difference to their lives.

1st
MARKS & SPENCER

M&S champions high-welfare food and raises the standard for other supermarkets. Animal welfare is at the heart of its business.

2nd
WAITROSE

Also leading the way, Waitrose has a strong track record on animal welfare and continues to make excellent advances.

3rd
THE CO-OPERATIVE FOOD

Committed to improving animal welfare, the Co-op shows animal-friendly products can be sold at affordable prices.

4th
SAINSBURY'S

Sainsbury's has made great strides in animal welfare and was the first of the 'big four' UK supermarkets to commit to going cage-free on all shell eggs and eggs in its own-label products by 2012.

5th
TESCO

The biggest supermarket, Tesco can change the lives of billions of farm animals when it improves welfare. It is strong on ensuring policies become reality through rigorous auditing.

6th
MORRISONS

Morrisons is developing its standard and is starting to take customers' concerns about animal welfare seriously.

7th and 8th
SOMERFIELD AND ASDA

ASDA refused to provide information, so its scores are from CIWF's 2005 survey. Shop more compassionately at Somerfield and ASDA by buying free-range or organic products.

What else can you do? Stop being a chicken and join a campaign

Last year, chefs Hugh Fearnley-Whittingstall and Jamie Oliver used their celebrity status to raise awareness of the appalling conditions suffered by intensively reared chickens and the grim reality of battery farming.

The exposé prompted a huge surge in demand for free-range poultry, meat and eggs in the UK, with many supermarkets reporting records sales. More than 160,000 people and over 250 politicians have since signed up to the Chicken Out! campaign calling for better welfare conditions for all farmed chickens in the UK.

The public's reaction highlights just how far removed many people are from the reality of livestock farming and the level of suffering endured by the animals that feed us. It also reveals the power of education and committed campaigning.

If you are outraged at the way animals are treated on UK farms write to your local paper, supermarket, or MP telling them about it. The more people voice their feelings about the issue the more likely standards will improve.

You could also join an animal protection group that campaigns for better conditions for farmed animals, such as Compassion in World Farming (CIWF) and People for the Ethical Treatment of Animals (PETA).

Hugh Fearnley-Whittingstall helped raise consumer awareness on battery farming

"Food seems an area where we're happy to save money, whereas it should be the most important thing. Some people will spend £30,000 on a car then go and buy a bumper pack of mince"

Hugh Fearnley-Whittingstall

IN PRACTICE:

Terre a Terre

'Mouthwatering vegetarian dinner' may be an oxymoron to meat-lovers, but with pressure from environmentalists to rein in our carnivorous tendencies, one Brighton restaurant might coax us from our cravings

Given the preoccupation celebrity chefs seem to have with meat- and fish-based banquets, you might think cooking a decent vegetarian meal is beyond them.

Gordon et al have whetted the nation's appetite for haute cuisine, but, when it comes to promoting meat-free dishes, they leave a lot to be desired.

Quality vegetarian food remains under the radar in many British restaurants, but there are plenty of veggie outlets providing nutritious nosh to enliven the tastebuds of even the most voracious meat eater. There is perhaps no better place to try than award-winning Terre à Terre, in Brighton.

It opened its doors to a somewhat dubious public in 1993 and, ever since, has been pushing the boundaries with astonishingly original menus. Today, its mix of intense flavours, sublime textures and daring combinations of ingredients lures diners back time and time again.

Terre à Terre has earned an international reputation for great cuisine and, this year, was voted the UK's best vegetarian restaurant in The Observer's Food Awards. But as a force for good in a society that craves meat at almost every meal, it is, perhaps, unparalleled.

Livestock production accounts for 18% of all human-induced greenhouse gas emissions around the world and this figure is expected to rise as developing countries introduce more meat into their diets. Many environmentalists claim cutting meat from our diets is the single most effective way of reducing our impact on the world – animal-rights campaigners and health experts have a few things to say for it, too. But such is our love of flesh in the UK that cutting down our daily intake might, to many, seem too much to swallow.

Terre à Terre proves eating vegetarian food is not only healthy and animal friendly, but also delicious. Olivia Reid, events and marketing manager for the restaurant, blames the 'great vegetarian barrier' on a mix of education, stereotypes, culture, time and interest.

'The secret is to deliver interesting, flavoursome food that offers all the requirements of a meal – texture, flavour, colour, nutrition – without falling into the stereotypes of fake-meat dishes or lentil stews,' she said.

'We have been raised in a culture of fast food and ready meals; more time to cook would, undoubtedly, improve the levels of home cooking – and, perhaps, increase curiosity when it comes to the unknown.'

Although not strictly an organic restaurant, much of Terre à Terre's produce is organically farmed and all of its wines are organic.

The restaurant uses local suppliers whenever possible and buys its vegetables and cheeses from Sussex and Kent farms, and gets its eggs from a farm that re-homes battery hens. Edible flowers, herbs and wild garlic collected from local independents and foragers are also used in the cooking, as is the fare from local allotments to promote 'grow your own' ventures.

Where? 71 East Street, Brighton BN1 1HQ
When? Open Tues-Fri (noon-10.30pm), Sat (noon-11pm), Sun (noon-10pm)
How much? Starters from £5.90, mains from £10.95. House wine, from £12.75 per carafe
Tel 01273 729051
Website *www.terreaterre.co.uk*

> **"The secret is to deliver interesting, flavoursome food that offers all the requirements of a meal"**

➤ Texture, flavour, colour, nutrition – and not a lentil in sight at Terre á Terre

Drinks

In the UK we devote a lot of attention to the health and social implications of drinking alcohol, but you barely hear a word spoken of its impact on the planet. Imported drinks makes up a large proportion of all drinks sold in the UK adding to the sector's carbon footprint. Here are some eco-friendly suppliers and ideas for drinking responsibly

Pure and simple

If you don't like the taste of your local tap water, invest in a water filter. Even if you splash out on an expensive filtration system, it will only be a matter of time before you start making savings.

WINE

The organic wine sector is growing quickly. Award-winning Vinceremos offers a wide range of organic wines and other alcoholic beverages (*www.vinceremos.co.uk*) and is a great place to start looking. Vintage Roots (*www.vintageroots.co.uk*) boasts being the UK's leading mail order supplier of organic wine, beer, cider, spirits, liqueurs and even soft drinks. The site has a user-friendly search facility where you can select different types of drinks from a range of countries, and even search specifically for vegan and biodynamic drinks only.

BEER

British-brewed bottled beer clocks up a fraction of the booze miles standard imports do, making them a popular environmental choice. However, traditional British beer and ale is often an acquired taste. If you really can't stomach it then there are a number of UK organic lagers which might suit your taste buds, including Freedom Organic, from Brothers Brewery in Staffordshire, and a range of bitters from Lancashire's Marble Brewery. Otherwise try Vinceremos or Vintage Roots for a selection of both domestic and imported organic beers.

SPIRITS

Try Juniper Green Organic gin (*www.junipergreen .org*), distilled in Clapham and a popular local tipple. Scotland's Bruichladdich brewery is also enjoying success with its organic single malt whisky (*www .bruichladdich.com*). Try Vinceremos or Vintage Roots for a wider selection of organic spirits from around the world. Otherwise the recently launched Icelandic eco vodka Reyka (*www.reykavodka.com*) boasts some fairly convincing eco-credentials.

Try taking a look too at The Slow Food movement's website (*www.slowfood.com*).

WATER

Doesn't it seem wrong that hundreds of millions of people across the world can only dream of having the quality of water we have on tap in the UK, and yet every year we spend billions of pounds on bottled water? There is no evidence that bottled water is any better for you than tap water, and in some cases it has been shown to be worse due to high sodium levels.

In terms of cost, bottled water is often several thousand times more expensive than tap water and typically costs even more than oil.

Buy Belu

If you really have to buy bottled water, buy Belu. All profits go to clean-water projects and the bottles are made from corn, which is compostable under the right conditions. Visit www.belu.org for more info.

FIZZY DRINKS

Carbonating drinks has proved an extremely successful formula and has resulted in some of the biggest brands on the planet. The organic fizzy drinks industry is completely dwarfed by the rest of the sector but nonetheless is beginning to establish its roots. Check for organic alternatives at your local supermarket or try Vinceremos or Vintage Roots which both stock a selection of soft drinks.

Alternatively, invest in a soda fountain (see below).

HOT DRINKS

Organic teas and coffees have become widely available in most large food shops and supermarkets, so consumers are spoilt for choice. A number of Fairtrade organic teas and coffees are also available, promoting fairer prices and better working conditions for producers and workers.

Great Scott!

In 2005, more than 5,000 tonnes of exported Scottish whiskey was reportedly imported back into the UK for resale!

Love fizzy water?
Get a Sodastream!

Back in the 1980s you would struggle to find a home without its very own soda fountain for making fizzy drinks. Today, they are tipped for a big revival as more and more families look for ways to reduce their waste.

Fountains work without electricity or batteries and gas cylinders are refillable so they are a far greater environmental option. Market leader Sodastream claims that over three years a family of four can cut their waste of soft drink-related packaging by over 90% with a soda fountain. Visit *www.sodastream.co.uk* for your nearest stockist.

IN PRACTICE:
The Ultimate Meal

GOLDEN GLOBE

WHOLE BRAISED GLOBE ARTICHOKES, SERVED WITH TOMATO BOUILLABAISSE, HARICOT BRANDADE AND FENNEL SEED BREAD

SERVES 4-6

BRAISED GLOBE ARTICHOKES

INGREDIENTS
- 4-6 small globe artichokes
- 2 bay leaves
- 1/4 tsp fennel seeds
- 1 star anise
- 20g parsley sprigs
- 20g basil sprigs
- 100g fennel, chopped
- 1 medium onion, chopped
- 6 garlic cloves
- 1 large tomato, chopped
- 125ml olive oil
- 125ml dry white wine
- 125ml white stock or water

METHOD:
First prepare the artichokes. Wash them in cold running water and discard any small or discoloured base leaves. Cut off the stems close to the base and remove the top quarter of the leaves, then plunge the artichokes into acidulated water (water with lemon juice/vinegar) to maintain their colour (add 2 tablespoons of lemon juice or vinegar per 200ml water). Peel away the fibrous outer layer to reach the tender part of the stem, which is edible and delicious. It is important you also remove the fuzzy choke from the centre - artichokes don't have that name for nothing! Spread the centre leaves until you reach the middle cone, then pull away the purple or thorny centre leaves. With a stainless steel spoon, scrape out the remaining purple tipped leaves and fibrous fuzz. Rinse the artichokes and keep in acidulated water until you are ready to cook them. Put the prepared artichokes and all the other ingredients into a large heavy based pan, cover and bring to the boil. Simmer for 30 minutes, remove from the heat and leave to cool in the liquor. Refrigerate until ready to use.

FENNEL SEED BREAD

INGREDIENTS
- 300g rye flour
- 300g strong flour
- 1/2 tsp salt
- 1 tsp caster sugar
- 12g dried yeast
- 1 tbsp fennel seeds
- 310ml warm water
- 3 tbsp extra virgin olive oil

METHOD:
Sift together the flours, salt and sugar and stir in the yeast and seeds. Add the water and oil to the flour mix and start working the dough together with a fork or spoon then, using your hands, work the mix into a firm but slightly sticky dough. If the dough seems tough just add a splash of water. Knead the dough for 5-6 minutes, then place in a bowl, cover with cling film and leave to prove until doubled in size. Now turn out the dough on to a lightly floured surface and knock back. Knead again for 2-3 minutes, then form the required loaf shape. Place the dough in a lightly oiled loaf tin, cover with cling film and leave to prove again until it has nearly reached the top of the tin. Bake at 180C/Gas Mark 4 for 30-40 minutes until the top of the loaf is golden brown. To check if the loaf is cooked through, remove it from the tin and tap the bottom. A hollow sounds means the loaf is ready. Allow the loaf to cool down on a cooling rack.

TOMATO BOUILLABAISSE

INGREDIENTS
- 100ml olive oil
- 150g onions, sliced
- 3 garlic cloves, finely chopped
- 1/2 tsp coriander seeds
- 2 bay leaves
- 1 tsp saffron
- 1kg tomatoes, roughly chopped
- 150ml dry white wine
- 35g parsley, chopped

METHOD:
Heat the olive oil in a saucepan and add the onions, garlic, coriander seeds, bay leaves and saffron. Cook until the onions are just softened. Add the tomatoes, wine and parsley and cook for a further 15 minutes. You now need to half fill a jug blender with the soup mix and blend it for 3 minutes, or until very smooth. Continue until you have blended it all, then strain through a fine sieve into a clean pan.

HARICOT BRANDADE

INGREDIENTS
- 50ml olive oil
- 50g onions, finely sliced
- 1/2 tsp chopped fresh sage
- 1 bay leaf
- 5 garlic cloves, finely chopped
- 250g cooked haricot beans
- 50ml dry white wine
- salt
- black pepper

METHOD:
Gently heat the olive oil and add the onions, sage, bay leaf and garlic. Cover and cook gently for 5 minutes. Add the haricot beans and the wine and cook, uncovered, until most of the wine has evaporated. Taste and season. Now blend the mixture in a food processor until smooth, and refrigerate until needed.

TO ASSEMBLE

- 2 tablespoons brandy
- 3 tablespoons pastis

Bring the bouillabaisse up to a simmer, add the brandy and pastis and stir well. Gently heat the artichokes in their liquor, drain (reserving the liquor) and put into warmed bowls. (The liquor is much too good to waste and can form the basis of another lovely soup.) Now heat the brandade in a small pan and spoon it into the centre of the artichokes. Pour the hot bouillabaisse into the bowls around the artichokes, and place a chunk of fennel bread beside each bowl, ready for mopping up the delicious juices. Serve with finger bowls and giant serviettes: messy, but well worth it!

Mondays meat free

On June 15 2009, Sir Paul McCartney launched the Meat Free Monday campaign, calling on us all to cut meat out of our diets one day a week and slow global warming McCartney's mission, which has drawn support from a star-studded ensemble of eco activists, is the latest in a long list of publicity fuelled campaigns to get us to bin our bad habits, from national no smoking days to walk to school weeks. And what a great idea it is. The former Beatle and lifelong vegetarian said that at a time when many people felt helpless in the face of environmental challenges, having a designated meat free day was a "meaningful change" that everyone could make. "Having a meat free day every week is a simple way to start making a real difference in the world," he said. "The more people who join in, the more difference we can make." A recent UN study estimated that meat production accounted for nearly a fifth of man's global greenhouse gas emissions and warned that consumption was set to double by the middle of the century.

Register your support for Meat Free Mondays at www.supportmfm.org

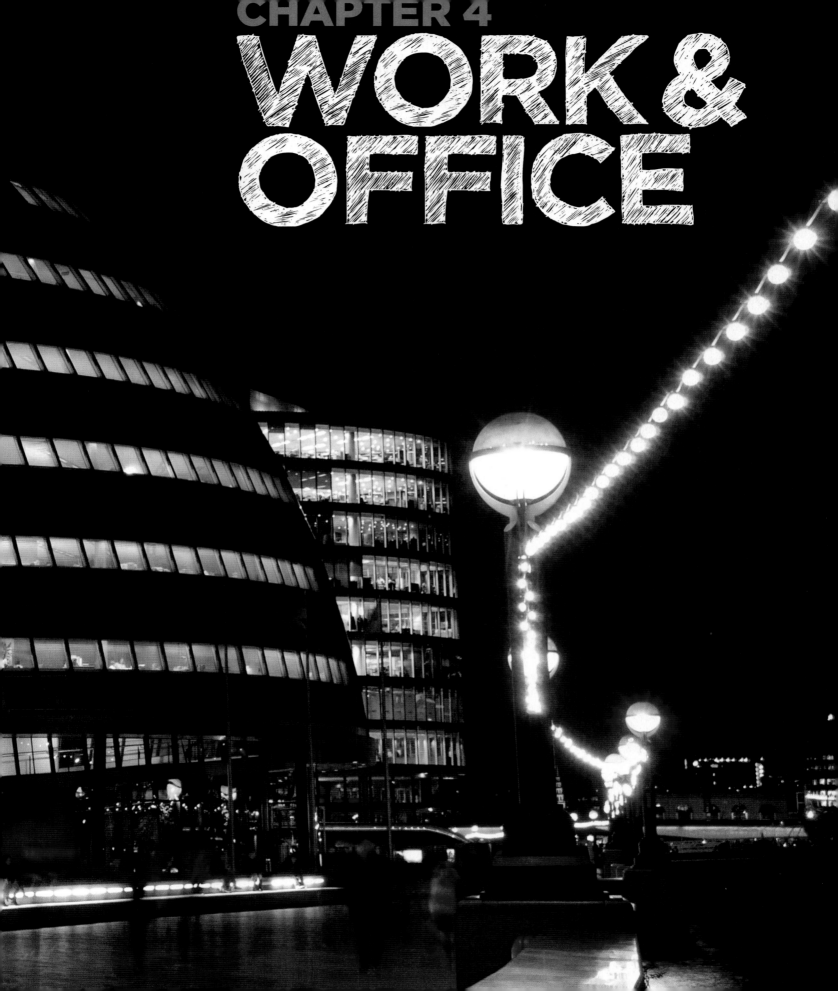

CHAPTER 4
WORK & OFFICE

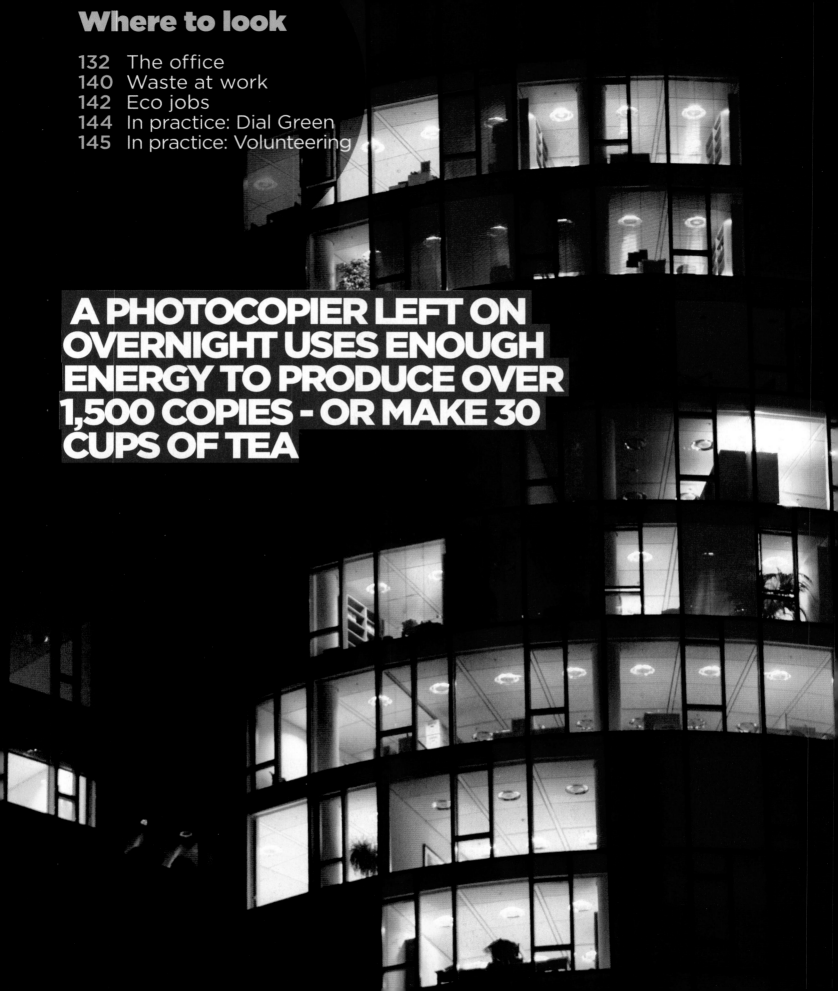

Where to look

A PHOTOCOPIER LEFT ON OVERNIGHT USES ENOUGH ENERGY TO PRODUCE OVER 1,500 COPIES – OR MAKE 30 CUPS OF TEA

WORK & OFFICE

While most of us have started to, quite literally, get our houses in order, going green at work is taking longer. But the pressure is mounting, and consumers are starting to take more notice of the eco-credentials of the companies they use. It's time to mind your business

Carbon Dioxide emissions

UK businesses are responsible for around 40% of all our carbon dioxide emissions, way more than all households put together, which account for 28%.

Yet the Carbon Trust claims that an astonishing 21% – or £2.4 billion – of the sector's total spent on energy is wasted.

There is huge untapped potential, therefore, for firms to make significant savings, not only in terms of greenhouse gas emissions, but financially as well.

It may sound too easy or simplistic, but by making small changes to what we do every day, like remembering to switch off the lights and workstations when we go home, we can make a big difference to the environmental impact of the sector as well as the company's bottom line. In fact, it is fair to say that the environmental and financial benefits of saving energy go hand-in-hand.

As well as cutting emissions and reducing costs, being green at work can do wonders to a

➤ **While it may sound like a cliche, the small changes you make around the office are a good place to start on your road to creating a green office.**

company's reputation and make the workplace a healthier environment for employees.

In reality, however, many businesses are failing to make the necessary changes to enact positive reductions in energy consumption and employers are often slated for paying lip-service to green ideas, but not actually doing anything about it.

A 2007 study of employees' energy-saving habits found that most people left good practice at home, lacking the incentive or encouragement from bosses to carry on at work.

Whilst most of us have

started to, quite literally, get our houses in order, going green at work is taking longer to get started. Too many companies are lacking the vision and the insight to make the small, but necessary changes to implement positive environmental policies and behavioural changes at work.

But the pressure is mounting. Consumers are starting to take more notice of manufacturer or retailer's eco credentials. Many commentators believe a business which turns its back on the environmental movement does so at its peril.

Low-energy PCs

www.ecopcs.co.
uk/ecopcshome.
html

www.go-green-
pc.co.uk

www.very-pc.
co.uk

Save Cash!
A computer and monitor left on all day costs over £50 a year to run. Switching it off and enabling standby features could cut this to £15

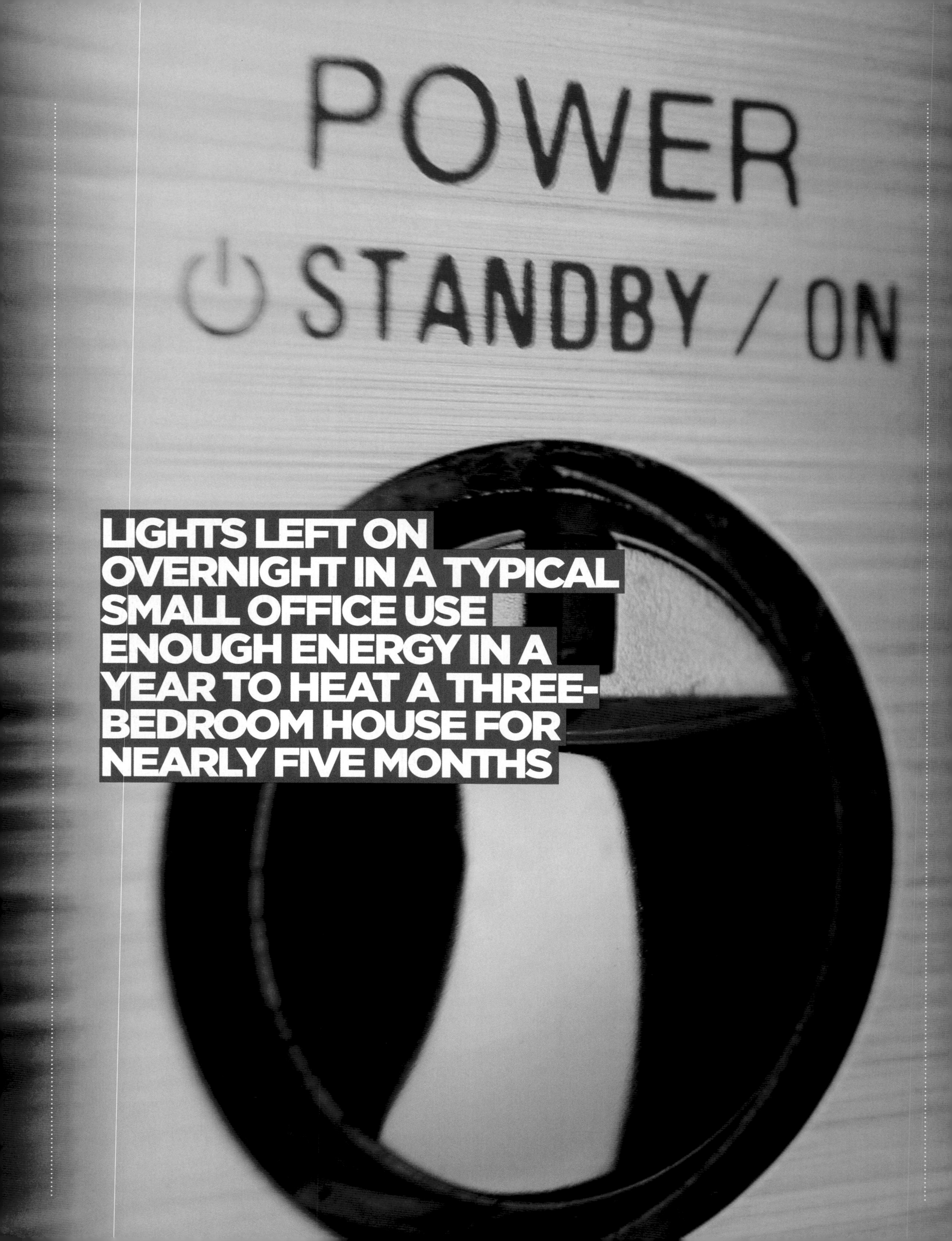

POWER

⏻ STANDBY / ON

LIGHTS LEFT ON OVERNIGHT IN A TYPICAL SMALL OFFICE USE ENOUGH ENERGY IN A YEAR TO HEAT A THREE-BEDROOM HOUSE FOR NEARLY FIVE MONTHS

The office

With all the equipment guzzling valuable energy in our offices, there are plenty of opportunities to cut back and help minimise our effect on the environment. Here's how...

COMPUTERS AND PERIPHERALS

When Pentium processors were introduced in the mid-1990s, the average computer system could operate on about a 140W power supply. Many of today's desktop systems use a 1,200W supply. According to the Carbon Trust, leaving a computer and monitor on round the clock costs more than £50 a year. But by taking simple energy-saving measures, such as enabling standby modes and switching things off at the end of the day, this figure can easily be reduced to around £10. That's a huge difference and, for larger offices, means potential savings of thousands of pounds.

Certification mark

ENERGY SAVING RECOMMENDED

This Energy Saving Trust initiative covers a wide range of electrical goods and appliances. Any product displaying this logo means it has been granted the Trust's seal of approval for energy efficiency. Although office equipment is not covered specifically, the logo is applied to a number of different product types you might expect to find in the office, including kettles, televisions, fridges and freezers.
Visit *www.est.org.uk* for more information.

ENERGY STAR

Products displaying the Energy Star logo have an energy consumption below an agreed level. For example: Energy Star computers will use 70% less electricity than computers without power management; monitors will use up to 60% less than standard models; printers use at least 60% less power and must automatically enter a lower power mode after a set period of inactivity.

EUROPEAN ECOLABEL SCHEME

The Ecolabel flower logo covers an increasingly broad spectrum of consumer products and is only awarded to goods and services which meet strict criteria limiting their environmental impact, from manufacture through to disposal.
Visit *http://ec.europa.eu/environment/ ecolabel/index_en.htm* for more information.

Eco Computing Systems

Eco Computer Systems is an innovative social enterprise offering IT recycling and refurbishment facilities to the private and public sector, including businesses of all sizes.

The London-based organisation also uses donated PCs to improve the computer skills of the unemployed and those on low incomes in its training centres, and gives free recycled PCs to a number of charities, social enterprises and individuals.

Eco Computer Systems will collect directly from offices on request and also has a drop off point in Sydenham for any unwanted PCs, printers and scanners.

All profits made through recycling are invested in providing the training courses and carrying out the social objectives of the enterprise.

Find out more at www.ecocomputersystems.org.uk.

Office Equipment

There's a huge number of flashing LEDs, beeps and buzzes in any office, and the prospect of reducing electricity use can seem almost impossible. Here are some simple checklists of the most effective tips and tricks for cutting energy waste – and saving money – in the office

COMPUTERS

- **Switch it off** It is a myth that turning on a computer uses a huge surge in energy. In reality, starting up your machine only uses as much energy as running it normally for just a few seconds. Whenever you are going to be away from your desk for a more than a few minutes, make sure you turn off your PC and monitor or turn it on to hibernation mode.
- **Enable automatic standby mode** It may not always be practical or convenient to turn your PC off during the day. Change the control settings on your computer so that the standby mode kicks in after a few minutes of inactivity, so that it's still running but using less power than normal.
- **Ditch screensavers** They use up unnecessary energy.
- **Make a commitment** Energy-efficient models could end up saving your company money in the long run and it's a good sign of your commitment to saving energy to employees.
- **Look out for the Energy Star logo** (see page 133) A reliable indicator of a product's energy efficiency.
- **Upgrade your PC rather than buy new** Most desktop and laptop computers can be upgraded with bigger hard drives, faster processors and greater memory capacity. When buying a new computer, make sure it can be upgraded at a later stage.
- **Choose flatscreen monitors** Not only do they use up to two-thirds less energy than CRT models, they also save space in the office, use far less packaging and are much lighter and so easier to transport.
- **Consider buying a laptop** Due to the nature of their use, laptops have been designed to be as energy efficient as possible. Docking facilities enables them to be easily connected to monitors and peripherals. However, be aware that laptops aren't as easy to upgrade as PCs.

◄ Laptops are designed with energy efficiency in mind

VENDING MACHINES

- **Turn them off** Wherever possible turn off vending machines at the end of the day. This may not be possible where the products need to be kept cool to stay fresh, but very often machines do not need to stay on to maintain their function. Invest in a timer from any DIY store to set the machine to come on in time for the start of the day.
- **Ask for what you want** Vending machines are often supplied by external catering companies. Make sure you demand the most energy-efficient and best-insulated models with no unnecessary lighting.
- **Minimise waste** When choosing a drinks machine make sure they can be used with ordinary cups and glasses to reduce waste, and that for hot drinks, they only heat the water required.

"Demand the most energy-efficient and best-insulated vending machines"

▼ When goods don't need to be kept refridgerated, turn off vending machines overnight to save power

PRINTERS

- **Switch it off** Most modern printers have far quicker startup times than older models, which means you don't need to spend ages hanging around waiting for it to warm up.
- **Enable standby modes**
- **Print in batches** Not surprisingly, printers use most energy when they are printing. However, they also use a lot of energy during the idling mode between printing and standby. If you try to print in batches you can reduce this idling time and the power used.

- **Default to duplex** Some printers offer duplex printing, which means they print on both sides of paper automatically. If your printer has this option, set it as the default setting. Also, choose the toner-saving mode as your default and only change to high-quality for important print outs.
- **Get more on a page** Save paper by expanding print margins.
- **Use inkjet** Try to go for inkjet models over laser ones, as they generally use less energy.
- **Look for the Energy Star logo**

FAX MACHINES

- **Use fewer machines** If there are multiple fax machines in your office, divert messages to one machine at night to reduce running costs and energy use.
- **Check standby energy consumption** When buying a new model, look for one that uses the least amount of energy in standby mode.
- **Default to draft** Set the default print setting to draft.
- **Stick to inkjets** Avoid laser fax machines where possible, as they use more energy.

"Divert messages to one machine at night to reduce energy use"

◄ Laser fax machines use more energy than inkjets

PHOTOCOPIERS

- **Copy in batches** Where possible, photocopy in batches and only ever copy what you need.
- **Default to duplex** As with printers, default to duplex printing where appliances allow.
- **What do you need it to do?** It sounds obvious, but buy a machine that does what you need. Photocopiers can be very expensive, and low-spec machines may offer all you need at a fraction of the cost of higher-end alternatives, and take far less energy to run.
- **Check the type of ink used** Look for models that allow low melting-point inks. Photocopiers work by heating components which fuse toner to paper. The lower the temperature that the ink melts, the less energy is used.
- **Check copy-to-standby times** Choose a photocopier that shifts quickly from copy mode to standby mode as this saves time in that energy-wasting idle mode.

A VISION OF THINGS TO COME

Every year, businessmen fly billions of miles around the world to attend meetings, spending precious time and money in the process and adding hugely to their carbon footprints. Telephone conferencing has become a popular and cost-effective way of involving several people in the same conversation from the comfort of their desks, but is limited as a purely auditory experience. Although video conferencing has gone some way to bringing the human touch to distance meetings, it remains a far cry from meeting in the flesh and has failed to catch on with great vigour.

So, what's the alternative? The focus is now on CAVE, a mind-boggling futuristic 3D simulator that promises to bring the virtual boardroom to life. The Cave Automated Virtual Environment (CAVE) was pioneered by a group of researchers at the University of Illinois in the late 1990s and works by back-projecting stereoscopic images onto the walls and floor of a small room, or CAVE. Wearing special glasses that make the images appear 3D and carrying a wand to track their movements, visitors can immerse themselves in this virtual world and, in theory, interact with other people in CAVEs across the world as though they were physically in the same room. The technology is already being adopted by car manufacturers, who can build and test their prototypes without the huge expense and time constraints of physical manufacture. Architects, astronomers and even archaeologists have also been keen to make practical use of the system.

Although the technology remains prohibitively expensive (the CAVE at University College London cost £888,000), advances in processing and graphical power mean the widespread use of CAVE in business could be closer than previously thought. Before long, businessmen could be pitching and presenting in cyberspace, socialising over a round of virtual golf and then making the short hop back to their desks to get on with other work.

> "Advances in processing and graphical power mean widespread use of CAVE in business could be closer than we thought"

▲ **CAVE technology allows remote participants to interact as if they were in the same space**

Good green buys

E-Cloth Screen Pack
The special E-cloth fibres attract and absorb all dirt particles into the cloth and away from the screen. The chemical free CleanSafe Spray, which is also included in the pack, is anti-static and is specially formulated for sensitive screens. It does not remove the screen coating, but forms a protective layer and repels dust from the screen. The pack is designed to be used for cleaning and protecting Plasma, TFT, LCD, and laptop screens. Available from www.footprint-es. com, priced £9.99

Evolve Business Recycled Paper
Most homes and many offices are into the habit of recycling. But buying products out of recycled materials is just as important. Evolve Business papers are made from 100% office waste and produced by a eco-friendly mill. They are suitable for both mono and colour laser and inkjet printing, and can be printed on both sides. The papers' brilliant whiteness is achieved using biodegradable cleaners, chlorine-free bleaches and Optical Brightening Agents. Available at www.greenstat.co.uk.

Ben the Bin
Made out of 100% recycled plastic and available in three different colours for easy sorting, Ben the Bin is perfect for at home or in the office recycling. The product was first seen on BBC's Dragons Den, where it was enthusiastically supported by investors Deborah Meaden and Theo Paphitis.. The bin works by reusing standard carrier bags held between its two handles
Available in blue, pink and green from www.footprint-es.com priced £6.99

Ecobutton
The ecobutton is a multi award-winning, power-saving device for your PC. Simply plug it into your computer via a USB cable and leave it by your keyboard. Whenever you leave your desk or take a call, press the ecobutton and it will send your computer into its most energy-saving mode, cutting carbon emissions and saving you money. And each time your computer is put into this 'ecomode' the ingenious ecobutton software records how much carbon, power and money you have saved by using it. Available at *www.footprint-es.com*, priced £14.99.

ENERGY-SAVING TIPS FOR YOUR OFFICE

01 KNOW WHAT YOU USE

Keep track of your bills, with attention to consumption rather than cost. It is also better to compare a period with the same period the year before.

02 SWITCH IT OFF

According to the Carbon Trust, the average UK office wastes £6,000 each year by leaving equipment on when it's not in use. Turn off computers and monitors at the end of the day.

03 SHOW YOUR COMMITMENT

Make energy-saving practices company policy and lead by example. Although most of us are getting better at saving energy at home, the same cannot be said for when we're at work.

04 WATCH THE LIGHTS

Try to avoid using excessive lighting and switch lights off when you leave a room.

05 WATCH THE HEATING

Only turn up the heating if you really need to. Turning up the thermostats by one degree pushes up your heating costs by 8%.

06 HELP WITH CAR SHARES

Start a lift-share scheme through which people living in the same areas can share lifts to work.

07 GIVE YOUR THERMOSTAT A CHANCE?

Keep the thermostat away from draughts or hot and cold areas as these will affect its performance.

08 MONITOR ENERGY USE

Buy an energy monitor to keep tabs on the company's actual, real-time energy consumption. Available from *www.footprint-es.com*, from £44.99.

09 TRAVEL SMART

Cut down on long-distance travel in favour of video conferencing (see opposite).

10 GREEN ELECTRICITY

Opt for the green electricity tariff from your power provider. If they don't have one, look for a company that does.

11 PRODUCT PLACEMENT

Don't put hot equipment, such as photocopiers and laser printers, close to cooling vents, as the cooling system will need to work harder.

12 GO BIKE-FRIENDLY

Improve facilities for cyclists (providing secure bike parking and showers) to encourage sustainable travel to work.

INTRODUCING THE CARBON TRUST

The Carbon Trust was set up to help the UK commercial and public sectors move towards a low carbon economy and is an extremely valuable resource for businesses of all shapes and sizes. Below is an overview of the key services you will find on its website at *www.carbontrust.co.uk*. Alternatively, call a Carbon Trust energy expert on 0800 085 2005 for more information and advice

Order a Starter Pack

The Carbon Trust sends out free Starter Packs written to cater specifically to different sectors including service organisations (such as healthcare, hospitality, retail and schools) and industrial companies (such as food and drink, agriculture and chemicals). Starter Packs include an Energy Saving Fact Sheet, with specific energy-saving tips relevant to your business, and a poster and stickers to help motivate your staff to take simple energy saving measures. It also details the free products and services the Carbon Trust offers to help you make further savings. To order your company's free starter pack visit *www.carbontrust.co.uk/energy/startsaving/starterpack.htm*.

Action Plan tool

This online service acts as an aid to developing a strong energy-saving action plan for your business. By simply selecting your business's sector and energy bill size from drop down menus, the online tool will identify a number of key actions most appropriate to your company, plus an indication of the cost and probable savings of each.

Carbon Surveys from the Carbon Trust

If your company's annual energy bills are more than £50,000 you could be eligible for a free carbon survey. The on-site audits are carried out by energy experts from the Carbon Trust who visit the company's premises and conduct an investigation to identify low- and no-cost ways to cut energy use and provide practical help on how to achieve them, usually in the form of a 10-step action plan.

Energy Efficiency Loans scheme

This year, the Carbon Trust bettered its own Energy Efficiency Loan scheme to help small- and medium-sized enterprises (SMEs) replace or upgrade their existing equipment with more energy efficient versions. The scheme provides interest-free loans of between £3,000 and £400,000 for up to four years for qualifying energy-efficiency projects. The loan is unsecured and interest-free. To find out if your company is eligible visit *www.carbontrust.co.uk/publicsites/loansform* and enter your details for evaluation.

A helping hand...

As part of its commitment to business, the Carbon Trust also offers a number of events ranging from introductions to its services to technical energy-efficiency training. The events are free and are held up and down the country; details of when and where are on their website. They also support events hosted by other organisations. If you are organising an event and would like support from the Carbon Trust, visit the Information for Event Organisers section on their website.

Carbon calculator

By calculating its carbon footprint, you can take a first step in a programme to reduce the emissions your company causes, irrespective of its size.

The Carbon Trust has developed a free and easy-to-use online calculator for businesses to quickly quantify their basic carbon footprint and understand where action might be required to cut emissions. The calculation covers the emissions the company is directly responsible for and some common sources of indirect emissions (for example from electricity usage and business travel). *www.carbontrust.co.uk*

THE LOWRY

Manchester's first ever five-star hotel has successfully merged green ethics with luxury

Asking hotel guests to opt out of having their towels washed in the interests of the environment might, cynically, be viewed as a cunning ruse to cut down on cleaning costs.

But one five-star hotel in Manchester has gone to great lengths to prove to its customers that it is serious about reducing its impact on the environment while not compromising on luxury.

The Lowry Hotel employs more than 200 staff, has 165 bedrooms and suites, a restaurant, spa, gym, sauna, health suite and event space for up to 400 people. From heating and cooling, to cleaning and catering, energy consumption quickly adds up.

Two years ago, the management team embarked on a plan to reduce the hotel's carbon footprint by 10% year on year – and to help them find the right solutions they applied for a carbon survey by the Carbon Trust.

Having put the Trust's recommendations into action, the hotel is saving 363.5 tonnes of CO_2 a year and making an annual financial saving of more than £37,000.

'It's not about the money, although that's an incentive, particularly given the increased

> "**Energy consumption can be efficiently managed, saving 207.5 tonnes of CO_2 per annum**"

cost of energy,' said marketing manager Helen Hipkiss. 'It's really about doing whatever we can to help the environment, without compromising the guest experience. The survey by the Carbon Trust made us realise how we could do this.'

The hotel created a green committee to oversee carbon-reduction initiatives. The first project was to put in place a building management system, allowing the hotel to monitor energy consumption and turn off lighting and air conditioning in areas that were not in use. This has resulted in annual savings of 207.5 tonnes of CO_2.

The hotel has saved a further 78 tonnes of CO_2 a year by changing lightbulbs to energy efficient alternatives.

Boilers have been fitted with a control system that makes them more energy efficient, saving 30 tonnes of CO_2 a year, while improvements to the air conditioning system have saved another 34 tonnes.

A host of other initiatives, including staff awareness training and improved recycling facilities, have further boosted the hotel's eco credentials. General manager Jason Harding said the changes had had a positive impact on business.

'The entire team here has been working hard to reduce the hotel's carbon footprint and we have been very pleased by how much interest our guests have shown in becoming greener and more environmentally friendly,' he said.

Cavan Bakery

A Middlesex bakery has saved lots of dough by raising its energy efficiency.

Until last year, The Cavan Bakery in Hampton Hill was haemorrhaging energy – and money – thanks to its two outdated, and massively inefficient, 1940s gas ovens and electric steam water boilers.

The company contacted the Carbon Trust and secured an interest-free Energy Efficiency loan of £31,000 to buy a new steam oven.

Today, the 80-year-old bakery is reaping the benefits of the new oven, which creates its own steam and has allowed the

bakery to get rid of the water boilers, thus creating far more working space.

The oven is saving the firm 1,000 units of gas and 500 units of electricity every month, which equates to an annual reduction in carbon dioxide emissions of 81 tonnes.

Managing director Jeff Greenall is very pleased with the help received, 'The Trust was very helpful and applying for the loan was incredibly straightforward. I kept thinking, 'what's the catch?'.'

The bakery's next focus is on finding an affordable, energy efficient alternative to its current fleet of delivery vans.

ENVIROWISE CLAIMS THAT BAD WASTE PRACTICES ARE COSTING UK INDUSTRY AT LEAST £15BN EACH YEAR

WASTE AT WORK

UK businesses produce around 25 million tonnes of waste every year, and of this only a third is recycled. Here are ways to better manage the waste generated at work

ELIMINATE WASTE

- Not producing any waste materials in the first place is the ultimate in waste management.

REDUCE

- It is not always practical or possible to eliminate waste entirely, but there is still a lot of unnecessary waste produced that could be cut out. For example, the amount of paper used for office printing is staggering. Adopting a company policy whereby you only print out emails and other documents when absolutely required is an effective way of reducing waste.

- Other common products and materials which can be reused are plastic vending cups, printer toners and drums for raw materials.

REUSE

- Finding a new use for waste materials is an effective method of reducing residual waste and can potentially save money. Packaging material like boxes, envelopes and bubble wrap can usually be used several times over – likewise old binders, rechargeable batteries and refillable printer toner cartridges – and you will save a huge amount of paper if you print on both sides.

- Encourage staff to re-use through staff awareness training and invite employees to make suggestions on what else the company can do.

RECYCLE

- Take a walk around your premises and identify the different types of material that can be recycled. Most businesses will generate common types of recyclable waste, such as paper, plastic bottles, vending cups, and packaging materials. But there are lots of other materials that can also be recycled including IT equipment, textiles, toner cartridge, construction waste and much more (see page 24 for other types of recyclable waste). You will then need to check with your local recycling centre what they will accept, as well as grade and type of material required and whether there is a minimum quantity for collection.

Separate materials

Cross-contamination of different wastes can lead to the whole lot having to be sent to landfill, which could cost you a lot more money. Make life easier for everyone by installing colour-coded recycling bins at appropriate sites around the premises.

Making money

Shop around for the best value-for-money recycling services in your area. There are a number of private and government recycling centres around that will be interested in your waste. Depending on the type and quantities, it could even become a source of revenue.

DISPOSAL

- By law, it is the responsibility of any business to ensure that any residual waste that cannot be reused or recycled is disposed of in an authorised and responsible manner. Check that your waste contractor is fully certified and that they provide you with a 'waste transfer note' or equivalent for each collection.

Know the law

Companies have to account for all waste under the Environmental Protection (Duty of Care) Regulations 1991. Companies must ensure waste is collected and disposed of in accordance with relevant legislation.

For more information contact the Environment Agency (*www.environment-agency.gov.uk*), Scottish Environment Protection Agency (*www.sepa.org.uk*) or Environment and Heritage Service (*www.ehsni.gov.uk*).

Make Cash!

Did you know your company could make money from recycling its waste? Hunt down a local firm or try your local council to see if such schemes exist in your area.

ECO JOBS

The development of a low-carbon future requires millions of individuals from all walks of life to cover the broadest reaches of employment, from ecology and conservation through to energy generation, resource management and sustainable transport planning

There is already a wealth of opportunities waiting for the eco-minded worker and a whole swathe of new jobs are being created. These pages give a flavour of some of the areas of work out there right now.

Ecology and Conservation

Conservation is about preserving and carefully managing the environment and the earth's natural resources including our forests, fisheries, habitats and biological diversity.

With environmental destruction across the world at its height the need for effective and wide reaching conservation programmes and strategies has never been more pressing.

Environmental Campaigning

Climate change might at last be reaching the top of the world's political agendas, but campaigners have been calling for action on global warming and environmental destruction for decades. Today the need is as great as it has ever been for activists to keep the pressure on decision makers and draw the world's attention to the many issues affecting the world and its communities today and in the future.

Renewable Energy

Clean, renewable and affordable energy sources are seen by many environmentalists as the key to successfully tackling climate change. Whether it is designing a revolutionary fuel cell, building a wind farm or simply installing a domestic solar hot water system, there is a vast and increasing array of jobs waiting to be filled in this sector.

Energy Efficiency

Preventing the unnecessary loss of energy is a fundamental way of reducing carbon emissions, and as such has already become a major source of employment. The UK government, for example, is investing hundreds of millions of pounds promoting the uptake of improved insulation and energy efficiency measures in our homes and public buildings and in the process is creating a wealth of job opportunities for installers, energy surveyors, insulation manufacturers, and many other sector specialists.

Recycling and resource management

Recycling is big news and big business, and there are many jobs out there to suit almost all levels of qualification.

Sustainable transport

Transport remains one of the main sources of carbon dioxide emissions in the world and is one of the greatest challenges in tackling climate change. Modern transport is so intrinsically linked to our way of life that it is simply not feasible to put a halt to it. But we do need a transport revolution which will see carbon emissions slashed through a mix of technological advances and increased uptake of public transport. From designing cutting edge eco cars to conjuring forward thinking town planning policies, there is tremendous scope for any budding environmentalist wanting to stamp their mark in this vital sector.

Climate change and sustainability

Understanding the complexities of climate change so that we can use this knowledge as the basis for calculated action has been the focus of thousands of climatologists' research for several years. But as well as improving our understanding of climate change, it is key to convey that knowledge to the public and to decision makers. Most councils now have a climate change and sustainability officer, and there are many businesses and community organisations which require up-to-date knowledge and advice to shape their policies.

> "There is a vast and increasing array of jobs waiting to be filled in this sector"

Useful links

www.environmentjob.co.uk
www.ecojobs.com
www.endsjobsearch.co.uk
www.greenjobsonline.co.uk
www.greenenergyjobs.com
www.greendirectory.net/jobs.

Case studies

Richard Farmer, Senior Reserves Manager, RSPB Former biology teacher Richard is responsible for all 19 RSPB reserves in Wales. His work includes managing staff and reserve objectives, planning the budget, developing big projects and finding new sites. He has been working for the RSPB for 20 years and has a degree in biological sciences.

"The thing I love most about my job is getting out and about and seeing that the things you have planned and organised have happened and produced results for conservation," he said. "I enjoy dealing with the people side of the job too; it's important to have good relationships and a good understanding with your staff when they're scattered far and wide.

"Part of my work involves interviewing job applicants. My advice for anyone who wants to get into this line of work is that qualifications and experience count for a lot, but the most important thing is a keen interest in conservation, natural history and land management."

Caroline Rams – PR executive, Energy Saving Trust Caroline landed her job with the Energy Saving Trust in December 2006 after applying through recruitment website www. environmentjob.so.uk. Much of her work involves responding to journalists' enquiries and providing them with statistics, press releases and statement for their stories. She has a BA in Environmental Management from the University of Leeds.

"I get a lot of satisfaction from my work, as I know I am helping the environment and carrying on with what I studied at university. I know it makes a difference when people are in their homes, making those little changes in their daily lives. I recommend that people looking to work in the environmental sector get the relevant qualifications, not only to show a move in to that area, but it's a very interesting subject to learn about. Confidence and creativity in the PR sector is a good trait, as you are looked upon for ideas and new ways of getting messages into the media."

David Blair, Regional and International Projects Co-ordinator, Trees for Cities Trees for Cities is an independent charity working with local communities on tree planting projects in urban areas, both in the UK and abroad. David started out working for the charity as a volunteer, then became a full-time member of staff. Today he is responsible for managing urban tree planting projects in seven UK cities and four overseas, as well as working with other team members and project partners on tasks including project proposals and fundraising, through to arranging planting events with local volunteers.

"The thing I like most about my job is the variety – working with project partners from Leeds to Peru means there's never a dull moment," he said. "On the other hand it can be a bit of a juggling act. I wouldn't say I dislike that, but I find it's the biggest challenge. I like the people you meet throughout the sector too – often I get the impression they'd be out planting trees anyway, and just consider themselves fortunate they're being paid to do it."

Be an Office Eco Angel

You don't have to work in the environmental sector to do your bit for the environment. Here are a few tips for the motivated office worker to make their work space more environmentally friendly:

- Become the office's self-appointed eco angel. At the end of the working day make it your responsibility to turn off all the lights and computers left on. Ideally, this role should be shared among a number of staff members to spread the responsibility and carried out on a rota basis.

- If the in-office recycling facilities are not up to scratch, put pressure on your employer or managers to make the necessary improvement.

- Work towards a paper-free office. Encourage colleagues to print on both sides of paper and only print out what is really necessary.

- Encourage your colleagues to behave more responsibly in the office by turning off machines when not in use and not overfilling the kettle unnecessarily at break time.

- Try to influence procurement procedures for your company, so that only sustainably sourced materials and energy efficiency devices are bought wherever possible.

For more tips on how you can make your office greener visit *www.carbontrust.co.uk*.

IN PRACTICE:
Dial Green

When it comes to being green, the telecoms industry is notoriously off colour and barely a week goes by when the sector does not create headlines for the wrong reasons. But Dial Green is the UK's first eco-friendly telecoms solution for small and large firms

Dial Green offers everything you would expect from a telecoms provider: line rental, calls, broadband, teleconferencing. However, unlike the industry's major players, the Devon-based company also provides customers with peace of mind that the carbon emissions associated with their calls are counter-balanced by reputable carbon-offsetting projects.

What's more, it won't cost you any extra with the company's Match Price Promise – and, nine times out of 10, it will actually save you money. In fact, the company is so confident it will reduce your telecoms bill that it promises to plant 10 trees if it can't.

David Wood, sales manager, believes any worthwhile environmental policy will involve a company 'greening its supply chain' and Dial Green fits that quest perfectly. 'We are able to ensure customers get the greenest service and, probably, save them money at the same time," he said.

Dial Green's offering hinges on the benefits of effective and responsible carbon offsetting, and the company has spent a lot of time seeking out services to suit its clients.

The chosen firm, UK-based Carbon Offsets Ltd, has created offsetting projects that are additional (i.e. they would not have happened without

offset funding) and these include a biomass plant in Brazil, a wind farm in India and an energy efficiency awareness initiative in South Africa.

To calculate the appropriate rate of emissions to offset, Dial Green used research conducted by British Telecom and Cable & Wireless to work out the amount of electricity used to power the average minute-long phone call and sought out an independent body to verify the calculations.

'Every quarter, we total up all of our customers' minutes, run that through the equation and use the resulting figure to offset the CO_2 tonnage using high-quality Certified Emission Reductions projects from Carbon Offsets Ltd,' said David.

Dial Green, an associate of Dial, which has been supplying telecoms solutions for 15 years, was launched last year and already has more than 500 customers – including local authorities and government agencies – and a turnover in excess of £1.5 million.

Besides looking after its customers' emissions, the company is committed to eradicating its own and is close to making its offices carbon neutral. It already has photovoltaic (PV) panels

and a 750W water turbine supplying electricity, solar panels for all of its hot water and a biomass boiler for heating. It has also recently started installing a 5KW wind turbine.

The company has planted more than 9,000 trees on land close to its North Devon offices and a plethora of small schemes and initiatives add weight to the firm's environmental standing.

These are too numerous to list, but include: weekly bench-marking of electricity and water usage; purchasing only FSC (Forest Stewardship Council) wood products and eco office supplies; and using a green electricity supplier, sensor-controlled LED office lighting, high levels of insulation, all-in-one networked printer solutions, double-sided printing, recycling bins, composting and company cars that run on bio-diesel.

'It's a great job here,' said David. 'Not only can we save people money, we are opening a debate about being green and pushing other businesses to look at their own actions.'

For more information, visit www. dial-green.co.uk or call 0808 141 0131.

Dial Green promises to reduce your telecoms bill. If it can't, the company will plant 10 trees.

IN PRACTICE:
Volunteering

Millions of volunteer posts exist for those wanting to get a rewarding job

If the idea of picking up litter or rebuilding stone walls doesn't take your fancy, maybe campaigning for Greenpeace or working on a marine conservation project in Tanzania might? Either way, there are thousands of environmental volunteer positions waiting to be filled. You won't get paid for your hard work, but other rewards can quickly add up.

What is volunteering?
Volunteering is giving your time for the benefit of something or someone, other than a close relative, without getting paid. In return, volunteers get the satisfaction of time and effort well spent, and, for many, it is a great way to meet new people and learn new skills.

What can I do?
The range of opportunities is vast – do-it.org.uk, the UK's national database of volunteering opportunities, boasts links to more than one million positions at home and abroad. Of course, the voluntary work available to you will depend on several factors. For many people, the biggest obstacle to volunteering is finding the time; another is age. But no matter how restrictive your circumstances, there will almost certainly be something to suit you.

How do I get involved?
As a first port of call, check out what is available

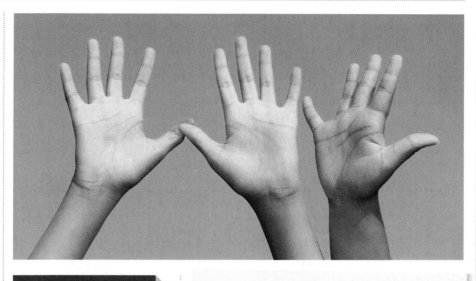

Did you know...?
Volunteering is worth more than £48 billion in England and Wales every year.

Useful links

Volunteering England
www.volunteering.org.uk

Volunteering Wales
www.volunteering-wales.net

Volunteer Centre Network Scotland
www.volunteerscotland.org.uk

Volunteering Development Agency (Northern Ireland)
www.volunteering-ni.org

in your area using the online database at www.do-it.org.uk. Its comprehensive, quick-search facility filters positions by area, category and time. Also try your local Volunteer Centre, details of which will be available on your country's volunteering website (see Useful Websites). It is also worth looking at your local newspaper and advertising notices to see what types of help are needed in your area.

Can I claim any expenses?
Volunteers do not get paid, but it is reasonable to expect payment for out-of pocket expenses such as travel. Check with the organisers before you start to avoid any awkward situations later. You should also expect appropriate training and support for your role.

Top Tips: Volunteering

✓ **Think about what you want from volunteering – new skills, fun, a chance to contribute to a cause?**

✓ **Think about what you have to offer – enthusiasm, work skills, life skills?**

✓ **Work out roughly how much time you have to give – and how many times a week or month.**

✓ **Browse. Check out the www.do-it.org.uk database, contact your local Volunteer Centre or scan the local newspapers and advertising boards.**

✓ **Remember, everyone can volunteer. Whatever your skills, experience or background, you should be able to find an opportunity.**

CHAPTER 5
TRANSPORT & MOTORING

EVERY YEAR, THE AVERAGE PERSON SPENDS NEARLY 16 DAYS TRAVELLING WITHIN THE UK. OVER A LIFETIME, THIS WORKS OUT AT ALMOST ALMOST THREE AND A HALF YEARS

TRANSPORT & MOTORING

Travel is a wonderful thing. It opens doors, broadens horizons, builds character and connects the world. As a nation of islanders, our prosperity and wellbeing has depended on it. The trouble with travel is transport and – more to the point – what it does to our environment. Here's our guide to getting around more cleanly and greenly

Rising emissions

When they came to power in 1997, the Labour Party pledged to reduce the UK's CO2 emissions to 20% below 1990 levels by 2010. While Defra maintains that we are still on track to meet this target, the Department of Trade and Industry has projected that we are on course for around a 10% reduction. Latest figures show that the UK's business sector has done well over time, cutting its CO2 emissions by around 14% since 1990. Residential emissions have fallen too, though by a more modest 4.5%. Further reductions have been seen across industrial, agricultural and public sectors.

The only sector to buck the trend is domestic transport, where, compared to 1990 levels, CO2 emissions have risen by nearly 12% to 157 million tonnes in 2006. This sector is now responsible for 28% of all our CO2 emissions and has overtaken the residential sector as the UK's second biggest emitter after business. Worst still is the fact that this figure only includes road, rail, domestic flights and domestic shipping, and does not take into account international aviation and shipping. Government figures actually show that emissions from aviation fuel more than doubled between 1990 and 2006.

In October 2008, the new Climate Change Act committed the UK to cutting greenhouse-gas emissions by 80% below 1990 levels by the middle of the century.

However, it is anticipated that by 2020, transport will have become the biggest source of greenhouse gases if current trends continue. This will put huge pressure on the other sectors to reduce their emissions enough to cancel out this rise in domestic transport and meet national reduction targets.

The way forward

Britain's love affair with its cars and foreign travel is deeply ingrained in the national psyche. The idea that we might voluntarily give it up, or even cut back significantly, is very unlikely. Unfortunately, industry's promises that technology will deliver sustainable transport are failing to deliver. Minor technological advances have largely been overshadowed by increased production rates, greater use and heightened performance.

While a small number of manufacturers, such as Honda and Toyota, strive for energy efficiency and sustainability in their designs, most manufacturers have so far failed to rise to these challenges and deliver the solutions the world so desperately needs. Meeting the greenhouse gas reduction targets of the 21st century will not be achievable by technology alone, and so the responsibility lies heavily with the individual to reduce their own carbon emissions through changes in behaviour and smart and informed consumer choices.

What is necessary is the rapid, widespread introduction of greener fuels and modes of transport, which must be coupled with a huge increase in the uptake of public transport. As oil prices continue to soar, changes are already occurring as people and organisations do their best to lower costs. Motorists are driving less and more slowly says the AA, airlines and ferry companies are cutting cruising speeds and train drivers are even being told to switch off their engines and coast downhill.

Of course, these changes aren't being made in response to climate change, but because of money. Nevertheless, they show how, with the right motivation, significant and fast-acting changes can be made.

> **"Business has done well, cutting CO2 emissions by 14% since 1990"**

Global issue

Rising emissions from transport are, of course, by no means a UK problem only. The US vehicle fleet, for example, emits more CO2 than all but three other countries' total emissions and is still increasing. And with the ongoing rapid economic expansion of China and India, massive emissions rises are anticipated as these nations become progressively more mobile.

A RETURN FLIGHT FROM HEATHROW TO SYDNEY IN AUSTRALIA PRODUCES 5.61 TONNES OF CO2 PER PASSENGER – THE SAME AMOUNT THE AVERAGE UK HOUSEHOLD PRODUCES IN A YEAR

AIR

For many, flying less is the single biggest thing they can do to tackle their impact on the climate. With dirt-cheap flights feeding our well-established love affair with international travel, cutting down on them will be hard, but here are some ideas to help reduce your aviation carbon footprint

Rapid rise of air travel

The unabated speed at which the UK's – and the world's – aviation industry is growing is terrifying environmentalists and infuriating people living along flight paths. And there's no sign of it stopping either. Currently, around a fifth of all international air passengers in the world are on flights to or from a UK airport. The British government is very eager to preserve this ratio, fearing, rightly or wrongly, that the economy will lose its competitive edge if we fail to meet rapidly increasing demand. To that end it predicts that the number of passengers will more than double to 475 million passengers a year by 2030 compared with 228 million in 2005.

In 1999, the world's top climate scientists at the Intergovernmental Panel on Climate Change published a detailed study of the impact of aircraft pollution which found that aviation contributed around 3.5% of global warming from all human activities. The scientists warned that this would rise to 15% by 2050 if aviation was not curbed.

Helping hands

Part of the reason why aviation has been able to grow so rapidly is due to the fact that airlines currently benefit from huge tax breaks, paying no tax at all on their fuel and no VAT on many of their operations. This has led to disproportionately cheap air tickets compared to other modes of transport, which has driven a huge surge in flights in recent years.

International aviation is also exempt from most international treaties on climate change because agreement has not yet been reached on how to allocate emissions. However, thanks to Friends of the Earth's Big Ask campaign, the ground-breaking Climate Change Act (2008) obliges the UK to cut its greenhouse emissions by 80% by 2050, including international aviation and shipping emissions.

What can be done?

The problems posed by aviation are by no means restricted to greenhouse gases and climate change. Noise pollution, road congestion around airports and damage to the countryside through airport expansion all add weight to the combined impact of the industry. Grounding all planes is not the solution, however. To do so would have catastrophic economic and social impacts on the world, since so many businesses and people rely on air travel to survive. The UN's World Tourism Organisation, for example, says that one in 10 people in the world works in the tourism industry, and that tourism is growing fastest in developing counties. Stopping flights to the poorest destinations would lead to widespread unemployment and poverty.

The government's view is that aviation is an international business and that controlling its effect on climate change demands international solutions. More specifically, it hopes emissions trading schemes will create the right incentives to reduce carbon emissions.

Ministers also cling to the hope that technology will provide a big helping hand. Yet the IPCC have repeatedly warned that improvements in aircraft and engine technology, as well as in air traffic management, will not offset projected growth. As consumers, it falls to us to make a stand by choosing to fly less by holidaying closer to home and looking for greener ways of travelling abroad wherever possible.

Protesters spend to save

Anti-expansion protesters have bought up land earmarked for the construction of Heathrow's third runway. Land the size of half a football pitch was purchased by a four-member Greenpeace coalition, which included actress Emma Thompson and impressionist Alistair McGowan.

Carbon offsetting

Almost everything we do uses energy which, either directly or indirectly, produces carbon dioxide emissions. From turning on the lights when we wake up to heating our homes at night, from driving to work to cooking our dinner; it all adds to our carbon footprint.

Carbon offsetting is seen as a way of compensating for CO2 emissions by preventing or removing an equivalent amount of the gas from the atmosphere elsewhere. The process involves calculating emissions from a particular activity, such as flying or driving, and then purchasing 'credits' from offsetting companies' emission-reduction projects to nullify them.

The nascent industry has grown rapidly as consumers, businesses, rock stars and even governments have spent millions of pounds trying to cancel out their own CO2 emissions by investing in green projects.

In 2008, for example, supermarket giant Marks & Spencer said offsetting would play a part in its effort to become the UK's first carbon-neutral supermarket, while a number of high-street travel agents have started selling carbon offsets alongside flights and package holidays. Former Prime Minister Tony Blair hit the headlines for all the wrong reasons in January 2007, when he publicly admitted that he had no intention of reducing his personal flights. Following a ferocious public backlash, he later announced that he would be offsetting his family's recent holiday to Miami, at an estimated cost of around £90. Even perennial rockers Bon Jovi partnered with a US energy firm to offset the carbon created by the band's Lost Highway 2008 tour – an estimated 5,000 tonnes that accounts for the band and crew's air and road travel and electricity and energy usage.

Does it work?

Despite its popularity, carbon offsetting has been shrouded in controversy ever since its inception. In theory, carbon offsetting is a practical solution to cancelling out unavoidable carbon dioxide emissions so that the overall effect is zero, or carbon neutral. Robust and responsible carbon offsetting projects can also offer a means of investment in clean technology in the areas which lack it the most, which can lead to low-carbon development across entire regions. And by calculating the CO2 emissions of common activities, these companies can help raise awareness of our impact on climate change.

What many environmental groups are quick to point out, however, is that carbon offsetting can too easily be seen as a substitute for cutting emissions and of 'buying out' of the problem of rising carbon emissions.

Tony Juniper, executive director of Friends

▼ Despite its popularity, carbon offsetting has always courted controversy

of the Earth, says offsetting has a small role in providing the solutions to global warming 'at best' and should be used as a last resort. He says: 'Carbon offsetting schemes are used as a smokescreen to avoid real measures to tackle climate change. We urgently need to cut our emissions, but offsetting schemes encourage individuals, businesses and governments to avoid action and carry on polluting.'

The industry also remains largely unregulated, prompting serious concerns over the environmental credibility of many of its schemes. Tree-planting initiatives, for example, have come to be seen as being particularly problematic, with large scale plantations leading to decreased biodiversity, people displacement and social disruption.

> **"Offsetting schemes encourage us to avoid action and carry on polluting"**

Facts and figures

- In 2005, the number of passengers at UK airports was 228 million compared with four million in 1954.
- The distance flown by UK airlines more than trebled between 1985 and 2005 from 80 billion kilometres to 287 billion. And the number of visits abroad made by UK residents also more than trebled since then, to a record 66.4 million visits in 2005. Two-thirds were holidays.
- More than 10% of passengers at UK airports in 2005 were travelling domestically.
- Europe is the most popular destination for UK residents, accounting for 80% of visits abroad in 2005. Spain is the most popular country to visit, followed by France.
- Friends of the Earth claims the UK taxpayer effectively forks out more than £300 a year to the aviation industry whether they fly or not.

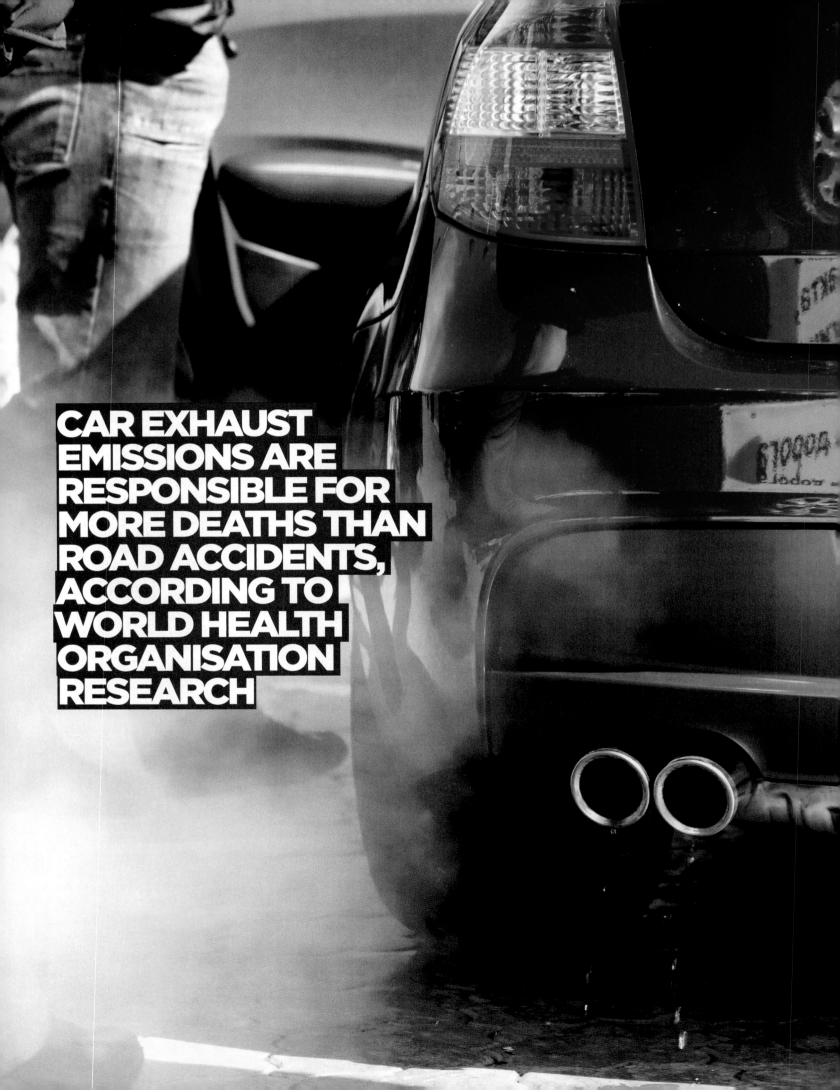

CAR EXHAUST EMISSIONS ARE RESPONSIBLE FOR MORE DEATHS THAN ROAD ACCIDENTS, ACCORDING TO WORLD HEALTH ORGANISATION RESEARCH

CARS

Cars. We love them. There's no escaping it. But cars and everything that goes with them – production, roads, noise, emissions – have heavily contributed to our worsening environment. Here are some green motoring tips for both the long-term and short-term

Green motoring

The development of greener cars is not just one of the most exciting areas of industrial development of the 21st century, it's also big business, and is spurred on by ever-rising fuel prices and fears over climate change. The race for developing the most efficient and cleanest cars has captured the world's imagination and at last the biggest manufacturers, such as Ford, are taking notice. Where once, focus was on greater speed and performance, there is now an increased interest in fuel efficiency and sustainability. For today's eco-conscious motorist there are a number of greener technologies already on offer. The Toyota Prius became the first mass-produced petrol-electric hybrid car to hit the market when it went on sale in 1997 and since then has topped more than one million sales. Further hybrids have since gone on sale, and there are a number of battery-powered cars available, as well as a variety of greener fuels that can be used in modified vehicles. It is hoped that within a few years, the world will see the launch of the first mass produced hydrogen-powered cars and other environmentally friendly alternatives.

Make the most of your car

While the future of road travel lies with renewable technologies, the reality is that for the time being we are going to have to make the best of what we have.

Many consumers may be reluctant to invest in new technologies until they have been proven, and adequate infrastructure, such as charging depots for electric cars, is in place. The important thing to remember is that all cars are not environmentally equal, and that we should choose those which have the lowest impact on the environment depending on our requirements. There are no points for guessing that the largest, fastest cars use a lot more fuel per mile than the smallest and lightest cars on the market. By opting for low-emission options we are not only taking steps to limit our own carbon footprints but bolstering the market for low-emission vehicles.

Diesel vs petrol

Although they are still very harmful to the environment, petrol-engine cars are much cleaner than they used to be after a 1992 law made it compulsory for manufacturers to fit catalytic converters, which remove many harmful emissions.

However, diesel-engine cars actually produce fewer harmful emissions in the first place and are more fuel efficient. The trouble with diesel is that it produces a lot more 'particulates' – very small particles of soot – than petrol when it is burned. These present a serious health hazard and are known to cause asthma and other respiratory diseases. Diesel cars can be fitted with particulate traps, though these are not yet mandatory.

Big car, little car?

Some people need their large off-road vehicles. If this is the case for you, try to find the least-polluting and most efficient options. Try *www.whatgreencar.com* for reviews and ratings on all 18,000 petrol, diesel, LPG & hybrid cars in the UK. Or try *www.vcacarfueldata.org.uk* for further fuel comparisons.

Noise maps

A government initiative launched earlier last year provides people living in the UK's noisiest areas with a 'snapshot' of environmental noise levels in their neighbourhoods. The online facility gives information on 23 urban areas covering 50,000 miles of roads, nearly 18,000 miles of major road networks and around 3,000 miles of railways.

The maps show noise levels over an average 24-hour period, as well as during the night, and can be searched for by postcode. The 23 urban areas available are: Birkenhead, Blackpool, Bournemouth, Brighton, Bristol, Coventry, Hull, Leicester, Liverpool, London, Manchester, Nottingham, Portsmouth, Preston, Reading, Sheffield, Southampton, Southend, Teeside, The Potteries, Tyneside, West Midlands and West Yorkshire.

To view the noise maps visit *http://noisemapping.defra.gov.uk.*

GREEN MOTORING:

DUAL OR FLEXIBLE-FUEL VEHICLES

These are vehicles with engines that can use more than one type of fuel, either mixed in the same tank or with separate tanks and fuel systems for each fuel. Drivers of vehicles with separate tanks can switch back and forth from petrol to the alternate fuel

ALTERNATIVE FUELS

Biodiesel

Biodiesel is a renewable fuel made from the oil of crops including oilseed rape, sunflowers and soybeans. It can also be made from waste cooking oils. Conventional diesel can contain a blend of 5% biodiesel and 95% diesel. However, pure biodiesel is available from some manufacturers.

Pros:
- Renewable
- Gives a 60% reduction in CO2 from well to wheel
- Highly biodegradable, meaning it does not accumulate and pollute soil and waterways if spilt
- Biodiesel receives a 20p/litre duty reduction. A 5% blend therefore gets 1p/litre duty reduction.

Cons:
- Oxides of nitrogen, a smog-forming gas, are slightly higher in biodiesel than with ultra-low sulphur diesel
- There are very few refuelling stations compared with petrol and diesel, and even LPG. Check *www .biodieselfillingstations.co.uk* for more info
- Most engines need to be modified to use 100% biodiesel and stronger blends. You could compromise your warranty if you don't conform to the EN 14214 biodiesel standard.

Bioethanol

Bioethanol is a renewable fuel made from starch plants, such as corn and wheat and sugar plants. It can be blended with petrol to concentrations of between 5% and 85%. It can also be used as a direct substitute for petrol in cars with appropriately modified engines. Brazil is the largest producer of bioethanol in the world. In the USA there are around six million E85 vehicles.

Pros:
- Depending on the production method and source, it is generally accepted that bioethanol gives a 70% carbon dioxide reduction
- Bioethanol gets a 20p/litre duty reduction.

Cons:
- Bioethanol vehicles cost around £500 more than the petrol equivalents
- 5% blend bioethanol is only available at a limited number of outlets, though this looks set to increase in the UK as car manufacturers begin to produce vehicles that can run on all blends up to 85%
- For details of the availability of higher blends check *www.green-car-guide.com/news/bioethanol-fuel-stations-in-uk.htm*.

Liquefied petroleum gas

Liquefied petroleum gas is a mix of propane and butane produced either as a by-product of oil-refining, or from natural gas (methane) fields. It is stored in an on-board pressurised tank.

Pros:
- Gives a 10 to 15% reduction in carbon dioxide emissions compared to petrol, and 80% less nitrous oxide emissions than diesel, along with zero particulate emission
- LPG vehicles cost approximately 30% less to run than their petrol equivalents
- 100% discount from the London Congestion Charge.

Cons:
- Globally, there are more than 10 million vehicles that run on LPG, although few manufacturers offer it as a factory-fitted option. To convert your existing petrol engine to run on LPG typically costs between £1,200 and £2,700. Some vans are available direct from manufacturers as LPG variants
- Not as widely available as petrol and diesel – of the 10,000 refuelling sites in the UK, around 1,200 offer LPG
- Loss of storage space to accomodate LPG tank.

TODAY'S OPTIONS

Battery-powered electric vehicles

Powered by onboard batteries charged from electrical sources, electric vehicles are by no means new to the UK. Most milk floats, for example, are battery powered to keep down on the early morning noise and during the 1920s Harrods used electric vans for deliveries.

Pros:
- No exhaust, so no direct emissions
- Can be up to 99% cleaner than petrol vehicles and cut greenhouse emissions by 70%, even when charged using electricity from conventional power stations
- Cheaper to power and maintain
- Very quiet
- Exempt from congestion charge and road tax.

Cons:
- Generally slower than normal cars. However, the Tesla Roadster (pictured) tops 130mph, does 0-62 in less than four seconds and has a range of around 220 miles. But it's not available in the UK
- More expensive to buy, though this is expected to fall as sales increase
- Limited choice for buyers at the moment, though this is increasing
- Limited range, with latest models

Hybrid electric vehicles

Hybrids combine a small combustion engine with an electric motor and battery to reduce fuel consumption and exhaust emissions. Models include the Toyota Prius, the world's first and best-selling hybrid, as well as the Honda Hybrid Civic.

Pros:
- Hybrids work by capturing energy lost during braking and return it to the battery, a process known as 'regenerative braking'
- More efficient and cleaner than combustion engines alone
- Can cut smog pollution by more than 90% when compared with even the cleanest conventional cars
- Anticipated that future models will cut greenhouse gas emissions by more than half
- Tax benefits
- Exempt from London congestion charge.

Cons:
- A new hybrid electric vehicle costs around £1,000 - £3,000 more than a conventional vehicle. However, this will be cancelled out over the course of the vehicle's life by reduced running costs
- Hybrids will never be true zero-emission vehicles, because of their

Carbon dioxide emissions: Making sense of the figures

Establishing the level of CO2 emissions generated by different modes of transport is difficult for a number of reasons, not least because of the very many variables involved. What is an 'average' car, for example? A coach travelling with a single passenger is an extremely inefficient form of transport, whereas if the coach is full, it becomes one of the most efficient. Below is a worthy attempt by *The Ecologist* to quantify the main methods of transport, using a number of available sources.

GRAMS OF CO2 PER PASSENGER KILOMETRE

1,611	**Transatlantic luxury cruise liner**
300	**Domestic short-haul flights**
248	**International short-haul flight**
210	**Average petrol car**
201	**International long-haul flights**
199	**Average diesel car**
107	**Motorbikes**
89	**Bus**
60	**Rail**
20	**Coach**
0	**Walking**

Sources: *Heat: How to Stop the Planet Burning* by George Monbiot (£22, Allen Lane); Passenger Transport Emissions Factors, 2007 report by Defra; Aviation and the Global Atmosphere, 1999 report by IPCC.

TOMORROW'S WORLD

THE FUTURE'S BRIGHT...

As science fiction slowly but surely becomes science fact, more and more exciting technologies enter the market place – not only capable of getting us from A to B, but also protecting the planet that both A and B are on. Look to the future...

ON THE HORIZON

Compressed-air cars

Compressed-air cars use the expansion of compressed air stored in a very strong lightweight carbon-fibre tank under high pressure to drive their pistons. Although the idea for compressed-air cars has been around since before the Second World War, they are now being researched and developed by a number of large manufacturers. However, reports of impending production have to date proven wholly overoptimistic in the sector.

Pros:

- Air-powered vehicles are ultimately powered by electricity used to compress the air, which means there are no exhaust emissions, making it easier to focus on reducing pollution from one source
- Production costs are lower compared with conventional engines because there is no need to build a cooling system, spark plugs or silencers
- Compared with the limited life expectancy of electric vehicle batteries, compressed-air storage tanks have far greater longevity
- There's a predicted lower initial cost than battery electric vehicles when mass produced
- Compressed-air is not currently subject to fuel tax
- Air-turbine technology is well developed and simple to achieve with low-tech materials.

Cons:

- Operating problems associated with colder temperatures
- Lack of torque provided by the compressed gas
- Low top speeds and range compared to conventional cars
- Storage tanks can take up to four hours to fill when charging at home, though commercial refilling stations could take as little as three minutes
- Governments are likely to adapt their taxation strategies to

Fuel cell vehicles

For many years, scientists and environmentalists have hoped the fuel cell would bring a new dawn to motoring. That day is getting closer.

Fuel cell vehicles create electricity through the reaction of hydrogen and oxygen, with water the only by-product created. Cells can run on hydrogen, eliminating harmful exhausts, or other fuels, such as methanol, which reduces greenhouse gas emissions but is not as clean as hydrogen.

In February 2006, the then mayor of London, Ken Livingstone, announced plans to introduce 70 new hydrogen vehicles into the capital by 2010. However, new mayor, Boris Johnson, has scaled this back to just 10 buses.

Pros:

- Pure hydrogen fuel cells have no emissions
- Unlike battery-powered cars, fuel cells generate electricity on board, which means there are no charging problems
- Very quiet
- Same range as conventional cars and trucks.

Cons:

- The production of pure hydrogen is an energy-intensive process. Producing hydrogen using fossil fuels cancels out much of the benefits of the fuel cell. A lot of further research is needed to produce hydrogen sustainably
- Production is more or less limited to prototypes at the moment, so it is impossible to predict costs. However, a number of major manufacturers are investing heavily in hydrogen technology, which is an indication of their belief in its mass marketability
- Widespread uptake of hydrogen vehicles will need huge and costly changes to the nation's fuelling infrastructure
- Fuel cells that run on hydrocarbons do not have the same

GREEN OPTIONS: Take a look at some of the alternatives

NEW TOYOTA PRIUS

The Toyota Prius is perhaps the most famous eco car in mass manufacture today and includes Arnold Schwarzenegger and Leonardo DiCaprio among its 1.2 million owners.

Although not without its critics, the Prius has helped pave the way for a new, cleaner market for today's driver – the hybrid motorcar. Hybrids combine a conventional internal combustion engine propulsion system with an electric propulsion system to deliver greater fuel efficiency and lower carbon emissions.

The third generation Prius was launched this summer and according to What Car? was the cleanest mass produced car on sale at that time.

And despite boasting an average 72mpg and just 89g/km of CO2 (a considerable improvement on the 65.7mpg and 104g/km of CO2 of its predecessor) its power has increased by 22% thanks to a larger engine and reduced overall weight.

Prices start from £18,390.

Delivering 72mpg, the Prius equates to huge savings in fuel costs.

ESCOOTER CLASSIC

The eScooter Classic from Xero Technology is a retro designed electric scooter that enables its rider to be environmentally and economically aware without compromising on style.

With top speeds nudging 30mph, an overnight charge time of 8 hours and a range of approximately 50 miles, the eScooter is perfect for the urban commuter.

The vehicle is powered with a maintenance free brushless DC 1000W hub motor with a lead-acid silicone sealed battery, and includes a battery power indicator and a digital controller

Available in green, pink, black, silver and white. Prices start at £14,999.

Car stats

• 72% of Britons aged 17 and over are licensed to drive.

• Between 1987 and 2007, motoring costs in the UK measured by the Retail Prices Index (RPI) rose by 85%, while the cost of public transport fares and other travel costs rose by a massive 130%.

• As we went to press, British drivers were paying £502 per 100 litres of petrol in duty and tax, compared to just £353 in Ireland and £436 in Italy.

MEGA CITY 2+2

This is the best selling electric car from the NICE Car Company, London's leading electric vehicle supplier and the trading arm of AIXAM-MEGA Ltd.

With a top speed of 40mph and a range of up to 60 miles on a single charge the four-seater Mega City 2+2 is an ideal city commuter car but is also large enough for the school run.

It is exempt from the congestion charges and road tax and is eligible for free parking in many London locations, which means it significantly cuts down on the annual costs of running a car in the city. A full charge costs approximately £1 via any standard 13amp domestic wall socket and takes about five hours.

Thanks to the upsurge in roadside charging stations throughout central London and in many shopping centre and council run car parks you can now charge when out and about as well.

To arrange a test drive visit *www.nicecarcompany.co.uk.* Prices start from £12,564

ECO DRIVING TIPS: Save fuel and money

The AA teamed up with *Auto Express* to study the potential savings of adopting different driving habits. Fifty employees took part in the experiment, with the average saving 10% on fuel, and best saving a whopping 33%. Here are the results...

To maximise your fuel efficiency follow these top tips:

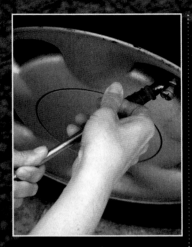

Save cash!
Save up to a month's worth of fuel by following the advice below

MAINTENANCE

- **Get serviced**
  Get your car serviced regularly to maintain engine efficiency
- **Oil**
  Use the right engine oil (refer to the handbook for the exact specification)
- **Tyre pressure**
  Check tyre pressures regularly and before long journeys. Under-inflated tyres create more rolling resistance and so use more fuel. Refer to the handbook as pressure will normally have to be increased for heavier loads.

BEFORE YOU GO

- **Lose weight**
  The more the car weighs, the more fuel is used. Take out anything you don't need for the journey.
- **Streamline**
  Roof racks and boxes create extra wind resistance and so increase fuel consumption. If you don't need it take it off; if you do, pack carefully to reduce the extra drag.
- **Don't get lost!**
  Plan unfamiliar journeys to reduce the chance of getting lost. Try the AA Route Planner or consider investing in a sat nav system if you regularly drive unfamiliar routes. Check the traffic news before you go too.
- **Combine short trips**
  Cold starts are inefficient so it pays to combine errands such as buying the paper, dropping-off recycling, or collecting the kids into one trip.
- **Leave the car at home**
  If you're making a short journey consider walking or cycling rather than taking the car, as fuel consumption is worse when the engine is cold and pollution will be greater too until the emissions control system gets up to normal temperature.

ON THE WAY

- **Don't leave the car idling**
  Turn on the engine when you are ready to leave. If it's icy, use a scraper for the windows rather than leaving the car on to melt it.
- **Drive smoothly**
  Accelerating and decelerating nice and gently, and reading the road ahead to avoid unnecessary braking, will not only save you fuel and money, but will reduce the risk of accidents too.
- **Keep on rolling**
  If you can keep the car moving all the time, so much the better. Stopping then starting again uses more fuel than keeping rolling.
- **Change up a gear earlier**
  Try changing up at an engine speed of around 2,000rpm in a diesel car or around 2,500rpm in a petrol car. This can make a big difference to fuel consumption.
- **Use air-con sparingly**
  Air conditioning increases fuel consumption at low speeds, but at higher speeds the effects are less noticeable. Open the windows around town and save the air conditioning for high-speed driving.
- **Turn it off**
  Any electrical load increases fuel consumption, so turn off your heated rear windscreen, demister blowers and headlights, when you don't need them.
- **Stick to the limits**
  The faster you go the greater the fuel consumption and the greater the pollution too. The most efficient speed depends upon the car in question but is typically around 45 to 50mph.

The need for speed?
According to the Department for Transport, driving at 70mph uses up to 9% more fuel than at 60mph and up to 15% more than at 50mph. Cruising at 80mph can use up to 25% more fuel than 70mph.

Information courtesy of the Automobile Association (www.theaa.com)

IN PRACTICE:

Mean, Not Green

The story of how an influential petrol-head transformed his house into a low-energy eco-home as an economic investment

There may be many compelling reasons to adopt a sustainable lifestyle, but for Harry Metcalfe there is none greater than saving money.

The father-of-two from Oxfordshire is the founding editor of the award-winning motoring magazine Evo and is a committed petrol-head. With a fleet of super-cars in his possession, the former farmer readily admits there is "absolutely nothing" which could ever persuade him to give up his motors for environmental reasons, describing such an action as nonsense.

But despite this unwavering reluctance to go green on the roads, Harry has spent a considerable fortune turning his Cotswolds' farmhouse into a model of environmental sustainability, cutting his running costs by two thirds and saving an estimated 15,000 litres of oil a year.

Six years in the making, the revamped and extended 1939 farmhouse now incorporates the latest in renewable technologies, including a £20,744, 28kW ground-source heat pump for heating and a whopping £18,000, 6kW wind turbine for electricity.

The home is also super-insulated throughout, has an air-source heat-pump to warm the swimming pool and a rainwater harvesting system feeding a 6,500-litre underground tank which provides the family with around a half of its water needs.

There may still be room for improvement, but Harry has certainly pulled out the stops to get his home this far.

"It wasn't a matter of going green as such, more it was a case of do we create a house that is no longer dependant on oil as I was sure the price was only going to be going one way in the future," he explains. "I then got more into it and realised heat-pumps were the way forward and if I could create the power via wind-power then the running costs would be minimal.

"I'm mean, rather than green." Nevertheless, Harry said he would like to see a rise in fuel duty to stop people wasting this "valuable commodity" and is keen to point out that the entire emissions from his car fleet are dwarfed by the savings from his home. His Pagani Zonda, for example, may struggle to achieve more than 17mpg, but then it is only driven around 2,000 miles a year.

"That means it only consumes 530 litres of petrol a year, nothing in comparison," he argues. "I also have a Fiat Panda that does 12,000miles/year at 40mpg using 1,350 litres of petrol.

"I'm not a greenie, but even I can see how new technology has meant I've made a massive difference to my carbon emissions and my lifestyle hasn't changed in the process. That's important to me and my family."

Soaring motoring costs and heightened concerns over climate change have prompted many drivers to look for new ways to slash their bills. By providing members with quick and easy access to cars without the extra hassles of ownership, car clubs allow people to just that.

Car clubs

When Claire Smart first heard about car sharing she was filled with trepidation. But she overcame her misgivings and, today, is one of the scheme's keenest ambassadors.

'The first time I heard about car sharing was about five years ago, when I was approached by a colleague in our transport unit.

'I had some reservations at first, worried about losing my independence and that I wouldn't get on with my car sharers. But, after the first day, those concerns were shown to be completely unfounded.

It wasn't just the money I was saving and the satisfaction of being green, it really was nice to have companionship. We started off strangers, but we soon become very close friends.

'I couldn't believe what a very simple process car sharing is either. People contact you through the site and you simply arrange a suitable time to do your first journey. I am a complete technophobe and if I say it's easy, believe me, it really is.

'If anyone is thinking about joining a scheme, I would say do it. The worst that can happen is you don't like it and you stop, having lost nothing. However, I think you'll find you'll be hooked.

'Car sharing has taken the stress out of going to and

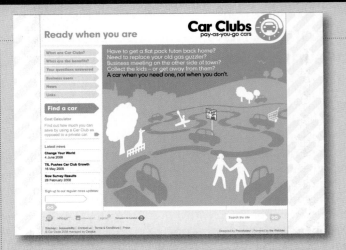

from work. We have great fun chatting or listening to each other's music – we even tried to learn Spanish on our journey.

'It's introduced me to new friends who live locally. It's also safer: when the evenings are dark, I always have someone meeting me in the car park; cheaper: over five years, my car sharer and I have probably saved more than £6,800 between us based on the standard 40p per mile; and, of course, it's greener. What's not to like?'

Claire is director of strategic procurement at Gloucestershire County Council. Her car share scheme is provided through Liftshare.com.

Car sharing

Liverpool businessman Alan Brown sold his car to join a car club two years ago and has never looked back.

'I live and work in the city centre, so owning a car was a bit more hassle than it was worth by the time I paid parking costs, as well as car tax, insurance and maintenance," said Alan, managing director of The Design Division.

'We're based in the city centre and many of our clients are within walking distance. However, we often have meetings with clients in the wider region and WhizzGo is a great resource for our team to use to travel to those.'

WhizzGo is a national network of low-emission cars that are ready to be picked up on the street at any time of the day or night, for as little as an hour or for as long as you want. Members are charged only for the time they use the cars, so there is huge

potential for saving compared with owning your own vehicle.

'The WhizzGo concept is really flexible and fantastic for people who only need a car for a few hours at a time. My wife and I used to have two cars, but we have got rid of them both and just use WhizzGo cars to go to meetings or to visit family and friends.'

Find out how to join WhizzGo at *www.whizzgo.co.uk*.

Did you know...?

The benefits of car sharing can really be put into perspective when you consider that every day there are 10 million empty seats on Britain's roads.

CARS: GREEN VS NOT SO GREEN

Here's a list of the ten best and worst new cars on the market according to the Environmental Transport Association's Car Buyer's Guide. Cars are ranked using a statistical combination of power, carbon dioxide emissions, fuel consumption and noise

The best of the best ✓

1. Honda Insight
2. Toyota iQ
3. Toyota Yaris
4. Nissan Pixo
5. Suzuki Alto
6. Honda Civic Hybrid
7. Ford New Fiesta
8. Toyota Auris
9. Mazda Mazda2
10. Toyota Prius

Honda Insight

Green Rating: ★★★★★
Description: 1.3 IMA ES
Category: Small family
Transmission: Continuously variable automatic
Fuel: Petrol hybrid
Engine Capacity: 1339cc
Combined Fuel Consumption: 64.2mpg
Emissions: 101g/km
Cost: £725 per 12,000 miles

IN PRACTICE :

Mean, Not Green

The story of how an influential petrol-head transformed his house into a low-energy eco-home as an economic investment

There may be many compelling reasons to adopt a sustainable lifestyle, but for Harry Metcalfe there is none greater than saving money.

The father-of-two from Oxfordshire is the founding editor of the award-winning motoring magazine Evo and is a committed petrol-head. With a fleet of super-cars in his possession, the former farmer readily admits there is "absolutely nothing" which could ever persuade him to give up his motors for environmental reasons, describing such an action as nonsense.

But despite this unwavering reluctance to go green on the roads, Harry has spent a considerable fortune turning his Cotswolds' farmhouse into a model of environmental sustainability, cutting his running costs by two thirds and saving an estimated 15,000 litres of oil a year.

Six years in the making, the revamped and extended 1939 farmhouse now incorporates the latest in renewable technologies, including a £20,744, 28kW ground-source heat pump for heating and a whopping £18,000, 6kW wind turbine for electricity.

The home is also super-insulated throughout, has an air-source heat-pump to warm the swimming pool and a rainwater harvesting system feeding a 6,500-litre underground tank which provides the family with around a half of its water needs.

There may still be room for improvement, but Harry has certainly pulled out the stops to get his home this far.

"It wasn't a matter of going green as such, more it was a case of do we create a house that is no longer dependant on oil as I was sure the price was only going to be going one way in the future," he explains. "I then got more into it and realised heat-pumps were the way forward and if I could create the power via wind-power then the running costs would be minimal.

"I'm mean, rather than green." Nevertheless, Harry said he would like to see a rise in fuel duty to stop people wasting this "valuable commodity" and is keen to point out that the entire emissions from his car fleet are dwarfed by the savings from his home. His Pagani Zonda, for example, may struggle to achieve more than 17mpg, but then it is only driven around 2,000 miles a year.

"That means it only consumes 530 litres of petrol a year, nothing in comparison," he argues. "I also have a Fiat Panda that does 12,000miles/year at 40mpg using 1,350 litres of petrol.

"I'm not a greenie, but even I can see how new technology has meant I've made a massive difference to my carbon emissions and my lifestyle hasn't changed in the process. That's important to me and my family."

Soaring motoring costs and heightened concerns over climate change have prompted many drivers to look for new ways to slash their bills. By providing members with quick and easy access to cars without the extra hassles of ownership, car clubs allow people to just that.

Car clubs

When Claire Smart first heard about car sharing she was filled with trepidation. But she overcame her misgivings and, today, is one of the scheme's keenest ambassadors.

'The first time I heard about car sharing was about five years ago, when I was approached by a colleague in our transport unit.

'I had some reservations at first, worried about losing my independence and that I wouldn't get on with my car sharers. But, after the first day, those concerns were shown to be completely unfounded.

It wasn't just the money I was saving and the satisfaction of being green, it really was nice to have companionship. We started off strangers, but we soon become very close friends.

'I couldn't believe what a very simple process car sharing is either. People contact you through the site and you simply arrange a suitable time to do your first journey. I am a complete technophobe and if I say it's easy, believe me, it really is.

'If anyone is thinking about joining a scheme, I would say do it. The worst that can happen is you don't like it and you stop, having lost nothing. However, I think you'll find you'll be hooked.

'Car sharing has taken the stress out of going to and

from work. We have great fun chatting or listening to each other's music – we even tried to learn Spanish on our journey.

'It's introduced me to new friends who live locally. It's also safer: when the evenings are dark, I always have someone meeting me in the car park; cheaper: over five years, my car sharer and I have probably saved more than £6,800 between us based on the standard 40p per mile; and, of course, it's greener. What's not to like?'

Claire is director of strategic procurement at Gloucestershire County Council. Her car share scheme is provided through Liftshare.com.

Car sharing

Liverpool businessman Alan Brown sold his car to join a car club two years ago and has never looked back.

'I live and work in the city centre, so owning a car was a bit more hassle than it was worth by the time I paid parking costs, as well as car tax, insurance and maintenance," said Alan, managing director of The Design Division.

'We're based in the city centre and many of our clients are within walking distance. However, we often have meetings with clients in the wider region and WhizzGo is a great resource for our team to use to travel to those.'

WhizzGo is a national network of low-emission cars that are ready to be picked up on the street at any time of the day or night, for as little as an hour or for as long as you want. Members are charged only for the time they use the cars, so there is huge

potential for saving compared with owning your own vehicle.

'The WhizzGo concept is really flexible and fantastic for people who only need a car for a few hours at a time. My wife and I used to have two cars, but we have got rid of them both and just use WhizzGo cars to go to meetings or to visit family and friends.'

Find out how to join WhizzGo at *www.whizzgo.co.uk.*

Did you know...?

The benefits of car sharing can really be put into perspective when you consider that every day there are 10 million empty seats on Britain's roads.

Get a copy of
THE WEEK
absolutely
FREE

You may well have heard about The Week, but if you have never seen the magazine, why not allow us to send you a copy **absolutely FREE.**

The Week has over 145,000 subscribers who obtain everything they need and want to know from the week's news in only one hour of their time.

See for yourself, call the hotline number below and **claim your free copy today.**

" The one way to keep abreast when all other news sources fade away. "
Jon Snow, News Presenter

" The Week is the ideal paper for those who are too lazy or too busy. I am both and proud of it. "
Dawn French, Comedienne

CALL NOW ON
0845 357 3003

Quote reference: GREEN LIVING

UK only offer

CARS: GREEN VS NOT SO GREEN

Here's a list of the ten best and worst new cars on the market according to the Environmental Transport Association's Car Buyer's Guide. Cars are ranked using a statistical combination of power, carbon dioxide emissions, fuel consumption and noise

The best of the best ✓

1. Honda Insight
2. Toyota iQ
3. Toyota Yaris
4. Nissan Pixo
5. Suzuki Alto
6. Honda Civic Hybrid
7. Ford New Fiesta
8. Toyota Auris
9. Mazda Mazda2
10. Toyota Prius

Honda Insight

Green Rating: ★★★★★
Description: 1.3 IMA ES
Category: Small family
Transmission: Continuously variable automatic
Fuel: Petrol hybrid
Engine Capacity: 1339cc
Combined Fuel Consumption: 64.2mpg
Emissions: 101g/km
Cost: £725 per 12,000 miles

The worst of the rest

1. Dodge SRT10
2. Lamborghini Murcielago
3. Bentley Motors Brooklands
4. Bentley Motors Arnage
5. Bentley Motors Azure
6. Aston Martin Lagonda V12 Vantage
7. Aston Martin Lagonda DB9 08MY
8. Lamborghini Gallardo
9. Cadillac Escalade
10. Bently Motors Continental

Dodge SRT10

Green Rating: 0 (no stars!)
Description: Cabriolet
Category: Sports
Transmission: 6-speed manual
Fuel: Petrol
Engine Capacity: 8285cc
Combined Fuel Consumption: 13.4mpg
Emissions: 488g/km
Cost: £3,583 for 12,000 miles

Lambo CEO:

"Being a supersports car is all about accelerating and top speed. If you want to go fast, you consume, and if you consume, you have emissions. You will never come to the average emissions of the average car."

SOURCE: INTERNATIONAL HERALD TRIBUNE

BENTLEY

LAMBORGHINI MURCIELAGO

DODGE SRT10

IN PRACTICE:
Driving Wind

From its humble origins inside a Norfolk garage, a wind-powered electric supercar is poised to set the car world – and the record books – alight

Imagine 100,000 speed-crazed electro-heads crammed into Brands Hatch to bear witness to death-defying racing between the world's elite drivers and the crème de la crème of manufacturing brilliance.

The lights go green, engines scream and the world's biggest race tears off at lightning pace – leaving nothing but fresh air and a 'whoosh' in its wake. Now, wouldn't that be something? A green Grand Prix may sound too good to be true, but, if the efforts of maverick eco entrepreneur Dale Vince are anything to go by, science fiction might soon be reality.

Former hippy Vince is the founder of green electricity supplier Ecotricity. Last year, he set a team of British motorsport engineers the challenge of creating an 'out-and-out sports car' powered by the wind – well, powered by electricity created by wind turbines. The result would be a zero-carbon-emission supercar to 'blow the socks off Jeremy Clarkson and smash the stereotype of electric cars'.

Now close to completion, it is claimed the converted, second-hand Lotus Exige is capable of doing 0-60mph quicker than a V12 Ferrari, has a top speed of more than 100mph and can do about 150 miles on a single charge.

It seems Great Yarmouth-born Vince and his team have done in a matter of months – and with a budget of just £200,000 – what the car giants have failed to do in years and with millions of pounds at their disposal.

Vince has chronicled the creation of the Nemesis on his blog site, www.zerocarbonista. com. 'The acceleration is astonishing,' he tells his many followers. 'I had a run up and down with John Miles [former Lotus F1 man] at the wheel. If you've ever been on Oblivion at Alton Towers – that feeling you get in the pit of your stomach as you go over the edge and rush groundward – that was exactly the feeling, and it was relentless. It's incredible.'

Vince – whose company's success as a green energy supplier earned him 657th place

in this year's Sunday Times Rich List, with an estimated worth of £85 million – insists the car is not a gimmick. He hopes it will become an 'exotic and desirable' choice for customers in the high-end car market.

The creation of the world's first wind-powered car has coincided with an emergent interest in electric cars as a green solution to motoring. Earlier this year, the Government unveiled the largest co-ordinated trial of environmentally friendly vehicles as part of a £25m effort to accelerate the introduction of electric cars and establish the UK as a world leader in adopting the technology.

London mayor Boris Johnson also wants to make the city the 'electric car capital' of Europe by introducing 100,000 electric cars and building an infrastructure of 25,000 charging points. But, as Vince points out, while electric cars that run off the grid are a big improvement on internal combustion engines, they remain a far cry from their potential.

'Electric cars that run on wind energy are the ultimate in sustainability and zero emissions, using a fuel source that will never run out,' he said.

> **"Electric cars that run on wind energy are the ultimate in sustainability and zero emissions"**

▼ The Nemesis is said to accelerate faster than a V12 Ferrari and have a top speed of more than 100mph

IF YOU DITCH YOUR CAR...

Any plausible attempt to reduce car and air travel demands a reliable, safe and integrated public transport system. Here we examine the state of our public transport and how things are expected to change

On the buses...

When you're out and about, travelling by bus or coach is a far greener option than going by car. Of course, this may not be the case when comparing a passenger packed car with an empty 32-seater, but generally speaking the benefits of bus and coach travel outstrip the automobile by a significant margin. However, the number of people travelling by bus has nearly halved since 1970 as more and more people have got behind the wheel. On the plus side, the actual number of journeys has been rising steadily since the late 1990s and has jumped nearly 10% in the last five years alone though this is predominantly due to increases in bus travel in London: the capital accounts for well over a third of all UK passenger bus journeys. Elsewhere in England numbers have continued to fall.

The Government is working with local authorities and bus companies to boost bus travel by improving facilities, ensuring reliability and providing better access to traveller information and timetables.

... For free

Since April last year, anyone aged 60 or over living in England is entitled to free off-peak travel on local buses anywhere in the country. This statutory entitlement, extended to eligible disabled passengers, has been a welcome help to around 11 million people. The scheme, supported by a £212 million a year fund from the Government, is the latest in a series of bus concessions aimed to improve independence and accessibility for the elderly and disabled. In 2000, half-price off-peak local bus travel became the statutory minimum concession and in 2006 this was extended to free off-peak local bus travel. Off-peak is 9.30am to 11pm on weekdays and anytime on weekends and Bank Holidays. The concession does not cover national coach travel or other modes of transport.

For further information, including details on how to register, contact your existing pass provider. If you are unsure who this is log on to *www.direct.gov.uk/buspass*.

> "**The bus concession has helped around 11 million people**"

Did you know...?

Ten hydrogen-fuelled buses will hit the capital's streets next year as part of a transport plan put forward by former mayor Ken Livingstone.

Public perceptions

According to a 2007 survey by the Office for National Statistics Omnibus on public attitudes to bus travel, the main reason people don't use buses was the perceived convenience of travelling by car instead. However, around a quarter of infrequent/non bus users said that many of their short car journeys could already be made as easily by bus and almost half said they'd travel by bus at least monthly if improvements were made to services. Among regular bus users, satisfaction was on the up, rising from 54% in 2003 to 64% in 2006. Respondents were particularly impressed with the level of frequency and the number of destinations.

RAIL

The rail industry has been enjoying something of a renaissance. Much of the network has been restructured and punctuality is better than ever, with latest figures showing 90% of passenger trains arriving on time. The number of passengers in 2005/06 reached 2.2 billion as rail freight levels increased by 60% over the past decade. National rail and London Underground accounted for 49% and 44% of all rail journeys respectively in 2005/06, though the number of passenger boardings on light rail systems continues to rise, accounting for 171 million boardings in the same period.

The Government says it is committed to investing in the future of rail, with an immediate priority on increasing capacity by 22.5% over five years with longer trains and platforms.

Transport Direct

This invaluable online resource was set up by the Department of Transport in 2004 and provides comprehensive door-to-door travel advice integrating all public transport services in the UK.

- Find the quickest way of making a particular journey by public transport or car simply by entering the address you are leaving from and your destination.
- Find routes and times for specific modes of transport including coaches, buses and trains, and buy train and coach tickets.
- Use the CO2 calculator to find the level of emissions your journey will produce.
- Use PDAs and mobile phones to get departure and arrival times for railway stations throughout Britain and for some bus or coach stops.
- Find a car route that takes into account predicted traffic levels at different times of the day so that you can make informed decisions about when to travel
- Get an estimate of the cost of a car journey, which you can compare with the cost of using public transport

Visitors will soon also be able to mix a car journey with public transport so they can plan a 'Drive and Ride' journey more easily.

Visit *www.transportdirect.info.*

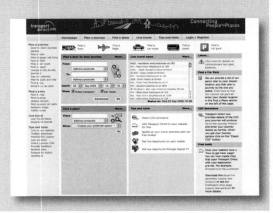

Need a taxi? Try traintaxi.co.uk

Quite often public transport will get you very close to your destination, but not quite close enough. Traintaxi lists all train, metro, tram and underground stations in Britain and provides information on whether they have a taxi rank or nearby cab company. Visit *www.traintaxi.co.uk* or call 01733 237037. Alternatively, try National Rail Enquiries on 08457 484950 for information on local taxis.

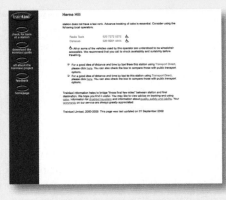

Staying at home

- Teleworking is a rapidly growing trend in business and typically results in a reduction of between two and six home-to-work journeys.
- Teleconferencing typically reduces business travel by between 10% and 30%.
- Home shopping currently accounts for less than 5% of the grocery market and is expected to reach 10 to 15% in the next decade, leading to potential reductions of 7% to 11% of all food shopping traffic.

▼ Staying at home can save you time and money – and help the planet

BIKES

Selling the car in favour of a bike – or at least supplementing it with one – is one of the most environmentally progressive steps a motorist can make. It can also save you a lot of money and help keep you fit and healthy. Dedicated cycle lanes are springing up all over towns and cities, and bike-parking facilities are improving all the time.

Bicycle design has come a long way too, as manufacturers have looked to cater for the requirements of modern day needs. Today, it is not so much a question of 'Should I get a mountain bike or racer?', but, 'Should I get a mountain bike, racer, hybrid, folding or electrical?' – see over the page for an explanation of the main varieties. Here we've tried to pull together all the practical info you need, from staying safe to choosing the best bits of kit.

Cycle safety

They say you never forget how to ride a bike, but that does not mean you can't get a little rusty. If you feel in need of a refresher course, or are starting from scratch, contact National Cycle Training Helpline on 0844 7368460 or email cycletraining@ctc.org.uk.

As with cars, your bicycle brakes will get worn out, tyre treads thin and gears wonky. Make sure you get your bike fully serviced at least once a year to keep it in tiptop condition.

Get kitted out

Besides the various bits of safety equipment such as helmets and lighting gear, there are a host of biking accessories available. If you get the basics, like a puncture-repair kit, tyre pump, trousers clips and a lock, you're off to a good start.

Depending on the type of cycling you have planned, you may also want to splash out on panniers, padded shorts and gloves, sunglasses, mudguards, child seats and much more besides.

Planning your route

If you would like to know more about cycling routes in your area, contact your local council to see whether they produce cycle maps. Alternatively, visit the Sustrans website at *www.sustrans.org.uk*, which maps the UK's National Cycle Network, or visit CTC's maps at *www.ctc-maps.org.uk* for its extensive database.

CHOOSING THE RIGHT BIKE

Racing bike

Also known as a racer, this is designed for road cycling and is therefore lightweight and aerodynamic. It is chiefly characterised by its thin wheels and drop handlebars, which are positioned lower than the saddle to maximise the aerodynamic posture of the rider. Due to their design they are inappropriate for off-road cycling and are generally less popular than mountain bikes for recreational use. In terms of cost, a new entry-level racing bike starts at around half the price of an entry-level mountain bike.

Mountain bike

This is designed for off-road use, either on dirt trails or other unpaved terrain. They are characterised by their wide, knobbly tyres, which offer superior traction and shock absorption, a sturdy frame, robust brakes and lots of gears. To suit their use, most mountain bikes are now built with front suspension and an increasing number also include rear suspension. Mountain bikes can be used on-road, though their robust design makes them sluggish compared with more slender alternatives. Mountain bikes are very popular and widely available.

Touring bike

This has been designed for, or modified to handle, extended cycling trips or tours. To cater for all the equipment required for such a trip, the bikes include numerous pannier racks mounted on the front and rear of the frame, and sometimes on the forks of the wheels as well. Bikes typically have a longer wheelbase for stability and heel clearance, additional water bottle mounts, front and rear mudguards and wide, puncture-resistant tyres.

There is a far greater variety of bikes available now than ever before, ranging from as little as £100 up to well into four figures. But how to choose the one that's right for you? We've rounded up the basic information on the six main varieties to give you a decent guide helping you pick out the best from the rest

Hybrid bike

This is a mix between a mountain bike and a racer. Like a racer, the centre of a hybrid's tyres is smooth to make cycling on roads easier and faster. However, the outer edges of the tyre are roughened, making it suitable for cornering on less stable surfaces. Although hybrids generally retain the basic features of a mountain bike in terms of frame, seat and gears, there can be a wide variation between different models, with some tending to favour off-road cycling and others favouring on-road.

Folding bike

These have come a very long way over recent years. Gone are the chunky, hard-to-ride and slow-to-fold models, and in their place are an inviting range of streamlined and lightweight varieties. You can fold them up and store them in a cupboard or take them onto a train, bus, ferry and even plane usually at no extra cost and without having to book in advance. Folded size is important to consider when buying, as is folding speed. The smaller it folds the greater flexibility you have to take it places, while the quicker it folds makes it better for regular use. Heavier models (14kg or more) cost in the region of £200 or less, whereas for the lightest bikes (10kg or so) you are looking at £1,000 or more.

Electric powered bike

These take the physical edge off riding a conventional bike by providing motorised support when you need it. The bikes are powered by an on-board battery charged from the mains. Some will also recharge while you are pedalling. Although they generally cost more to buy (expect to pay £400 to £1,200) and run than standard bicycles, electric bikes are great for commuters who don't want to sweat on their way to the office. Electric bikes use very little energy to run, working out at between 800 to 2,000mpg. And being electric, they can be made carbon-neutral by using electricity from a green tariff or creating your own electricity domestically. For advice, reviews and information on stockists and prices visit *A to B* magazine's website at *www.atob.org.uk*.

IN PRACTICE:
Brompton Bicycles

Taking your bike on the train or the bus? You don't get much greener than that. And UK's Brompton is a leader in its field

When it comes to best of British design and manufacturing expertise, there is little to beat Brompton's folding bicycle. The West London-based engineering company is a world leader in its field, having built its solid reputation on quality design and superior workmanship. Its bicycles are enjoyed by tens of thousands of owners the world over, from city commuters to round-the-world cyclists.

There are three types of Brompton on the market which have all been designed to be functional, light and a pleasure to use, without compromising handling or safety. Each bike has around 1,200 parts and is built by hand.

Emerson Roberts, marketing manager at Brompton, said folding bicycles took the environmental advantages of cycling and public transport a stage further.

'At Brompton, we believe we offer a personal transport solution – a bike that's as easy to take with you as it is to ride, allowing people to rethink, vary and adapt their journeys at will, to take control and make their trips greener,' he said. 'And at journey's end, it fits under a desk, safe from rain and thieves.'

The environmental impact of Brompton's operations has featured heavily in its decision-making from the beginning. Under founder and inventor Andrew Ritchie, the company supports UK-based suppliers where practical and retains as much production in-house at its 22,000ft London factory as it can. It has also adopted various efficiency initiatives to minimise the impact of its production operations on the environment.

In October 2007, the company moved electricity supply to green electricity provider, Ecotricity, and is working with Cranfield University to calculate the carbon footprint of its operations which will tell customers how far they would have to pedal to offset the carbon emissions that went into the manufacture of their Brompton.

Find out more at www.brompton.co.uk.

"We allow people to take control and make their trips greener"
Emerson Roberts, marketing manager

▲ **Brompton's reputation is built on quality design and superior workmanship**

IN PRACTICE:
Woking Council

All talk and no action is a common complaint of our politicians. But nothing could be further from the truth in Woking, where borough councillors are blazing a trail for governments and communities to follow

For more than a decade, Woking Borough Council has been putting its money where its mouth is.

While many local authorities are only just getting to grips with improving their recycling services, and some not even that, councillors in Woking have long been advocating – and implementing – changes to support the local and wider environments.

From establishing effective policies to cut down on motorised transport to investing in technologies to create clean energy from renewable sources, the town's leaders have shown a commitment to sustainable living.

Indeed, the council is one of the first UK local authorities to have adopted a comprehensive climate change strategy aligned to the UK Climate Change Act's target of an 80% cut in greenhouse gas emissions by 2050.

The council might well give itself a pat on the back, but there is not the slightest hint of complacency as it rolls out one groundbreaking initiative after another.

As far back as 2001, the council was recognised for its pioneering approach to sustainability and granted the Queen's Award for Enterprise. More recently, it's been awarded Beacon status for sustainable energy, promoting sustainable communities through the planning process and tackling climate change.

In light of this, the council has been visited by groups from across the globe keen to learn about its achievements at a local level.

Beryl Hunwicks, a member of the council's Climate Change Working Group, says the authority is committed to taking a proactive role in tackling climate change.

'As soon as we had taken on board the threats posed by climate change, we decided not to hold back and wait for others to start taking action,' she said.

'We didn't want to sign up to something in essence – we wanted to really get things moving in practical ways. It has always been about being proactive, rather than doing

▲ **The wind and the sun power these street lights.**

> **"The borough secured £1.82 million from Cycling England to improve cycling facilities"**

something reactively, when it might be too late.'

Woking's strategy for tackling climate change has three aims: to reduce greenhouse emissions, to adapt to climate change and to promote sustainable development.

Among the changes and improvements to have taken place in the Surrey town so far are the installation of a 200KWh hydrogen fuel cell, which provides heating and power for a public swimming pool and leisure centre; one of the UK's first commercially operated combined heat and power energy stations; and the adoption of energy-saving techniques for council-owned buildings and public places – the savings from which have been reinvested in other environmental measures to further improve energy efficiency.

In the town centre, eco-friendly hybrolights use the wind and sun to provide renewable street lighting, waterless urinals in public toilets cut down on water waste, and a photovoltaic canopy near the railway station is capable of generating 81KWp of renewable energy.

The council is also committed to adopting a target of buying 100% of its electrical and thermal energy from sustainable sources – and 20% from renewable sources by 2010/11 – and has created a schools' awareness programme to increase knowledge about the issues.

Transport is a major issue in Woking and promoting an environmentally friendly system is one of the town's greatest challenges.

The council has come up with a host of ideas to reduce vehicle movements in the town and to encourage drivers to opt for more eco-friendly cars. Among these are the introduction of a car club, an emissions-based car-park tariff and an environmental levy of 5p per visit to a car park. The revenue generated is invested in carbon-offset schemes and environmental improvements for the borough.

Residents are also encouraged to get on their bikes and, last year, the borough secured £1.82 million from Cycling England for the improvement of cycling facilities.

Mrs Hunwicks said communicating all of the initiatives to local people was key to their success, but admitted things were not always easy. 'I don't think people woke up and just aspired to what we are trying to do,' she said. 'There was a certain amount of resistance initially, but most of the residents are aware of what we are doing and, increasingly, support us.'

CHAPTER 6
FASHION & BEAUTY

In the UK we spend an estimated £38 billion on clothes every year

CLOTHING

Saturday shopping sprees have become a favourite national pastime, as the rise of unfathomably cheap garments has enabled us to refresh our entire wardrobes for less than a week's wages. But, sadly, as with most bargains, the low price tag hides enormous environmental and social costs

The Environment

According to the Office of National Statistics, we buy around two million tonnes of clothing and textiles every year, and this is increasing year on year. Between 1995 and 2005, the rate at which we bought clothes rose by more than 34%.

The EC's Environmental Impact of Products investigation in 2006 reported that, due to the high volume of clothes we are buying, clothing and textiles account for between 5% and 10% of the EU-25 entire environmental impact.

In terms of carbon dioxide and other green house gas emissions, the sector was responsible for 3.1 millions of CO_2 equivalent in 2006 alone, with most of these generated from washing and drying, the processing of fossil fuels into synthetic fibres and the widespread use of manmade fertilisers and irrigation systems for conventional cotton growing.

Cotton production alone accounts for 25% of the world's pesticide use and the WWF has estimated that to produce a single kilogram requires 20,000 litres of water. Synthetics are no better. Nylon, for example, accounts for around 50% of all nitrous oxide emissions and, like most synthetic fibres, is derived from petroleum.

Cheap imports from the Far East have led to the almost disposable nature of clothes, with more and more people now wearing a garment just a few times before giving it to a charity shop, recycling it or even throwing it in the bin.

Indeed, textiles are discarded at such an astonishing rate that the wholesale price of used clothing dropped by 80% between 1997 and 2002.

The market for donated second-hand clothes has also fallen significantly in the UK, due in no small part to the low price of brand-new clothing in this country. A pair of old jeans, for example, may only cost you a couple of pounds in your local charity shop, but you can get a new pair for much the same in the "bargain" outlets. Consequently, as little as 10% of donated clothes are now finding their way into high-street charity shops, with the rest being sold to developing countries where they are in danger of undercutting local textile manufacturers. In Zambia, for example, 51 out of 72 clothing firms closed between 1985 and 1992 partly because of foreign competition. So, what may be seen as a humanitarian act could actually be doing more harm than good.

Social injustice

As we cough up a few pounds for a T-shirt, thousands, if not millions, of workers from developing countries are being paid a pittance to work in appalling conditions to meet our demands. In the worst cases, suppliers are forcing young children to work in their sweatshops, paying them next to nothing for their labours. Recent exposure of the use of child labour by high-street giants such as Primark and Gap has brought the issue very pressingly to the world's attention. Companies that have shown a flagrant disregard for the production history of their garments in the past are starting to realise the importance of corporate social responsibility in sustaining their share of the market in increasingly ethics-conscious times. As consumers we have a vital role to play in the fight against exploitation, both of people and the environment, by refusing to buy from companies who breach the rules and questioning the true cost of low priced goods before we purchase them.

Shocking but true...

An investigation by the News of the World revealed how Indonesian workers producing England's World Cup 2012 competition kit, were earning poverty wages and toiling in terrible conditions. Around 2,000 workers were employed at the sweat-shop, earning 16p an hour, working 12 hours and forced to work under intense pressure to complete the order for UMBRO.

TOP TIPS FOR A MORE ECO-FRIENDLY WARDROBE

01
BUY FEWER CLOTHES
but spend more on quality. Well-made clothes will not only stand the test of time, they will usually have a higher resale value for charity shops. It also makes a statement to retailers that you are not in the market for cheap clothes

02
BUY SECOND-HAND
Charity shops have borne the brunt of cheap clothing in the UK, with sales falling year on year. Buying from them extends the life of clothes and supports this worthy sector

03
GIVE AWAY CLOTHES
This is particularly relevant for baby clothes which are outgrown very quickly. Or why not try hosting a clothes-swapping party where you invite friends over to exchange clothes?

04
BUY FAIRTRADE CLOTHING
Although the Fairtrade Foundation does not currently cover all stages in the production line, investing in Fairtrade cotton clothes will ensure that at least the growers are guaranteed a fair deal

05
TRY ALTERNATIVE MATERIALS
Hemp, bamboo and soy all make great products – read over the next few pages to find out why

06
READ AROUND THE GLOSSIES
Fashion mags may tell you all you need to know about what's hot and what's not, but gathering information from other sources such as Labour Behind the Label and No Sweat will give you the fuller picture

07
WASH CLOTHES WHEN DIRTY
Washing clothes uses lots of water and energy; underwear might require a wash after every use, but think twice about whether that jumper really needs a wash after 2 days

08
DON'T IRON UNNECESSARILY AND NEVER TUMBLE DRY
A washing line or clothes horse is perfectly adequate and allows clothes to dry naturally.

09
BUY ORGANIC COTTON CLOTHING
There are plenty of companies sourcing organic cotton for their ranges. A simple search online will bring up some surprising names

10
AVOID CLOTHES WHICH NEED TO BE DRY-CLEANED
Most dry-cleaners use a fluid called tetrachloroethylene, which causes long-term pollution if it escapes into the waterways. Many articles whose tags ask for the dry clean treatment can actually be hand washed, especially silk, wool and linen. As an alternative to conventional dry-cleaning, an increasing number of dry-cleaners are now using Green Earth Cleaning solution, which is made from liquid silicone and is non-toxic. Visit *www.greenearthcleaning.com* for more information

In focus: Conventional versus organic cotton

Cotton is the most popular textile fibre in the world, accounting for around a third of all global textile production. It may be marketed as clean, fresh and natural, but conventional cotton farming is a very dirty business. Globally, it accounts for 25% of all pesticide use, causing widespread damage to local environments and eco-systems and significant health problems for unprotected workers. Seven of the 15 pesticides used on cotton are considered possible human carcinogens according to the US Environmental Protection Agency.

It also uses huge amounts of fertiliser, land and water. In Ethiopia, for example, 60% of the fertile Aswan river valley has been devoted to cotton production, forcing local people onto fragile uplands and thereby contributing to the deforestation that has been partly responsible for Ethiopia's ecological crisis.

Organic cotton is becoming big business and your patronage will only serve to bolster this emerging industry. Many of the biggest retail chains, including M&S and Tesco, now stock an ever-increasing range of organic cotton products so finding them is easy.

M&S and Tesco now stock an increasing range of organic cotton products

Hemp

Until the 18th century, hemp was one of the most important crops known to mankind. Its seeds were eaten and its fibres were used for making papers, clothing and strong ropes used in ships. It was only with the introduction of cotton at the end of the 1700s that hemp was gradually phased out of the textile industry and cheaper fibres were sourced for making paper. Since the 1990s there has been a noticeable revival in hemp cultivation as farmers have capitalised on the biodegradable and non-toxic qualities of the easy-to-grow plant to meet a rising demand for ethical and environmentally friendly textiles, body-care and health products.

Today, every part of the plant, from its core, fibres, seeds and flowers, is used commercially to make all manner of products from bags, books and health products to insulation, fabrics and clothing.

There are many environmental benefits of growing hemp. Under the right conditions it grows to maturity in 100 days, is ideal in rotation and conditions the soil for future crops with its long root systems. Hemp is also one of the most robust fibre crops on Earth and can be grown across a wide range of climates, including the UK. Mass cultivation requires very little in terms of input and is especially easy to grow organically. Fabrics made from hemp are extremely durable, very comfortable to wear and they "breathe" due to the porous nature of the fibres, which makes them ideal for hot weather. Supporters also claim hemp clothing naturally stops up to 95% of the sun's harmful UV light, and have strong anti-fungal and antibacterial properties.

Unfortunately, hemp cultivation remains illegal in many countries because its leaves and flowers become marijuana. However, low narcotic cannabis varieties have been developed and many of these countries are relaxing their laws to allow the cultivation of the plant for commercial reasons.

Where to go for hemp clothing
www.thtc.co.uk
www.braintreehemp.co.uk
www.clothworks.co.uk
www.getethical.com

"Hemp produces a strong, clean yarn, with a structure that makes the cloth cool in summer, and warm and comfortable in winter"
Giorgio Armani

Bamboo and other alternative fabrics

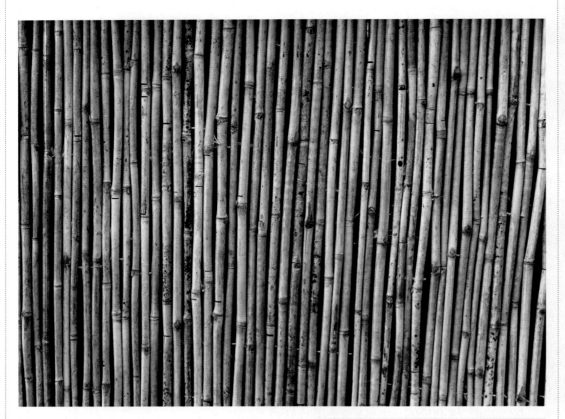

Labour Behind the Label

Many eco-conscious designers are now using the likes of bamboo, soy, coconut and even corn fabrics in their collections. Whilst these fabrics are regularly touted as having major environmental benefits over conventional ones, there are some downsides to be aware of. Bamboo crops, for example, mature very quickly and do not require pesticides to grow, which is a major plus. The fabric is also very strong, is antibacterial and breathable, which means it works well as a body insulator, keeping you cool in summer and warm in winter. It also has a drape quality similar to that of silk, which means it 'floats' on your body, yet is stronger and washing-machine safe.

The drawback with bamboo is that the commonly used process of turning bamboo into a fabric relies on the use of dangerous chemicals, which can be harmful to manufacturing workers if they are not provided with adequate protection and can cause environmental damage if spilt. Since virtually all of the world's bamboo fabric comes from China where workers' rights are negligible, it is feared that many people are suffering acute health problems directly linked to the production of bamboo fabric. In this sense, bamboo is no better than conventionally farmed cotton.

Furthermore, with the increased demand for bamboo some Chinese manufacturers are turning ancient forests over to bamboo

plantations and are even starting to use fertilisers to enhance their crop growth.

Soy, coconut and corn fabrics are also emerging fabrics within the clothing industry, though less is known about their true environmental costs. For the conscientious consumer, looking for environmentally-friendly clothing can be tricky. The current lack of international accreditation systems and regulatory controls in these areas mean that very often you cannot be sure what has gone into the process of growing a crop and turning it into clothing. It is generally accepted, however, that these alternatives are an improvement on conventionally farmed cotton and synthetic fabrics. If you want peace of mind, for the time being stick to Fair Trade organic cotton, but keep an eye out for further developments in this area.

Bamboo towels and linens are available from *www.nigelsecostore.com*

Labour Behind the Label is a campaign that supports the efforts of garment workers around the world to improve their own working conditions. It does this by raising awareness, providing factual information about and from within the clothing industry and encourages international solidarity between workers and consumers. The campaign is the UK arm of the Clean Clothes Company, which is an international collective of organisations and campaign groups which strive to improve the working conditions of factory workers making clothes and footwear.
Labour Behind the Label works with trade unions, consumer organisations, campaign groups, and charities towards the following four aims:

- **Raising public awareness and mobilising consumers**
- **Putting pressure on companies to take responsibility for workers' rights across the entire supply chain**
- **Supporting workers to organise and improve their own working conditions**
- **Campaigning for governments to take responsibility by legislating on corporate responsibility and in the procurement of workwear**

Pledge your support at *www.labourbehindthelabel. org*

ECO-CHIC
Eco alternatives for even the most fashion-conscious consumers

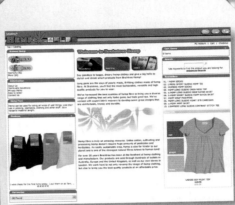

TRAIDremade

TRAIDremade is an award-winning recycled fashion label that uses textile waste that would otherwise be sent to landfill to make stylish alternatives to high street fashion.

Founded in 2000, TRAIDremade is an offshoot of Textile Recycling for Aid and International Development (TRAID), the UK-based charity committed to protecting the environment and reducing world poverty through recycling and delivering educational programmes and campaigning within the UK.

Through a combination of mixing, matching, ripping, cutting, sewing and printing, TRAIDremade's capable designers give a new lease of life to scraps of old clothing.

And since the designers are working exclusively with donated materials, each and every piece of TRAIDremade product is unique. TRAIDremade is available in TRAID's Brighton, Brixton, Shepherds Bush, Westbourne Grove and Wood Green shops. A limited range of accessories is available on *www.getethical.com*. For more information visit *www.traid.org.uk/remade.html*.

Brain Tree

Braintree is an established manufacturer of hemp clothing, selling through hundreds of retail outlets across Australia, mainland Europe and the UK. The company prides itself on working with expert designers, weavers and manufacturers to create high-quality, stylish clothing with minimal environmental impact in fair and ethical conditions. Having recently branched out into soy and bamboo fabrics, the company offers a full collection of clothes using alternative fabrics, from its hardwearing hemp jackets and antibacterial socks, to its bamboo pashminas and soft soy dresses. Visit *www.braintreehemp.co.uk* to shop online, or call 020 7354 7374 for this season's catalogue.

Greenfibres

This Devon-based clothing firm began trading in 1996 and has been pushing its ecological standards and its range ever since. From organic shirts to latex mattresses, Greenfibres offers one of the most comprehensive selections of eco products in its field. Search its online shop at *www.greenfibres.com* for everything from beds to bathrobes and hairbrushes to hand creams. Greenfibres is committed to only sourcing the highest quality organic and natural textiles and to minimising the use of synthetics. It also supports local textile production and manufacture in the UK.

As an ethical company, Greenfibres is dedicated to the principles of fair trade, and guarantees to pay a fair price for goods or services, and to use local labour wherever possible.

Hippy Shopper
Hippy Shopper is a superb green consumer blog that reviews ethical fashion and much more. Visit www.hippyshopper.com

EDUN

EDUN is a socially conscious clothing company whose mission is to create beautiful clothing while fostering sustainable employment in developing countries.

Launched in spring 2005 by U2 lead singer Bono and his wife Ali Hewson, the company is founded on the premise of trade, not aid, as a means of building sustainable communities. The EDUN range is currently produced in India, Peru, Tunisia, Kenya, Uganda, Lesotho, Mauritius and Madagascar, where the company works on a micro-level to help build the skill sets of factories, whilst bringing them up to the highest standards of fair wages and good working conditions. EDUN also exists to encourage the fashion community to do business in Africa and thereby help bring the continent out of extreme poverty. The company maintains that if Africa could regain just an additional 1% share of global trade, it would earn $70 billion more in exports each year, which is several times more than what the continent currently receives in international assistance. Whilst EDUN focuses primarily on fair trade, it is working towards environmental sustainability by introducing more organic materials in its collection whenever possible, which in turn provide healthier conditions for workers. Currently, all EDUN T-shirts are made from 100% organic cotton. Visit *www.edunonline.com*.

People Tree

People Tree is the fair trade pioneer of the clothing industry, putting people values at the forefront of all of its operations. Founded by Safia Minney in 1991, People Tree works with 50 fair trade groups in 15 developing countries to improve the lives and environment of the artisans and farmers who work to produce its wear.

One of People Tree's first suppliers was Assisi Garments in India. Set up by Franciscan nuns, it provides employment for deaf, mute and poor women who are considered unfit for marriage by their families. Assisi offers a haven for these women to live in, and a safe and supportive working environment. They are paid a fair wage and receive a lump sum paid after five years of employment to start a home. People Tree also pioneers ecologically sound methods of production to minimise environmental impact. Almost all of its cotton is certified organic, and all clothes are dyed using safe and natural dyes. As many products as possible are sourced locally, choosing natural and recycled products over toxic, synthetic and non-biodegradable materials. In 2006, clothing giant Topshop became the first high-street store to stock People Tree products at its store in London's Oxford Street. Visit *www.peopletree.co.uk*.

Terra Plana's Worn Again shoes

Terra Plana has been making eco-friendly shoes in the UK, Italy, Portugal, Spain, Romania, Morocco and Mexico since 2003. In 2004, it teamed up with Anti-Apathy, an organisation which promotes and supports people who take creative approaches to social and environmental issues, to make good-looking, guilt-free shoes.

The trouble with making shoes in the conventional way is that it's destructive, both environmentally and socially. From the sourcing of materials, to the treatment of the people who put them together, to transporting the finished product – shoemaking is a very resource-intensive, polluting and toxic industry. To address these problems, the makers of the Worn Again range set about collecting everything from old suits to car seats and granddad shirts to prison blankets, and then used their considerable expertise to fashion these fabrics into fantastic trainers. A proportion of the money the consumer spends on Worn Again shoes goes directly to alternative energy projects and sustainable development. Shop online at *www.workagain.co.uk*.

IN A STUDY OF 34 WELL KNOWN COSMETIC PRODUCTS, NEARLY 80% WERE FOUND TO CONTAIN PHTHALATES, A FAMILY OF SYNTHETIC CHEMICALS LINKED TO DECREASED FERTILITY AND REPRODUCTIVE DEFECTS

TOILETRIES & COSMETICS

Sneak a peek inside a typical bathroom cabinet and you will most likely find all manner of potions and lotions. Understanding what goes into making these products enables consumers to make informed choices. Below is a list of some of the most common types of chemicals you are likely to find in many toiletries

Parabens

Used as antimicrobial preservatives, parabens are synthetic chemicals commonly found in toiletries such as deodorants, moisturisers and baby wipes. Research has indicated that the widespread use of propylparabens could be partly to blame for men's significantly reduced fertility over the last sixty years. Common parabens include methylparaben (E number E218), ethylparaben (E214), propylparaben (E216) and butylparaben.

Phthalates

Phthalates are widely used plasticisers, which are substances added to plastic to increase its flexibility. They are most commonly used to make PVC, but are also found in hairsprays, perfume and nail polishes. Some phthalates are known hormone disrupters. In lab tests, toxic effects on the liver, kidneys, heart, lungs and blood have also been observed. To avoid all phthalates, choose products which specifically state they are phthalate-free.

Triclosan

Triclosan is an antibacterial agent which stays on surfaces after cleaning, thus providing long-lasting action against germs. It is used in a wide range of applications, including toothpaste, mouthwashes and acne treatments. However, in tests, when mixed with chlorinated water, triclosan produced chloroform gas. Popular brands which contain triclosan include Clearasil Daily Face Wash, Dentyl mouthwash, the Colgate Total range, Crest Cavity Protection and Right Guard deodorant.

Toulene

Toulene is a solvent derived from crude oil and commonly found in lacquers and nail polishes. Other uses include paint thinners, silicone sealants and disinfectants. Low to moderate levels of toluene can cause tiredness, confusion, weakness, memory loss, nausea, loss of appetite and hearing. High levels of toluene over a short period of time can make people feel light-headed, dizzy, or sleepy. In extreme cases it can cause unconsciousness and even death.

Xylene

Also found in lacquers and nail polishes, the solvent xylene (aka xylol) has been linked to skin and respiratory problems, as well as liver damage. High levels of exposure over short periods can cause headaches, lack of muscle coordination, dizziness, confusion, and changes in one's sense of balance. Exposure to high levels of xylene over short periods can also cause irritation of the skin, eyes, nose, and throat; respiratory difficulties; delayed reaction time; memory difficulties and stomach trouble.

Formaldehyde

Formaldehyde has a wide range of uses including as a disinfectant, germicide, fungicide, defoamer and preservative. It is commonly found in deodorants and nail varnish, yet is a known human carcinogen, triggers asthma symptoms and is an irritant to the eyes and respiratory system. Further evidence suggests that formaldehyde can damage DNA.

Alkylphenol Ethoxylates

These chemicals are synthetic surfactants, which means they allow liquids to foam or penetrate solids. They are found in some shampoos, hair dyes and shaving gels. Alkylphenol ethoxylates, also known as octoxynol or nonoxynol, are known hormone disrupters and are bio-accumulative, which means they build up in body fat faster than they can be broken down. They are also toxic to fish. Although some progress has been made in phasing out alkylphenol ethoxylates, many industries are still using them.

Acetone

Acetone is a solvent commonly used in nail polish remover and some perfumes. It is toxic if ingested and irritates the lungs. Acetone is consumed by microorganisms and does not build up in soil, animals, or waterways. However, it may pose a significant risk of oxygen depletion in aquatic systems.

COSMETIC SUPPLIERS

You've seen how certain synthetic chemicals can affect your body. Here is a range of skin-friendly alternatives

Being Organic

This family-run business was established after the new-born son of its founders developed a skin rash which they felt was due to a reaction to ingredients in conventional baby products. Frustrated by the lack of retailers selling solely organic certified health and beauty products they decided to go it alone and fill this whole in the market. The web-based company only sells organic products that have been certified by the Soil Association or are certified by another certifier and are up to Soil Association standards. This means that if a product is certified by a foreign certifier but the ingredients do not meet the Soil Association's stringent criteria then Being Organic will not stock it. Product categories include skincare, body and child, bath and shower, health and for men. Visit *www.beingorganic.com*.

Honesty Cosmetics

Honesty Cosmetics has been manufacturing cruelty-free skin and hair products for more than 20 years and adheres to among the most rigorous standards in the industry. All of its own-brand products are endorsed by The Vegan Society, BUAV Humane Cosmetics Standard, the Ethical Company Organisation 'Good Shopping Guide' and the Naturewatch Compassionate Shopping Guide. All products sold through the company are suitable for vegetarians, containing no animal derived ingredients whatsoever. Honesty Cosmetics deals mainly with smaller businesses whose products are not widely available on the high street, with the aim of providing the choice and service to make ethical shopping easy and enjoyable. Visit *www.honestycosmetics. co.uk* or call the helpline on 01629 814 888 for free advice.

Origins

Origins was established in 1990 to promote beauty and wellness through good-for-you products and feel-good experiences. The company's three collections, The Genius of Nature, Dr Andrew Weil for Origins and Origins Organics, covers skin care, bath and body, colour, sensory therapy and fragrance. Origins Body Pampering Massage Oil was this year's winner of the Soil Association's Best Organic Bodycare Product Award. Although not all of Origins products are organic, the company is committed to only selecting ingredients from renewable and sustainable sources and never uses plants that are on the endangered species list. None of its products have ever been formulated with phthalates, petroleum, paraffin, dyes, mineral oil, the chemical sunscreen PABA or animal ingredients (except cruelty-free honey and beeswax). Origins tests its products only on volunteer panels. Origins is sold in around 60 department and speciality stores in the UK as well as in 26 countries around the world. You can also shop online at www.origins.co.uk.

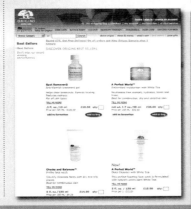

Spiezia Organics

The award-winning skincare range from Spiezia offers one of the most extensive selections of organic produce in its category. Handmade in Cornwall, every single item has Soil Association certification, demonstrating the company's commitment to only ever using the highest quality certified organic ingredients. Even the recycled glass jars and bottles are made at the company's workshop to cut back on its environmental impact. The company website www.spieziaorganics.com includes a comprehensive database of all of the ingredients found in Spiezia products and their uses, as well as an introductory guide to how all the products are made. A list of Spiezia Organics' stockists is listed on their website. Alternatively, you can buy through the online shop directly.

Razors

Disposable razors represent a huge waste of plastic and metal. A decent reusable razor with replaceable blades may cost more up front but in the long-run could save you money and will certainly cut down on all the thrown-away plastic that you are responsible for. Better still are well-made electric razors which cut out the wasted steel blades as well. You can even buy solar rechargeable electric razors, which means you can power up your razor using the renewable energy of the sun. Alternatively, buy reusable twin-blade razors made from recycled yoghurt pots, available from www.ecotopia.co.uk.

ANIMAL WELFARE

There are an estimated 8,000 established ingredients that have been passed as safe for use in cosmetics. Although there is still concern that some are damaging, the majority are widely recognised as being harmless. One might think this was more than enough to work with, yet every year tens of thousands of animals in the EU alone are subjected to lives of pain and suffering as scientists try to find yet more ingredients to pamper our vanity.

Dogs, rabbits, pigs, mice, rats, guinea pigs, fish and birds are all routinely tested for reactions to new ingredients, from skin and eye irritations to poisoning, genetic damage and birth defects. But animal tests for cosmetics or household products are not specifically required by European law; there are alternative approaches companies could choose, or they could use ingredients that have already been established as safe for human use. Countries such as the US and Japan do require that all new ingredients must be animal tested to ensure safety, however.

Some companies are making claims that their final products have not been tested on animals, when in reality the ingredients used to make them have been tested on animals by their suppliers, or even parent companies. In response to this, the Humane Cosmetics Standard (HCS) and the Humane Household Products Standard (HHPS) were set up to provide a guarantee for conscientious consumers. These accreditation schemes recognise the reality that almost all chemical ingredients have been tested on animals at some point. However, accredited companies must ensure that they neither conduct nor commission animal tests on their products, and that they only use ingredients which have not been tested on animals, according to the fixed cut-off date principle. Accredited companies will feature the HCS/HHPS leaping bunny logo on their products.

Although the UK and a few other countries have introduced a whole or partial ban on cosmetics animal testing, such practices continue in the rest of Europe and around the world, meaning many ingredients in products on sale in the UK have been tested on animals.

Thankfully, that is soon to come to an end. After a 10-year battle the EU finally agreed to a Europe-wide ban on the use of animals to test cosmetics in 2003 coming into effect in 2009. Not only that, but no beauty and hygiene products tested on animals outside the bloc may be sold inside the EU. Though there are exemptions condemned by animal rights groups. Animal testing for toxicity or effect on fertility will be allowed until 2013. And even then if the scientists are still stumped the deadline could be extended.

> "WHEN IT COMES TO HAVING A CENTRAL NERVOUS SYSTEM, AND THE ABILITY TO FEEL PAIN, HUNGER, AND THIRST, A RAT IS A PIG IS A DOG IS A BOY," **INGRID NEWKIRK, PRESIDENT, PETA**

Little Book of Cruelty Free

The British Union for the Abolition of Vivisection (BUAV) Little Book of Cruelty Free is packed with info on where to find products not tested on animals. Or visit www.gocrueltyfree.org/ companies.php

▽ **Some sanitary products can contain synthetic, plastic and chemical ingredients**

Feminine hygiene

In the UK, women buy more than three billion disposable feminine hygiene products every year. This results in a huge amount of waste that ends up incinerated or in landfill, or appears in our seas and rivers. But despite the environmental problems associated with menstrual products, there are some known health risks too. Most modern products are made from a mix of cotton and synthetic materials, and are often so absorbent that they create a breeding ground for Toxic Shock Syndrome (TSS). Many women may also find that they experience skin allergies, irritation, soreness and itching, due to contact with synthetic, plastic and chemical ingredients found in most sanitary products. An increasing number of women are now turning to natural and organic alternatives which avoid the use of chlorine bleaching, other chemicals and plastics. These include washable cotton pads or menstrual cups, as well as organic cotton tampons. For more information and advice visit the Women's Environmental Network's website at *www.wen.org.uk.*

Did you know...?

Symptoms of toxic shock syndrome can include fever, low blood pressure, and confusion, and can progress to coma, and multi-organ failure. The characteristic rash resembles sunburn.

IN PRACTICE:
Beanbag Natural Health Shop

A family-run business caught the eye of the judges at this year's Natural & Organic Products Fair to win the coveted Independent Retailer of the Year Award. Here's its secret...

The worst thing that can be said about Beanbag Natural Health shop is that there isn't one in every town. This is hardly a criticism, of course, and the idea of becoming a chain would no doubt churn the stomachs of its owners. But with everything Beanbag has to offer, as a health shop and eco store, unless you live in Witney you're missing out.

Beanbag lies amid an eclectic collection of independent shops in the Cotswold market town and has been in the hands of the Bright family since 1987. Over the past 22 years, John and Joan Bright, and their daughters Jane and Lisa, have kept faithful to their objective of carrying out ethical business while meeting the needs of the customer.

They have evolved the shop and its product range to meet the ever-changing needs of the market. Most recently, this has meant focusing on natural and chemical-free bodycare products, a move that helped earn Beanbag the Independent Retailer of the Year Award at this year's Natural & Organic Products Fair in London.

'We have become fanatical about the quality of bodycare products we sell and are committed to not selling anything that contains chemical nasties,' said Jane. 'Our whole range is truly chemical-free.'

Beanbag also operates a strict policy of not selling products that have involved vivisection in their development.

Today, the shop has everything you would expect to find in a health store and more. You'll find herbal teas, nuts, seeds, cereals, beans and pulses; gluten-free and dairy-free

Beanbag sells eggs, honey, skincare products and raw chocolate made in the local area

alternatives; supplements, aromatherapy oils, bodycare lotions, feminine-hygiene products and reusable nappies. There is also an expanding range of eco products.

Eco-friendly cleaning range Ecover is well represented and the shop offers refills, thus reducing waste and saving the customer money. There is also all manner of products made from recycled materials, including aluminium foil, baking paper, kitchen towel, baking cups and scourers.

Beanbag supports local producers and sells eggs, honey, skincare products and raw chocolate made in the area. It is also a weekly drop-off point for a vegetable box scheme.

But Beanbag would not be half the shop it is without its great team of workers, who have more than 115 years' experience between them. They regularly put on in-store events offering expert advice, demonstrations and tastings, as well as providing leaflets and handouts with up-to-date information.

'We love our shop and genuinely love working together as a team, offering superb, personal customer service,' said Jane. 'We are passionate about the ethical nature of our industry and what it should stand for. We will not compromise on quality or effectiveness for profit – and we believe this has led to Beanbag Natural Health's success.'

JEWELLERY

Although giving precious jewellery is meant to be an expression of love and devotion, your gift may very well be hiding a grotesque history that, if ever known, would no doubt weigh heavily on the wearer

If ever there was any one symbol of the injustices of this world it must surely be the blood diamond. Blood, or conflict diamonds, as they are also known, are diamonds that have been implicated in horrific human rights violations including diamond-fuelled violence, child labour and environmental destruction.

Smuggled across borders and blended into the legitimate diamond market, these precious stones are no different from any other diamond except they leave a trail of brutality and misery. The profits are often used to fund corrupt governments, civil wars and rebel forces, paying for arms that sustain violence and oppression.

An estimated 3.7 million people have died in Angola, the Democratic Republic of Congo (DRC), Liberia, and Sierra Leone in conflicts fuelled by diamonds. Even though the wars in Angola and Sierra Leone are now over and fighting in the DRC has decreased, the problem of conflict diamonds remains.

Amnesty International and Global Witness claim consumers have the power to effect industry-wide change by demanding their diamonds are clean. In a joint statement, they recommended people asked their jewellery retailer the following questions before buying:

- Do you know where your diamonds come from?
- Can I see a copy of your company's policy on conflict diamonds?
- Can you show me a written guarantee from your diamond suppliers which states your diamonds are conflict-free?
- How can I be sure that all of your jewellery is conflict-free?

Of course, this is not to say that conventional diamond mining is not fraught with problems. The exploitation of the workforce is rife within the industry and the health and safety standards are often criminal. Some industry commentators claim all diamonds are blood diamonds.

To make a simple gold ring requires around five tonnes of water and generates up to 20 tonnes of rocks and debris

Environmental damage

Diamond mining, like other gemstone and precious metal mining, is extremely destructive. Around a fifth of the world's diamonds come from alluvial mines, which involves digging up riverbed deposits and violating eco-systems. Other diamonds come from more conventional open-pit and underground mines. Mining for precious stones and metal destroys thousands of acres of habitat and creates huge amount of waste. To make a simple gold ring requires around five tonnes of water and generates up to 20 tonnes of rocks and debris. Some mining and refining processes require the use of toxic chemicals as well. It is estimated that the gold mining industry is responsible for hundreds of tonnes of mercury entering the ground every year. Cyanide is another commonly used toxin in the processing of gold ore, and arsenic, which occurs naturally and is often found among gold and silver bearing minerals, is released upon extraction and can pollute water sources.

What can I do about it?

Wearing precious jewellery has been entrenched in human culture for thousands of years. But as consumers we have a duty to make sure that when we buy our glitzy adornments they have not left destruction in their wake. Look for socially responsible jewellers who source precious metals and gemstones in an ecologically and socially responsible manner. Although mining is always going to be destructive, there are mining companies which make greater effort to minimise environment damage and are committed to treating workers fairly. Alternatively, rather than buy a new ring or necklace, think about buying one or two second-hand rings and taking them to a jeweller to make into something new.

- Download Global Witness's ethical consumer guide, 'Are you looking for the perfect diamond?', at www.globalwitness.org/pages/en/what_you_can_do.html

DIRECTORY

Home & Garden

DEPARTMENT FOR COMMUNITIES AND LOCAL GOVERNMENT (DCLG)
www.communities.gov.uk
0207 9444400

ENERGY SAVING TRUST
www.est.org.uk
0800 512 012

ENVIRONMENT AGENCY
www.environment-agency.gov.uk
08708 506506

SUSTAINABLE DEVELOPMENT COMMISSION
www.sd-commission.gov.uk

LOW CARBON BUILDINGS PROGRAMME
www.lowcarbonbuildings.org.uk
0800 915 0990

OFWAT
www.ofwat.gov.uk
0121 6251300

Bubble House Worms

Bubble House Worms breeds worms for composting and makes hand made wormeries, using components manufactured out of recycled plastic in the UK. As environmental solutions are a core part of the business, Bubble House Worms mobilised its investors, employees, suppliers and customers to achieve low carbon operations.

The company's Herb Garden Wormery was designed with small spaces in mind (40x75cm). An efficient wormery topped with a practical planter for growing herbs, it perfectly complements container gardening and is not limited to, but well suited to courtyards, roof-gardens or balconies. Hand made in the UK using recycled plastic components and supplied with hand harvested and home-bred worms.

For more info, visit
www.bubblehouseworms.com
or call 01886 832559

Family & Children

COUNCIL FOR THE PROTECTION OF RURAL ENGLAND (CPRE)
www.cpre.org.uk
020 7981 2800

DISCOVER IRELAND
www.discoverireland.com
0800 039 7000

DISCOVER NORTHERN IRELAND
www.discovernorthernireland.com
028 902 31221

ENJOY ENGLAND
www.enjoyengland.com
020 8846 9000

FORESTRY COMMISSION
www.forestry.gov.uk
0131 334 0303

FREECYCLE
www.freecycle.org

INTERNATIONAL ECOTOURISM SOCIETY
www.ecotourism.org
001 202 347 9203

NATIONAL TRUST
www.nationaltrust.org.uk
0844 800 1895

UN'S WORLD TOURISM ORGANISATION
www.unwto.org

VISIT BRITAIN
www.visitbritain.co.uk
020 8846 9000

VISIT SCOTLAND
www.visitscotland.com
0845 225 5121

VISIT WALES
www.visitwales.co.uk
0870 830 0306

CAMPAIGN AGAINST CLIMATE CHANGE
www.campaigncc.org
020 7833 9311

FRIENDS OF THE EARTH
www.foe.co.uk
020 7490 1555

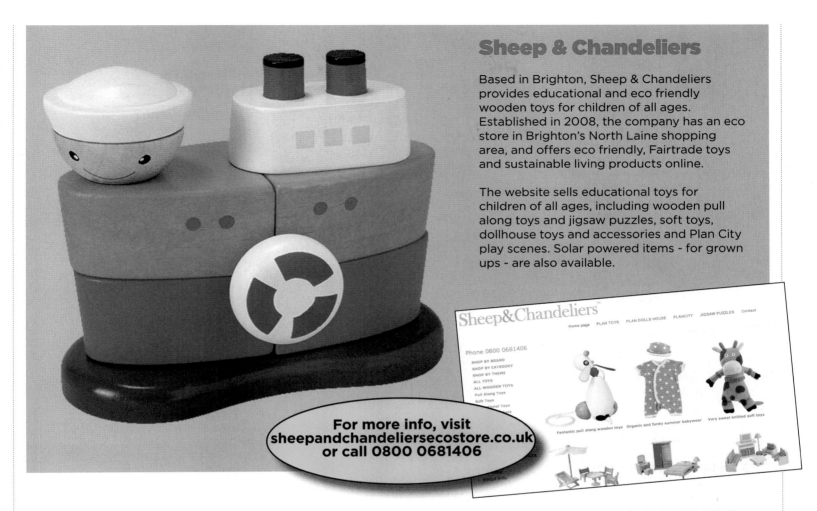

Sheep & Chandeliers

Based in Brighton, Sheep & Chandeliers provides educational and eco friendly wooden toys for children of all ages. Established in 2008, the company has an eco store in Brighton's North Laine shopping area, and offers eco friendly, Fairtrade toys and sustainable living products online.

The website sells educational toys for children of all ages, including wooden pull along toys and jigsaw puzzles, soft toys, dollhouse toys and accessories and Plan City play scenes. Solar powered items - for grown ups - are also available.

For more info, visit sheepandchandeliersecostore.co.uk or call 0800 0681406

GREENPEACE
www.greenpeace.org.uk
020 7865 8100

PEOPLE AND PLANET
www.peopleandplanet.org
01865 245678

STOP CLIMATE CHAOS
www.stopclimatechaos.org
020 7729 8732

WORLD WILD FUND FOR NATURE (WWF)
www.wwf.org.uk
01483 426444

Food & Drink

ANIMAL AID
www.animalaid.org.uk
01732 364546

BIO-DYNAMIC AGRICULTURAL ASSOCIATION (UK6)
www.biodynamic.org.uk
0131 552 6565

BRITISH ASSOCIATION OF FAIR TRADE SHOPS www.bafts.org.uk
07866 759201

COMPASSION IN WORLD FARMING (CIWF) www.ciwf.org.uk
01483 521950

DEPARTMENT FOR ENVIRONMENT, FOOD AND RURAL AFFAIRS (DEFRA)
www.defra.gov.uk
020 7238 6951

FAIRTRADE FOUNDATION
www.fairtrade.org.uk
020 7405 5942

FOOD AND AGRICULTURE ORGANISATION (FAO)
www.fao.org
The UN's leading international efforts to
defeat hunger

IRISH ORGANIC FARMERS AND GROWERS ASSOCIATION (UK7)
www.iofga.org
00 353 043 42495

ORGANIC FARMERS AND GROWERS LTD (UK2)
www.organicfarmers.org.uk
01939 291800

ORGANIC FOOD FEDERATION (UK4)
www.orgfoodfed.com
01760 720444

ORGANIC TRUST LIMITED (UK9)
www.organic-trust.org
00 353 185 30271

PEOPLE FOR THE ETHICAL TREATMENT OF ANIMALS (PETA)
www.peta.org.uk
020 7357 9229

QUALITY WELSH FOOD CERTIFICATION LTD
01970 636688

RSPCA
www.rspca.org.uk
0300 1234555 (advice line)

SCOTTISH ORGANIC PRODUCERS ASSOCIATION (UK3)
www.sopa.org.uk
0131 333 0940

SOIL ASSOCIATION (UK5)
www.soilassociation.org/certification
0117 914 2406

WORLD HEALTH ORGANISATION
www.who.int

GROW WILD ORGANIC PRODUCE

Since 1998, The Grow Wild team has worked strongly with local organic growers and suppliers to offer a fantastic range of quality produce to customers. The award-winning company brings in fresh, organic produce several times a week, and warehouse staff quality control, pack, and organise customer orders. With the ever increasing range of general groceries, fresh local dairy, bakery and Scottish meat and poultry products, getting all things organic delivered to your door has never been easier. These are

distributed by delivery drivers Ian, Les and Stuart direct to customers in Edinburgh, Glasgow, West Lothian and Central Scotland.

For more info, visit
www.growwild.co.uk
or call 01506 656544

Work & Office

BRITISH COUNCIL FOR OFFICES
www.bco.org.uk

THE CARBON TRUST
www.carbontrust.co.uk
0800 0852005

DEFRA
www.defra.gov.uk
08459 335577

DEPARTMENT FOR BUSINESS ENTERPRISE AND REGULATORY REFORM (BERR)
www.berr.gov.uk

ENVIRONMENT AGENCY: BUSINESS
www.environment-agency.gov.uk/
business
0870 850 6506

ENVIROWISE
www.envirowise.gov.uk
0800 585794

INTERNATIONAL ORGANISATION FOR STANDARDISATION (ISO)
www.iso.org

LOW CARBON BUILDINGS PROGRAMME (PHASE 2)
www.lowcarbonbuildingsphase2.org.uk
0870 423 2313

NETREGS (ENVIRONMENT AGENCY)
www.netregs.gov.uk
0870 850 6506

Public Transport Information

ACT TRAVELWISE
www.acttravelwise.org

BUS PASS
www.direct.gov.uk/buspass

BUSWEB
www.busweb.com

DEPARTMENT FOR TRANSPORT
www.dft.gov.uk
0207 9448300

NATIONAL RAIL ENQUIRIES
www.nationalrail.co.uk
0845 7484950

NSCA (NATIONAL SOCIETY FOR CLEAN AIR)
www.nsca.org.uk
01273 878770

PLUSBUS
www.plusbus.info

RAIL FUTURE
www.railfuture.org.uk

SCHOOL RUN
www.school-run.org
08700 780225

SUSTRANS' SAFE ROUTES TO SCHOOLS
www.saferoutetoschools.org.uk

THE TRAINLINE
www.thetrainline.com

TRAINTRACKER
0871 2004950

TRANSPORT DIRECT
www.transportdirect.info

TRANSPORT FOR LONDON
www.tfl.gov.uk
0207 2221234

TRANSPORT IMPACT CALCULATOR
www.travelcalculator.org
01273 878781

Fashion & Beauty

AMNESTY INTERNATIONAL
www.amnesty.org
020 7413 5500

CARE INTERNATIONAL
www.careinternational.org.uk
020 7934 9334

GLOBAL MARCH AGAINST CHILD LABOUR
www.globalmarch.org

GLOBAL WITNESS
www.globalwitness.org
020 7272 6731

LABOUR BEHIND THE LABEL
www.labourbehindthelabel.org

NO SWEAT
www.nosweat.org.uk

OXFAM
www.oxfam.org.uk
0300 200 1300

TRAID
www.traid.org.uk

ANIMAL AID
www.animalaid.org.uk

BRITISH UNION FOR THE ABOLITION OF VIVISECTION (BUAV)
www.buav.org

GO CRUELTY FREE
www.gocrueltyfree.org
020 7700 4888

PEOPLE FOR THE ETHICAL TREATMENT OF ANIMALS (PETA)
www.peta.org

THE VEGAN SOCIETY
www.vegansociety.com
0121 523 1730